The Travels of William Wells Brown

The Travels of William Wells Brown

including

Narrative of William Wells Brown,
A Fugitive Slave

and

The American Fugitive in Europe.
Sketches of Places and People Abroad

edited by

PAUL JEFFERSON
Haverford College

 Markus Wiener Publishing, Inc.
New York

Second Printing, 2017.
© Copyright 1991 for the introduction and commentary by Paul Jefferson.

For information, write to: Markus Wiener Publishers
231 Nassau Street, Princeton, NJ 08542
www.markuswiener.com

Library of Congress Cataloging-in-Publication Data

Brown, William Wells, 1815-1884.
    The travels of William Well's Brown: Narrative of William Wells Brown, a fugitive slave, and
    Sketches of places and people abroad / by William Wells Brown;
edited by Paul Jefferson.
    Reprint (1st work). Originally published: 2nd ed., enl, Boston:
Anti-slavery Office, 1848.
    Reprint (2nd work). Originally published: Boston: John P. Jewett, 1855.
    lncludes bibliographical references.
    ISBN 978-1-55876-043-1 (pbk.)
    I. Brown, William Wells, 1815-1884. 2. Fugitive slaves—United States
—Biography. 3. Great Britain—Description and travel—1801–1900.
4. France—Description and travel—1800–1918. 5. Fugitive slaves—
Travel—Great Britain. 6. Fugitive slaves—Travel-France.
I. Jefferson, Paul, 1944-   . II. Brown, William Wells, 1815–1884.
Narrative of William W. Brown, a fugitive slave, 1991.
III. Brown, William Wells, 1815–1884. The American fugitive in Europe.
Sketches of Places and People Abroad, 1991. IV. Title.
E450.B883A3 1991
305.5'67'092—dc20   91-8667
                          CIP

Markus Wiener Publishers books are printed on acid-free paper, and meet the guidelines for permanence and durability of the Committee on Production Guidelines for Book Longevity of the Council on Library Resources.

WILLIAM WELLS BROWN
at the age of thirty-six

CONTENTS

INTRODUCTION

I

William Wells Brown, the black nineteenth-century man of letters, is best known for the *Narrative of William Wells Brown, A Fugitive Slave* (Boston, 1847), a once popular and now classic autobiography;[1] *Clotel; or, The President's Daughter* (London, 1853), the first novel published by an African-American;[2] and several works of history, among them *The Rising Son; or, The Antecedents and Advancement of the Colored Race* (Boston, 1873), the most important book by a black historian until George Washington Williams' *History of the Negro Race in America, 1619–1880* (New York, 1883). Brown's other writings include a compilation of anti-slavery songs, published lectures, a five-act play, and English and American editions of the first travel sketches published by a black American.

Brown's writings exhibit the thematic richness and formal variety of nineteenth century black literature at its best. As a pioneering architect of a black counter-discourse, an ambiguously subversive literary tradition whose complexity is now appreciated, his work warrants the closer reading it is beginning at last to receive.

II

The future William Wells Brown was born a slave in Lexington, Kentucky in 1814. His mother, Elizabeth, was one of forty slaves owned by Dr. John Young, a gentleman farmer and practising physician who had migrated from Virginia. Brown's father, George Higgins, was his master's

1

cousin. In 1816, when William was two years old, Young moved his goods and chattels to Saint Charles County in the Missouri Territory. Eleven years later, Young relocated his household to St. Louis, after buying a farm near the city. Here William was hired out successively as a tavernkeeper's helper, a steward on a Mississippi River steamboat, a servant to a hotel-keeper, and a boy Friday in the printing office of Elijah P. Lovejoy, then part-owner and editor of the *St. Louis Times*.[3] Before he escaped from slavery, three years and two owners later, William would work once more as a steamboat steward, a fieldhand, a house-servant and general factotum, a part-time physician's assistant, a carriage-driver, and a gang-boss for his nemesis, the slave-trader James Walker.

On January 1, 1834 the young Missouri bondsman slipped off a steamboat at Cincinnati, Ohio, and set out toward Canada and freedom. Taking the name of Wells Brown, a Quaker benefactor who assisted him on his way, he entered history as William Wells Brown, Fugitive Slave, a *persona* he exploited professionally until his freedom was certified in 1854.[4]

Brown reached Cleveland by the end of January 1834 and made it through the winter doing odd jobs. He had exhausted his scanty funds, and felt secure enough to bide his time. By spring he had obtained work on a Lake Erie steamboat, a position he exploited to help other fugitive slaves reach Canada by way of Buffalo, New York and Detroit, Michigan. In the summer of 1836 Brown himself moved to Buffalo, which had a larger black population, was closer to Canada, and was the terminus of the Lake Erie steamboat lines on which he worked each year from thaw to freeze. In Buffalo he made his home an important station on the Underground Railroad, and he got more deeply involved in the welfare of the free black community. He organized a black temperance society—one of the first in western New York—which became, in effect, an omnibus local reform association.

Brown met Frederick Douglass for the first time in August 1843 when the latter came to Buffalo to hold a series of anti-slavery meetings. He encountered Douglass again at a national convention of free Negroes which met in Buffalo later that month. At this tumultuous five-day gathering Brown was introduced to a wider network of black leaders and anti-slavery workers. That fall Brown became a traveling lecturer for the Western New York Anti-Slavery Society. He was soon one of its most successful agents.

In May 1844 he attended an interstate convention of abolitionists in New York City. At this meeting the American Anti-Slavery Society officially took the position that the Constitution was a pro-slavery document, and reaffirmed its opposition to attacking slavery through political action. Brown extended his widening contacts with white abolitionists, meeting William Lloyd Garrison and Wendell Phillips for the first time, and coming away committed more strongly than ever to the Garrisonian strategy of "moral suasion."[5] He continued his work for the Western New York Anti-Slavery Society over the next three years, recounting his experiences as a slave to audiences throughout New York State.

In May 1847, at the annual meeting of the American Anti-Slavery Society in New York City, arrangements were made for Brown to lecture in New England under the auspices of the Massachusetts Anti-Slavery Society. That summer he moved to Boston, which he made his permanent home.

In turning his precarious legal status as fugitive to personal profit, first on the lecture circuit and then in print, Brown followed the example of Frederick Douglass, with whom he was inevitably compared. His autobiography, the *Narrative of William Wells Brown, A Fugitive Slave* (Boston, 1847), was published two years after the success of Douglass' *Narrative of the Life of Frederick Douglass, An American Slave* (Boston, 1845) demonstrated the utility of such a venture. Boston abolitionist Edmund Quincy asserted, following its appearance, that Brown was the most valuable recruit to the cause since Douglass. "I do not know," he wrote, "that his intellectual power is equal to that of Douglass, but he is of a much higher character."[6]

In June 1849 Brown was selected by the American Peace Society as a delegate to an International Peace Congress to be held in August in Paris. He was so honored because one of the leaders of the American Peace Society had established in 1846 a sibling organization, the League of Universal Brotherhood, thus linking the peace and anti-slavery movements.[7]

At this time the American anti-slavery fraternity learned that an agent of the American Colonization Society was in England winning support for its cause—the mass emigration of free American Negroes to Africa. This utopian program—subsidized privately by national benevolent associations and church groups, and publicly by grants from state legislatures—was being marketed to different constituencies, white and black, northern and southern, as a solution to the "Negro problem" of the day. The American Colonization Society insisted that the United States was a white man's country, that free blacks would fare better elsewhere, and that, were owners financially compensated and the nation assured that mass emigration would follow emancipation, slavery itself could be gradually abolished and the national honor restored. The program was a dangerously seductive one which had won wide support.[8]

In July 1849, a meeting of black and white abolitionists in Boston voted to have Brown counter the propaganda of the American Colonization Society's overseas agent when Brown went abroad in his official capacity as American Peace Society delegate.[9]

In a note to the fourth edition of the *Narrative* (Boston, 1849), Brown recalls that in visiting Great Britain he had two related objects in view—to parade his person widely, and to explain his point of view. In demonstrating by his presence as Peace Society delegate that a black person and fugitive slave could be elected to so honorable a position, he could dramatize the progress of abolitionist principles. At the same time, Brown indicates, "I wished to follow up the work of my friends and fellow-labourers, Charles Lenox Remond[10] and Frederick Douglass, and to lay before the people of Great Britain and Ireland the wrongs that are still committed upon the slaves and the free colored people of America."

The importance of Brown's dual function was emphasized by British journalist William Farmer in introducing *Three Years in Europe: or Places I Have Seen and People I Have Met* (London, 1852), the original English edition of Brown's travel sketches. Speaking on behalf of the trans-Atlantic abolitionist community, Farmer wrote that "[i]t was thought desirable always to have in England some talented man of colour who should be a living lie to the doctrine of the inferiority of the African race; and it was moreover felt that none could so powerfully advocate the cause of 'those in bonds' as one who had actually been 'bound with them.' "[11]

The utility of such living witness had been originally demonstrated by Frederick Douglass in his own visit to England four years before. As the second fugitive slave to function professionally as an anti-slavery publicist at home and abroad, William Wells Brown was as instrumental as his more famous contemporary in establishing the multiple parameters of the role.

The passage of the 1850 Fugitive Slave Law prolonged Brown's stay abroad by making it too dangerous for him to return to the United States.[12] Ironically, the threat the law posed caused him to recant a principle he had once invoked to distinguish himself from Douglass. In 1847 Brown had sent a copy of the *Narrative* to Enoch Price, the owner from whom he had escaped. Price wrote Edmund Quincy in reply, acknowledging that Brown was in fact who he claimed to be, and offering to provide Brown with free papers were Price's Boston agent remitted half of Brown's original purchase price. This letter—which worked to confirm Brown's identity and establish his veracity as author—was included in the third edition of the *Narrative* (Boston, 1848), along with Brown's response.

Unlike Douglass who had been prevailed upon to allow well-wishers to buy his freedom, Brown would not, he said, "accept Mr. Price's offer to become a purchaser of my body and soul. God made me as free as he did Enoch Price, and Mr. Price shall never receive a dollar from me or my friends with my consent." However, the Fugitive Slave Law caused Brown to rethink this admirable position. In 1854, like Douglass, he allowed his freedom to be purchased by friends abroad, so that he could return to the United States.[13] Though he might have remained in England, Brown felt that he could not in conscience do so while his countrymen languished in bondage. He returned as a moral soldier, he later explained, "for the express purpose of joining in the glorious battle against slavery, of which. . . . Negrophobia is a legitimate off-spring."[14]

For the next two years Brown traveled and lectured as an agent for the Massachusetts and the American Anti-Slavery Societies. He began to try his hand at other forms of anti-slavery argument. After presenting an earlier version on the lecture circuit, he wrote *The Escape; or, A Leap for Freedom: A Drama in Five Acts* (Boston, 1858), the first play to be published by an African-American. Four years later the first of four editions of an historical work, *The Black Man, His Antecedents, His Genius, and His Achievements* (Boston/New York, 1863), appeared.[15] In his preface, Brown made the rhetorical purpose of the book explicit. Targeting the "calumniators and traducers" of black Americans, the book was meant to counter assertions of the natural inferiority of the Negro by providing sketches of "individuals who, by their own genius, capacity, and intellectual development," Brown explained, "have surmounted the many obstacles which slavery and prejudice have thrown in their way, and [have] raised themselves to positions of honor and influence."[16]

During the Civil War—following the Emancipation Proclamation and Lincoln's decision to enlist black troops in the Union army—Brown helped recruit enlistees for the famous Massachusetts 54th and 55th Regiments, which were led by white officers.[17] At the same time, he lobbied energetically but unsuccessfully for the right of black soldiers to be led by officers of their own race. During the war, he worked to secure equal pay for black and white troops alike, and he called attention to the need for improved medical services for black units too often used as shock troops.

Following the Civil War—from a black point of view, the conflict was brought to a conclusion only upon the ratification of the 15th Amendment in 1870—Brown again took up the temperance cause. He continued to lecture and write, publishing his most ambitious work of history, *The Rising Son; or, The Antecedents and Advancement of the Colored Race* (Boston, 1873), three years later. After a unique variety of experiences as a fugitive and a free man, Brown's later years were less eventful. He died quietly in Boston, Massachusetts on November 6, 1884, a respected elder statesman for his race. Having been successively a temperance reformer, an anti-slavery lecturer, a versatile man of letters, and ultimately also a practising physician,[18] Brown lived—against all odds—a rich and instructive life.[19]

III

The texts reprinted here—the *Narrative of William Wells Brown, A Fugitive Slave* (Boston, Second Enlarged Edition, 1848) and *The American Fugitive in Europe: Sketches of Places and People Abroad* (Boston, 1855), the American edition of his account of his travels—are good examples of first-person retrospective prose narratives,[20] the most eloquent of forms in nineteenth century black literature. They reveal the development of the author's distinctive voice and point of view as he fashions differently managed accounts of successive stages in his life. Reprinting them side by side enables the reader to follow the development of William Wells Brown from a humiliated slave to a racial ambassador and an eloquent man of letters.[21]

From one point of view, the first text—Brown's *Narrative*—may be read as travel literature, as well as autobiography. Mapping changing spiritual and physical geographies, the *Narrative* first chronicles Brown's life in bondage—disclosing aspects of slavery more various and disturbing than those registered in the *Narrative of the Life of Frederick Douglass*—and then follows Brown's pilgrim's progress north to freedom.

Read as autobiography, the *Narrative* witnesses a double act of self-creation. Brown invents himself both in making the escape the narrative recounts, and in recounting the escape he makes. In the first instance, he makes good his resolve to change his fate by becoming a fugitive slave. The act of fleeing is an existential act of self-creation. In the second instance, he recreates himself as author and as free man in the very act of constructing the *Narrative*.

For the reader, the larger story Brown tells includes as well the wonder of his hard-won capacity to tell it—like Frederick Douglass, he had no formal schooling.[22] In blurring the distinction between Brown as subject, the teller of a generic "free story,"[23] and Brown as fugitive slave, the object of the story he tells, the first-person *Narrative* increases our appreciation of the double achievement.

Just as the *Narrative* may be read as travel literature, *The American*

Fugitive may also be read as autobiography. But in contrast to the *Narrative*, in the latter work Brown plays his *persona* as fugitive slave off against his achieved self, especially in his encounters with European philanthropists and *literati*. As simultaneously author and object of a brief for emancipation, Brown functioned abroad as the professional man of letters and anti-slavery lecturer, on the one hand, and as the fugitive slave as case in point, on the other. Strategically exploiting his anomalous identity, as an acknowledged fugitive Brown was a living refutation of the very assumptions of black incapacity and the justice of slavery that he challenged discursively as publicist.

IV

The *Narrative* is constructed in a distinctive way, and its framing is an integral aspect of its desired effect. Structurally, Brown's autobiography proper is only one of the constituents of the *Narrative* as an affective and cognitive whole. The reader encounters first an open letter to the Quaker, Wells Brown, in which the author demonstrates a becoming gratitude to his "earliest benefactor" and "first white friend." This letter is followed by another from Edmund Quincy to the author Brown himself. Quincy, a Boston abolitionist, has been asked by Brown to serve as his editor and intermediary, and has been given permission by Brown to blue pencil the narrative. However, he would "be a bold man, as well as a vain one," Quincy tells the author, who would presume to improve upon the other's first-person testimony. Finally, there is a conventional preface by J. C. Hathaway, president of the Western New York Anti-Slavery Society, Brown's first employer in his capacity as anti-slavery lecturer.

This mode of external framing does double duty. It is meant to confirm the truthfulness of the account and to suggest in advance how to read it. The issues the *Narrative* is presumed to raise are clearly spelled out, and the reader's feelings are manipulated without apology. Edmund Quincy functions implicitly as Everyman, suggesting that only one response is possible to the facts Brown recounts. "[A] man must be differently constituted from me," Quincy asserts, "who can rise from the perusal of your Narrative without feeling that he understands slavery better, and hates it worse, than he ever did before." The reader is moved to sympathize with Brown the slave, Brown the fugitive, and Brown the man, whose authority as witness must be vindicated. To this end, J. C. Hathaway comments on the author's "simplicity and ingenuousness which carries with it," he says, "a conviction of the truthfulness of the picture [the author paints]."

Hathaway then addresses the reader directly—Reader, are you an Abolitionist? are you a Christian? are you a friend of the Bible?—and stipulates
unequivocally how Brown's text is to be read. To understand slavery better
is to understand it as theft and as sin, he insists; and to hate it worse than
before is to join the crusade to eliminate it.

The distinction between the textual substance of the *Narrative* and its
external packaging—even if editorially imposed—is not always a clear
one. This is truer still of the internal framing of the *Narrative,* which—
being Brown's own architecture—is more obviously a vehicle for his
argument. Such structural elements include the generic themes, memorable human types, and significant incidents or rites of passage which
would soon become conventions of the form. Brown, following Douglass,
is working to invent an insider perspective on the "peculiar institution" by
establishing the parameters of the literary genre, the slave narrative, which
is its privileged vehicle.

Typically, slave narratives dramatize a juxtaposition of the facts surrounding the cultural status of slaves as objects, and the fictions by which
masters monopolize the status of human subjects. The meta-themes of the
genre involve, on the one hand, the fundamental contrast between slavery
and freedom—a contrast so stark as to achieve metaphysical resonance—
and, on the other hand, the contradictions of principle and practice in a
society determined to expropriate the humanity of others and to spare its
own feelings while doing so.

The contrast between slavery and freedom is often represented, implicitly or explicitly, as that between life and death. This occasionally has
the textual consequence of yielding a pivotal narrative episode, a pro-
bative "dark night of the soul,"[24] through which the author must pass.
Brown refers obliquely to such an episode in the first paragraph of chapter
11 of the *Narrative:* "The love of liberty that had been burning in my
bosom, had well nigh gone out. I felt as though I was ready to die . . . my
thoughts were so absorbed in what I had witnessed [here alluding to the
last time he would see his mother], that I knew not what I was about half
of the time. Night came, but it brought no sleep to my eyes." The final
paragraphs of chapter 13 link the notions of physical and spiritual death in
another fashion: "I have ever looked upon that night as the most eventful
part of my escape from slavery. Nothing but the providence of God, and
that old barn, saved me from freezing to death. . . . The thought of death
was nothing frightful to me, compared with that of being caught, and again
carried back into slavery."[25]

The theme of the contradiction of principle and practice is typically exploited by turning the languages nineteenth century America used to explain itself—the languages of natural law, moral philosophy, and republicanism, on some occasions; and the languages of religion, liberal or evangelical, on others—against the idealized norms, sacred and secular, those cultural languages presumed. Brown's references in the *Narrative* to "slavery with its Democratic whips—its Republican chains—its evangelical blood-hounds, and its religious slave-holders" and his ironic invocations of the "paraphernalia of American Democracy and Religion" are unique only in their energy and pointedness.

There are particular human types whose strutting and fretting on stage also helps to structure the *Narrative*. The obscenity of slavery is dramatized, for example, in the persons of the Yankee overseer, the Christian slave-holder, and the predatory slave-driver—figures whose contradictory spiritual and cultural identities point up the unnaturalness of a social institution that reproduces human mutants. For example, Brown mentions the overseer, Friend Haskell, "a regular Yankee from New England," early in chapter 3, and suggests without comment that Yankees in that role were noted for their cruelty. He concludes chapter 4 with an eloquently spare account of the on-the-ground meaning of religion as but an alternative language of power. In this connection, he dryly notes that during the visit of Mr. Sloan, a young Presbyterian minister from the North, "[i]nstead of his teaching my master theology, my master taught theology to him." Having earlier "got religion," Brown observes, identifying the practical consequences of slave-holder Christianity, his master proceeded to regiment his slaves more strictly in the name of the Lord.

Finally, Brown's distaste for the "soul-driver" James Walker is so profound as to evoke a tortured lyricism. Walker represents the acme of villainy in the *Narrative*. He forces the chaste quadroon, Cynthia, into his bed; fathers four children on her; then sells both children and mother down the river. While driving a coffle of slaves to St Louis, Walker tears a crying child from a mother who is unable to sooth her. To spare himself annoyance, he leaves the child behind. In reporting this scene, Brown can capture the horror it inspires only by resorting to poetry. His time in Walker's service, he later reports, "was the longest year I ever lived." Introduced first by Douglass and Brown in their master narratives, figures of this sort stalk the pages of the genre.

The physical violence inherent in the relation of master-as-subject and slave-as-object is evident throughout the *Narrative*. Of the ten incidents witnessed in the brief text, the most unsettling involve deliberate attempts to bring male slaves to heel, that is, in the revealing words of an irate owner. "to tame the d---d nigger." The first such incident involves breaking the spirit of the slave Randall, a man of great strength who has not before been flogged. It takes the combined efforts of three white men and a pistol shot to overpower him. Just as the beating then administered by the overseer, Mr. Cook, puts Randall himself in his place, witnessing the incident through young William's eyes fixes an indelible impression of slavery in the reader's mind.

A second incident, described more briefly, is equally telling. The slave John, purchased by one Robert More for the express purpose of repaying an earlier slight, is thrown into irons and whipped three times a week for two months. There was no "more noble looking man" than John before he fell into More's hands, Brown reports; but after undergoing this taming process, there was no "more degraded and spirit-crushed" being on a southern plantation. In the zero-sum game logic of the master-slave relation—a logic at once political and psychological—the need to break the spirit of the slave was a systemic one. Making discussions of "slave-breaking" a convention of the genre becomes a useful means of deciphering the obscene logic of the "peculiar institution."

Finally, two incidents function in concert as devices of internal framing in the *Narrative*, to mark a rite of passage. Together suggesting what's in a name, they signal Brown's coming of age. In the first incident, young William is deprived of his given name as a child, when his master's nephew moves into their household. Because the white William preempts their common name, the black William is henceforth known as Sandford. Though Brown enjoys no property in himself in more basic ways, his resentment at being so brusquely expropriated remains alive throughout his years as a slave.

Brown's perspective on his double predicament as a slave appears later in the *Narrative* in a wry allusion to the distinction between appearance and reality, name and fact. I was "not only hunting for my liberty," he says, "but also hunting for a name; though I regarded the latter as of little consequence, if I could but gain the former." Depending on how it is taken, as the reader comes to see, this statement is both true and not true.

Following his escape, Brown represents himself in the *Narrative* as free in fact, when he is legally still a fugitive. In his characteristic few words, he suggests that this new state took some getting used to. At first "[t]he fact that I was a freeman—could walk, talk, eat and sleep as a man, and no one to stand over me with the blood-clotted cowhide—all this," he says, "made me feel that I was not myself." But his physical liberty is consolidated and confirmed by an assertion of spiritual autonomy.

In the second incident, William becomes his own man in the encounter with the Quaker, Wells Brown, when he chooses a name for himself. He repossesses his given name and takes on the name of this early benefactor. Staking his claim to the past and the future, Sandford becomes William Wells Brown. That acquiring the name of a free man was in fact a matter of some consequence is confirmed by the author's grateful dedication of the *Narrative* to Wells Brown, his "first white friend."

V

The external framing of the second text, *The American Fugitive in Europe* (Boston, 1855), serves in similar ways to reinforce and focus its argument. The book opens with the preface to the original English edition in which Brown makes ritual apology for the shortcomings of the text, reminding the reader that he had been twenty years a slave and was without formal schooling. Thus, the *persona* he assumes is thrown into high relief.

A note to the American edition follows. Here Brown confesses that he had published an earlier book of travels while abroad because it was "advantageous to my purse." However, this curious announcement is less off-putting than it appears. It anticipates mention of a circumstance in the "Memoir of the Author"—which introduces the text proper of *The American Fugitive*—that Brown thought was entirely to his credit.

Written by the British journalist, William Farmer—here unnamed—the "Memoir" was based closely on Brown's *Narrative*. It told readers who the fugitive slave was whose adventures they would share, and it brought the story of Brown's life as anti-slavery worker fully up to date. Farmer recounts that Brown had been careful to stress that unlike those who had preceded him to England—he meant unlike Frederick Douglass and Charles Lenox Remond, with whom he was associated in the minds of the trans-Atlantic anti-slavery fraternity and from whom he hoped to distinguish himself—he went as a professional man of letters, who as a matter of principle would be self-supporting. Brown thus implied that he disdained charity and would take his chances. By mentioning this fact Brown insinuated that it was an exercise of will—the mental faculty most highly esteemed by the moral philosophy of the day—which enabled him to fashion from unpromising materials a self that could move in European society without apology. His achieved self and his assumed *persona* would be simultaneously on display—the one played off the other—throughout his sojourn abroad.

The external framing of the text is completed by four pages of "Opinions of the British Press," which follow Brown's account of his travels and close the book. Here the rhetorical point of the volume is made clear past all mistaking. The very fact of its publication, says *The Literary Gazette,* constitutes "another proof of the capability of the negro intellect." William Wells Brown in person, the *Glasgow Citizen* agrees, is "a full refutation of the doctrine of the inferiority of the negro." Elsewhere there are references to the excitement created by the recent appearance of Harriet Beecher Stowe's *Uncle Tom's Cabin* (1852). The comments of a "real fugitive slave" deserve equal billing, *The Critic* suggests. Finally, the point is made that Brown's is a radical counter-discourse. His "doings and sayings," the *Morning Advertiser* confidently predicts, will be "among the means of destruction of the hideous abomination" of slavery.

As in Brown's *Narrative,* certain aspects of the internal structuring of *The American Fugitive* also warrant notice. For example, Brown takes particular care to highlight the occasions he encounters other black persons in Europe. He mentions a visit paid to Alexander Crummell, later a famous educator and missionary, then studying at Cambridge University. He indicates that in an hour's walk through London "one may meet half a dozen colored men, who are inmates of the various colleges of the metropolis." Elsewhere, Brown notes with pleasure the three black students he sees "seated upon the same benches with those of a fairer complexion" at the University of Edinburgh.

These encounters do significant rhetorical work in several respects. First, Brown represents the presence of black students at institutions of higher learning as a sign of progress in "the cause of the sons of Africa." Then he draws the appropriate moral lesson, demonstrating the justice— at once interpersonal and cultural—of a state of affairs so foreign to American readers. There "appeared no feeling on the part of the whites toward their colored associates," he said, "except of companionship and respect." Taking the high ground, Brown presses the point home, then twists the knife. "In the sight of God and all just institutions, the whites can claim no precedence or privilege on account of their being white; and if colored men are not treated as they should be in educational institutions in America, it is a pleasure to know that all distinction ceases by crossing the broad Atlantic." The lesson is an emphatic one.

Another encounter with a black person abroad, the most memorable and amusing of all, works rhetorically in an entirely different way. Departing from his normal procedure, Brown devotes an entire chapter to one Joseph Jenkins. Jenkins is "a good-looking man, [who is] neither black nor white." As a semi-comic figure of uncertain antecedents, he is a nineteenth-century *picaro,* a man on the move who has learned to make do.

Brown encounters Jenkins in London in the successive guises of Cheapside bill distributor; Chelsea street sweeper; street musician and vendor of religious tracts; Shakespearean actor; spell-binding store-front preacher, who inveighs against "the sale and use of intoxicating drinks and the bad habits of the working classes;" kidnapped putative African prince; and sometime professional band-leader. Jenkins is a protean figure, a benign early incarnation of the urban hustler, and, withal, "the greatest genius," Brown wryly observed, "that I had met in Europe." Brown has just spent the greater part of *The American Fugitive* dropping famous names; the point is well taken and seriously intended.

This chapter works rhetorically by counterpoint. In light of the myriad tasks Brown had performed as a slave, and the promiscuous talent he had displayed; in light of the revealing description of Jenkins as "a good-looking man, neither black nor white," a description which could fit Brown himself; and in light of his current obligation to be a model "race man," and its possible spiritual costs, it is as if Brown recognizes in Jenkins a repressed *alter ego*. Whether this is so or not, his whole-hearted response to Jenkins complicates the reader's sense of the author more than he might have wished. Appreciation of the picaresque Jenkins appears to compromise Brown's commitment to the middle-class values he elsewhere consistently espouses.

On the other hand, recall that Jenkins inveighs against "the sale and use of intoxicating drinks and the bad habits of the working classes." What Brown celebrates in Jenkins is not the negative "fact" that a black man will do everything he might want to do, but the positve "fact" that—if permitted—a black man is able to do anything he may have to do. Joseph Jenkins, like Benjamin Franklin, is a very well-educated man. Read in this way, this chapter points up Brown's conventionality on social issues apart from that of race. Education and character—their sociological vacuity notwithstanding—are, for Brown, terms to conjure with. Like most of his nineteenth-century counterparts, he looks to individual transformations rather than institutional ones when he seeks for social remedies.

Alain Locke's penetrating twentieth-century observation that "the Negro is radical on race matters, conservative on others, . . . a 'forced radical,' a social protestant rather than a genuine radical" quickly comes to mind.[26] Though the African-American counter-discourse Brown has a hand in creating is culturally subversive from the point of view of race, from other points of view it is ambiguously so.

We may wonder, for example, whether Brown's acceptance of a "divide and rule" model of social injustice is the price of lack of class-consciousness. He alludes repeatedly in *The American Fugitive* to differences in the material conditions of life of American slaves and European work-

ers. On three occasions he explicitly challenges the proto-Marxist argument that the poverty and insecurity of the white working class in
Europe—and, by implication, that of the factory worker in the northern
United States—make wage slavery harsher than the plantation slavery of
the American South.

Brown's need to challenge a staple pro-slavery argument of the day is
understandable. But by addressing the question in the terms in which it is
framed, he mistakes what is really at issue. Because the languages at his
disposal—the languages of natural law, moral philosophy, and republicanism, on the one hand; and of religion, on the other—yield no
structural insights, Brown does not understand that the question of relative victimization is beside the point. The implications of the fact that
hierarchies of race and class alike are institutionally reproduced, and
might at times be usefully analyzed together, are lost on him.

Elsewhere, the device of contrast serves Brown as well in *The American
Fugitive* as it did in the *Narrative*. He again plays England off against the
United States, ironically juxtaposing Enlightenment ideals and reaction-
ary racial attitudes. He marvels at one point that "no sooner was I on
British soil, than I was recognized as a man, and an equal." On another
occasion, he wryly suggests how curious it is that monarchical England
rather than Christian republican America should be the home of freedom.
The liberating difference distance makes is dramatized in a more human
idiom as well. Snubbed at home and on the trip over by a fellow American,
Brown has the pleasure of snubbing him in turn when he seeks an introduction to *literati*, like Victor Hugo, with whom Brown himself freely
mingles.

Finally, Brown opens and closes *The American Fugitive* with an eloquent ambivalence, the grounds for which have been established
throughout the account. The book opens with his anxiety at leaving his
native land—whose evils at least are familiar—for the hazards of foreign
travel. It closes with his uncertainty about returning to the land of his birth
five years later—where now he feels a stranger—from an England which
has made him feel at home. Going and coming, Brown strikes the perfect
note.

VI

The *Narrative* and *The American Fugitive* are extended cultural arguments. Printing them side by side invites the reader to consider more
closely the ways they affect their audiences. On the page, the texts work

rhetorically in a double or hybrid manner. They function at once epistemically—by mirroring the world of slavery and picturing the impact of racism; and politically or ideologically—by undermining their rationales.

One effective example of this occurs in the *Narrative* when William dupes a free black man into receiving a beating meant for himself, a slave. Brown recounts what happened, as an unimpeachable first-person witness. Then he interprets what happened. By commenting astutely on his own unseemly behavior, he indicts the "peculiar institution" itself for producing slaves to pattern. "This incident shows," he suggests—at once conceptualizing and subverting a "blame the victim" point of view—"how it is that slavery makes its victims lying and mean, for which vices it afterwards reproaches them, and uses them as arguments to prove that they deserve no better fate."

As arguments deriving from a single parent form—that of the first-person retrospective prose narrative—the *Narrative* and *The American Fugitive* exhibit a certain kinship. But as distinct species of a common genus—as an autobiography and a travel account—they work on the reader in ways peculiar to themselves. Brown's *Narrative*, for example, is simpler on the surface, but more sharply focused, and more deftly subversive of reader expectations.[27] *The American Fugitive*, in contrast, works rhetorically by attrition, painting a broader canvas, and multiplying opportunities to show Brown at his best in good company.

Were one to exaggerate the differences between the two books, one might read them as examples of alternative modes of representation, that of metaphoric realism and that of mimetic realism, respectively. So phrased, however, the distinction is ultimatley misleading. What is more to the point is their common rhetorical function. The *Narrative* and *The American Fugitive* are extended cultural arguments. As fully accessible first-person narratives—however they achieve their effects—they are best appreciated on their own terms, without further preliminaries.

Paul Jefferson

Haverford, Pennsylvania
January 1991

Editorial Note
Chapters VI, VII, X, XII, XV, XXIV, XXV, and XXIX of *The American Fugitive* (1854) have been omitted from the reprinted text as both less interesting to the modern reader—they include extended descriptions of landscapes, museum interiors, grave sites, and assorted monuments—and less central to the "argument" of the book.*

---

*The remaining chapters in the 1991 edition have been re-numbered consecutively.

ENDNOTES

1. Following its publication in July 1847, the *Narrative* went through three editions and eight thousand copies in less than eighteen months. A fourth American edition of two thousand copies was printed in August 1849. Between 1849 and 1853, while abroad, Brown arranged the publication of four English editions—one an illustrated version—and one Irish edition of the *Narrative*, bringing the total number of copies in print to more than fifteen thousand. See William Edward Farrison, *William Wells Brown: Author and Reformer* (Chicago: University of Chicago Press, 1969), pp. 114, 155–157.

2. Harriet Wilson's *Our Nig; or Sketches of the Life of a Free Black* (Boston, 1859) was the first novel published in the United States by an African-American. Brown's *Clotel* was published six years earlier, but published abroad.

3. Seven years later the Reverend Elijah P. Lovejoy became the first white abolitionist martyr. He was killed in Alton, Illinois in 1837 when a pro-slavery mob destroyed the printing presses of his paper, the *Alton Observer*.

4. See Farrison, *William Wells Brown* (1969), p. 8.

5. William Lloyd Garrison inaugurated the radical phase of the anti-slavery movement in the United States. The first issue of his Boston-based anti-slavery paper, the *Liberator*, appeared on January 1, 1831 and the New England Anti-Slavery Society was organized later that year. In 1833 the American Anti-Slavery Society—its Declaration of Sentiments written by Garrison—was founded in Philadelphia. In 1835 the patrician Wendell Phillips joined the movement. The Garrisonian position was that slave-holding was a sin, and that abolition should be immediate and unconditional. Because the Constitution was seen as a pro-slavery document, radical abolitionists were not to compromise their principles by working politically to end slavery. Garrison's unbending posture and his commitment to public agitation and "moral suasion" as a tactic are reflected in the famous words with which he closed the opening number of the *Liberator:* "I will not equivocate—I will not excuse—I will not retreat a single inch—and I WILL BE HEARD."

6. See Edmund Quincy to Caroline Weston, July 2, 1847, Anti-Slavery-

Weston Papers, Boston Public Library; cited in Farrison, *William Wells Brown* (1969), pp. 113.

7. The American Peace Society, founded in 1828, brought together within a national organization most of the existing state and local peace societies of the day. Its membership was made up largely of Congregational, Baptist, and Methodist ministers. Strangely, the Society of Friends as a body did not associate itself with the peace movement, perhaps because the American Peace Society equivocated on the admissibility of "defensive war." Elihu Burritt, a leader of the American Peace Society and prime mover behind the International Peace Congresses of 1848 and 1849, organized the League of Universal Brotherhood in 1846. See Merle Eugene Curti, *The American Peace Crusade, 1815–1860* (Durham: Duke University Press, 1929), *passim*.

8. The American Colonization Society was established in 1817. By 1830 its goals had been endorsed by national conventions of the Presbyterian, Methodist, Baptist, and Dutch Reformed Churches, as well as by regional conferences of Episcopalians, Congregationalists, and Quakers. Its wide support was reflected in the approval voted its program by the state legislatures of Connecticut, Delaware, Indiana, Kentucky, Maryland, Massachusetts, New Jersey, New York, Ohio, Pennsylvania, Rhode Island, Tennessee, Vermont, and Virginia. The best single expression of the Society's program and rationale is the letter written by Robert Goodloe Harper to Elias B. Caldwell, August 20, 1817. Caldwell was the first secretary of the American Colonization Society. See William H. Pease and Jane H. Pease, eds., *The Antislavery Argument*, (Indianapolis: Bobbs-Merrill Company, 1965); pp. 18–32.

9. In his official capacity as American Peace Society delegate, Brown gave a speech at the Paris Congress the following month protesting the war spirit by which slavery was maintained in the United States. Interestingly, his lecture was favorably noticed in the Paris newspapers, but sarcastically reviewed in the *London Times*. Brown would keep good company abroad. At the Paris Peace Congress, for example, he was introduced to the celebrated novelist and playwright, Victor Hugo, and to the wife of Alexis de Tocqueville, French Minister for Foreign Affairs.

10. Charles Lenox Remond was a free black anti-slavery lecturer renowned for his eloquence. He was the most widely heralded black spokesman of the early-mid nineteenth century, until Frederick Douglass upstaged him.

11. William Wells Brown, *Three Years in Europe; or, Places I Have Seen and People I Have Met* (London, 1852), p. xxi.

12. By multiplying the mechanisms for recapturing fugitives available under the original Fugitive Slave Law of 1793, the Fugitive Slave Law of 1850 endangered the security of free blacks as well. Under the later act putative slaves could be seized either with a federal warrant, as under the act of 1793, or without legal process, by oral affidavit. The certificates of rendition thus secured could be issued not only by federal judges, but also by a new class of "commissioners" appointed for the purpose, who earned a larger fee if they ruled that the fugitive was a slave than if they decided he was free. Alleged fugitives were prohibited from testifying in their own behalf and were denied *habeas corpus*. Those obstructing slave-catchers were liable to heavy fine and imprisonment. Federal marshalls were authorized to form posses of bystanders to help recapture fugitives, for whose safe return once apprehended said marshalls were personally liable.

13. It was to a Miss Ellen Richardson of Newcastle—ironically, a member of the family which had earlier purchased Douglass' freedom—that Brown was "mainly indebted for the redemption of my body from slavery." See William Wells Brown, *The American Fugitive in Europe: Sketches of Places and People Abroad* (Boston, 1855), p. 304; Farrison, *William Wells Brown* (1969), pp. 238–241.

14. Brown, *The American Fugitive in Europe* (1855), p. 314.

15. The book appeared in December 1862, the printed date of publication notwithstanding.

16. William Wells Brown, *The Black Man, His Antecedents, His Genius, and His Achievements* (Boston/New York, 1863), pp. 5–6.

17. Brown was joined in this task by Martin R. Delany, Frederick Douglass, Henry Highland Garnet, John Mercer Langston, and Charles Lenox Remond, arguably the six most celebrated and influential black leaders of the day. However, it is significant that only Douglass' role as recruiter is dramatized in the recent movie *Glory*. (1989).

18. Having spent much of his spare time since 1860 reading medicine and attending lectures, Brown set up shop as a physician in Boston in 1865. No state agencies then existed to set conditions for admission to the profession. Though the Harvard Medical School offered lectures and some clinical instruction, aspiring physicians were not obliged to attend a medical college. The usual route into the profession was through apprenticeship with an established practitioner. Brown's interest in medicine probably grew out of his experience while still a

slave as a part-time physician's assistant to his master, Dr. Young. See Farrison, *William Wells Brown* (1969), pp. 24, 399–401.

19. Brown's life is historically instructive precisely because, from today's point of view, he was a rather conventional person—notwithstanding the myriad things to which he turned his hand. Temperamentally and ideologically—apart from the issue of race—he was emphatically not a revolutionary. His attitudes and opinions were solidly middle-class. He believed in education, character, and hard work. The only fault he found with the structure and functioning of American society was the fact that black Americans were not allowed to participate freely in it. But in the nineteenth-century context, to be black, on the one hand, and to be sufficiently successful and to command enough cultural literacy to mouth plausibly the platitudes of the day, on the other hand, was so thoroughly to confound expectations as to be in its way revolutionary. In this respect, Brown's life was instructive for his white contemporaries as well.

20. William L. Andrews has recently distinguished seven forms of antebellum first person retrospective prose narratives—forms, we suggest, which are not entirely and invariably distinct. These include slave narratives, spiritual autobiographies, criminal confessions, captivity narratives, travel accounts, interviews and memoirs. See his *To Tell a Free Story: The First Century of Afro-American Autobiography, 1760–1865* (Urbana and Chicago: University of Illinois Press, 1988), p. 19.

21. Brown's later confidence and assertiveness are memorably captured in an incident he recounts in *The American Fugitive*. He spent one winter's night in an English hotel which supplied him with damp bedding. The next morning he threw his sheets out the window. When the landlady threatened to charge him for the ruined bedding, Brown threatened to send the bill to the *London Times*, so its readers would learn how poorly-run the establishment was. The landlady backed down, and apologized.

22. Like Douglass, Brown was largely self-taught. He reports in the *Narrative* that he acquired what little learning he obtained while in slavery working in the St. Louis printing office of Elijah P. Lovejoy. This was in 1830. However, two years later Brown is obliged to have a literate free black man read a note for him. Clearly, whatever "learning" he had acquired earlier as a slave was ephemeral. After escaping to Cleveland, Brown reports that in the spring of 1834 he purchased several books and subscribed to an anti-slavery newspaper. His biog-

rapher suggests that Brown taught himself to read at this time by working his way doggedly through such material. However, no fully trustworthy information is available. For Brown's implausible later accounts of how he first learned to read and write, see Farrison, *William Wells Brown* (1969), pp. 61–62. However, we can assume that having somehow acquired a basic literacy by 1843, Brown's finishing school was the organized anti-slavery movement. The comments of a fellow matriculant, Frederick Douglass, at the National Negro Convention in Cleveland, Ohio in 1848 were autobiographical, as well as hortatory: "We ask you to devote yourselves to this [anti-slavery] cause, as one of the first, and most successful means of self-improvement. . . . Many of the brightest and best of our number, have become such by their devotion to this cause, and the society of white abolitionists." See "An Address to the Colored People of the United States," *Report of the Proceedings of the Colored National Convention, Held at Cleveland, Ohio* (Rochester, 1848), pp. 18–19, reprinted in Howard Holman Bell, ed., *Minutes of the Proceedings of the National Negro Conventions, 1830–1864* (New York: Arno Press, 1969).

23. See Andrews, *To Tell a Free Story* (1988), pp. xi-xii, 1–31.

24. See Andrews, *To Tell a Free Story* (1988), pp. 8–9.

25. A related consequence of this reading of slavery—less in evidence in the laconic Brown text than in other slave narratives—is that resurrection imagery abounds. Negotiating a dark night of the soul may constitute a form of purgation and presage spiritual rebirth. At other times, talk of being a "new man"—an evangelical locution—may follow either the symbolic assertion of autonomy in resisting an overseer, or an actual escape from bondage.

26. Alain Locke, ed., *The New Negro* (New York: Albert and Charles Boni, Inc., 1925), p. 11. Chapter XXX of *The American Fugitive,* which describes a day in the House of Commons, highlights Brown's conventionality. In his stereotyped references to future Prime Minister Benjamin Disraeli as "the Jew," in his admiration for the splendid fortunes and social polish of the land-owning aristocracy, and in his vicarious pride in "this assembly of senators" of an expanding British Empire, we see that he has internalized the political and social prejudices of his day.

27. See Andrews, *To Tell a Free Story* (1988), pp. 22–29, 144–151, 176, 273–274, whose use of "speech-act theory" to explore how slave narratives, generally, and Brown's *Narrative,* in particular, work on their readers is unexcelled.

Narrative
of
William W. Brown

A FUGITIVE SLAVE

WRITTEN BY HIMSELF

Is there not some chosen curse,
Some hidden thunder in the stores of heaven,
Red with uncommon wrath, to blast the man
Who gains his fortune from the blood of souls?
                                        Cowper

SECOND EDITION, ENLARGED

NOTE TO THE SECOND EDITION

The first edition, of three thousand copies, of this little work was sold in less than six months from the time of its publication. Encouraged by the rapid sale of the first, and by a demand for a second, edition, the author has been led to enlarge the work by the addition of matter which, he thinks, will add materially to its value.

And if it shall be instrumental in helping to undo the heavy burdens, and letting the oppressed go free, he will have accomplished the great desire of his heart in publishing this work.

LETTER FROM EDMUND QUINCY, ESQ.

Dedham, July 1, 1847.

To William W. Brown

My Dear Friend:—I heartily thank you for the privilege of reading the manuscript of your Narrative. I have read it with deep interest and strong emotion. I am much mistaken if it be not greatly successful and eminently useful. It presents a different phase of the infernal slave-system from that portrayed in the admirable story of Mr. Douglass,* and gives us a glimpse of its hideous cruelties in other portions of its domain.

Your opportunities of observing the workings of this accursed system have been singularly great. Your experiences in the Field, in the House, and especially on the River in the service of the slave-trader, Walker, have been such as few individuals have had;—no one, certainly, who has been competent to describe them. What I have admired, and marvelled at, in your Narrative, is the simplicity and calmness with which you describe scenes and actions which might well "move the very stones to rise and mutiny" against the National Institution which makes them possible.

You will perceive that I have made very sparing use of your flattering permission to alter what you had written. To correct a few errors, which appeared to be merely clerical ones, committed in the hurry of composition under unfavorable circumstances, and to suggest a few curtailments, is all that I have ventured to do. I should be a bold man, as well as a vain one, if I should attempt to improve your descriptions of what you have seen and suffered. Some of the scenes are not unworthy of De Foe himself.

I trust and believe that your Narrative will have a wide circulation. I am sure it deserves it. At least, a man must be differently constituted from me, who can rise from the perusal of your Narrative without feeling that he understands slavery better, and hates it worse, than he ever did before.

I am, very faithfully and respectfully,

Your friend,

EDMUND QUINCY

---

*Narrative of the Life of Frederick Douglass, an American Slave, Written by Himself (Boston, 1845).

PREFACE

The friends of freedom[1] may well congratulate each other on the appearance of the following Narrative. It adds another volume to the rapidly increasing anti-slavery literature of the age. It has been remarked by a close observer of human nature, "Let me make the songs of a nation, and I care not who makes its laws;" and it may with equal truth be said, that, among a reading people like our own, their books will at least give character to their laws. It is an influence which goes forth noiselessly upon its mission, but fails not to find its way to many a warm heart, to kindle on the altar thereof the fires of freedom, which will one day break forth in a living flame to consume oppression.

This little book is a voice from the prison-house, unfolding the deeds of darkness which are there perpetrated. Our cause has received efficient aid from this source. The names of those who have come from thence, and battled manfully for the right, need not to be recorded here. The works of some of them are an enduring monument of praise, and their perpetual record shall be found in the grateful hearts of the redeemed bondman.

Few persons have had greater facilities for becoming acquainted with slavery, in all its horrible aspects, than WILLIAM W. BROWN. He has been behind the curtain. He has visited its secret chambers. Its iron has entered his own soul. The dearest ties of nature have been riven in his own person. A mother has been cruelly scourged before his own eyes. A father—alas! slaves have no father. A brother has been made the subject of its tender mercies. A sister has been given up to the irresponsible control of the pale-faced oppressor. This nation looks on approvingly. The American Union sanctions the deed. The constitution shields the criminals. American religion sanctifies the crime.[2] But the tide is turning. Already, a mighty under-current is sweeping onward. The voice of warning, of remonstrance, of rebuke, of entreaty, has gone forth. Hand is linked in hand, and heart mingles with heart, in this great work of the slave's deliverance.

The convulsive throes of the monster, even now, give evidence of deep wounds.

The writer of this Narrative was hired by his master to a *"soul-driver,"* and has witnessed all the horrors of the traffic, from the buying up of human cattle in the slave-breeding states, which produced a constant scene of separating the victims from all those whom they loved, to their final sale in the southern market, to be worked up in seven years, or given over to minister to the lust of southern *Christians.*

Many harrowing scenes are graphically portrayed; and yet with that simplicity and ingenuousness which carries with it a conviction of the truthfulness of the picture.

This book will do much to unmask those who have "clothed themselves in the livery of the court of heaven" to cover up the enormity of their deeds.

During the past three years, the author has devoted his entire energies to the anti-slavery cause. Laboring under all the disabilities and disadvantages growing out of his education in slavery—subjected, as he had been from his birth, to all the wrongs and deprivations incident to his condition—he yet went forth, impelled to the work by a love of liberty—stimulated by the remembrance of his own sufferings—urged on by the consideration that a mother, brothers, and sister, were still grinding in the prison-house of bondage, in common with three millions of our Father's children—sustained by an unfaltering faith in the omnipotence of truth and the final triumph of justice—to plead the cause of the slave; and by the eloquence of earnestness carried conviction to many minds, and enlisted the sympathy and secured the cooperation of many to the cause.

His labors have been chiefly confined to Western New York, where he has secured many warm friends, by his untiring zeal, persevering energy, continued fidelity, and universal kindness.

Reader, are you an Abolitionist? What have you done for the slave? What are you doing in his behalf? What do you purpose to do? There is a great work before us! Who will be an idler now? This is the great humanitary movement of the age, swallowing up, for the time being, all other questions, comparatively speaking. The course of human events, in obedience to the unchangeable laws of our being, is fast hastening the final crisis, and

"Have ye chosen, O my people, on whose party ye shall stand,
Ere the Doom from its worn sandal shakes the dust against our land?"

Are you a Christian? This is the carrying out of practical Christianity; and there is no other. Christianity is *practical* in its very nature and essence. It is a life, springing out of a soul imbued with its spirit. Are you a friend of the missionary cause? This is the greatest missionary enterprise of the day. Three millions of *Christian,* law-manufactured heathen are longing for the glad tidings of the gospel of freedom. Are you a friend of the Bible? Come, then, and help us to restore to these millions, whose eyes have been bored out by slavery, their sight, that they may see to read the Bible. Do you love God whom you have not seen? Then manifest that love, by restoring to your brother whom you have seen his rightful inheritance, of which he has been so long and so cruelly deprived.

It is not for a single generation alone, numbering three millions— sublime as would be that effort—that we are working. It is for Humanity, the wide world over, not only now, but for all coming time, and all future generations:—

> "For he who settles Freedom's principles,
> Writes the death-warrant of all tyranny."

It is a vast work—a glorious enterprise—worthy the unswerving devotion of the entire life-time of the great and the good.

Slaveholding and slaveholders must be rendered disreputable and odious. They must be stripped of their respectability and Christian reputation. They must be treated as "MEN-STEALERS—guilty of the highest kind of theft, and sinners of the first rank." Their more guilty accomplices in the persons of *northern apologists,* both in Church and State, must be placed in the same category. Honest men must be made to look upon their crimes with the same abhorrence and loathing with which they regard the less guilty robber and assassin, until

> "The common damned shun their society,
> And look upon themselves as fiends less foul."

When a just estimate is placed upon the crime of slave-holding, the work will have been accomplished, and the glorious day ushered in—

> "When man nor woman in all our wide domain,
> Shall buy, or sell, or hold, or be a slave."

J. C. HATHAWAY

Farmington, N.Y., 1847.

CHAPTER I

I was born in Lexington, Ky. The man who stole me as soon as I was born, recorded the births of all the infants which he claimed to be born his property, in a book which he kept for that purpose. My mother's name was Elizabeth. She had seven children, viz.: Solomon, Leander, Benjamin, Joseph, Millford, Elizabeth, and myself. No two of us were children of the same father. My father's name, as I learned from my mother, was George Higgins. He was a white man, a relative of my master, and connected with some of the first families in Kentucky.

My master owned about forty slaves, twenty-five of whom were field hands. He removed from Kentucky to Missouri when I was quite young, and settled thirty or forty miles above St. Charles, on the Missouri, where, in addition to his practice as a physician, he carried on milling, merchandizing and farming. He had a large farm, the principal productions of which were tobacco and hemp. The slave cabins were situated on the back part of the farm, with the house of the overseer, whose name was Grove Cook, in their midst. He had the entire charge of the farm, and having no family, was allowed a woman to keep house for him, whose business it was to deal out the provisions for the hands.

A woman was also kept at the quarters to do the cooking for the field hands, who were summoned to their unrequited toil every morning at four o'clock, by the ringing of a bell, hung on a post near the house of the overseer. They were allowed half an hour to eat their breakfast, and get to the field. At half past four a horn was blown by the overseer, which was his signal to commence work; and every one that was not on the spot at the time, had to receive ten lashes from the negro-whip, with which the overseer always went armed. The handle was about three feet long, with the butt-end filled with lead, and the lash, six or seven feet in length, made of cow-hide, with platted wire on the end of it. This whip was put in requisition very frequently and freely, and a small offence on the part of a slave furnished an occasion for its use. During the time that Mr. Cook was overseer, I was a house servant—a situation preferable to that of a field hand, as I was better fed, better clothed, and not obliged to rise at the ringing of the bell, but about half an hour after. I have often laid and heard the crack of the whip, and the screams of the slave. My mother was a field hand, and one morning was ten or fifteen minutes behind the others in getting into the field. As soon as she reached the spot where they were at work, the overseer commenced whipping her. She cried, "Oh! pray—Oh! pray—Oh! pray"—these are generally the words of slaves, when imploring mercy at the hands of their oppressors. I heard her voice, and knew it, and jumped out of my bunk, and went to the door. Though the field was some distance from the house, I could hear every crack of the whip, and every groan and cry of my poor mother. I remained at the door, not daring to venture any further. The cold chills ran over me, and I wept aloud. After giving her ten lashes, the sound of the whip ceased, and I returned to my bed, and found no consolation but in my tears. Experience has taught me that nothing can be more heart-rending than for one to see a dear and beloved mother or sister tortured, and to hear their cries, and not be able to render them assistance. But such is the position which an American slave occupies.

My master, being a politician, soon found those who were ready to put him into office, for the favors he could render them; and a few years after his arrival in Missouri he was elected to a seat in the legislature. In his absence from home everything was left in charge of Mr. Cook, the overseer, and he soon became more tyrannical and cruel. Among the slaves on the plantation was one by the name of Randall. He was a man of great strength and power. He was considered the most valuable and able-bodied slave on the plantation; but no matter how good or useful a slave may be, he seldom escapes the lash. But it was not so with Randall. He had been on the plantation since my earliest recollection, and I had never known of his being flogged. No thanks were due to the master or overseer for this. I have often heard him declare that no white man should ever whip him— that he would die first.

Cook, from the time that he came upon the plantation, had frequently declared that he could and would flog any nigger that was put into the field to work under him. My master had repeatedly told him not to attempt to whip Randall, but he was determined to try it. As soon as he was left sole dictator, he thought the time had come to put his threats into execution. He soon began to find fault with Randall, and threatened to whip him if he did not do better. One day he gave him a very hard task—more than he could possibly do; and at night, the task not being performed, he told Randall that he should remember him the next morning. On the following morning, after the hands had taken breakfast, Cook called out to Randall, and told him that he intended to whip him, and ordered him to cross his hands and be tied. Randall asked why he wished to whip him. He answered, because he had not finished his task the day before. Randall said that the task was too great, or he should have done it. Cook said it made no difference—he should whip him. Randall stood silent for a moment, and then said, "Mr. Cook, I have always tried to please you since you have been on the plantation, and I find you are determined not to be satisfied with my work, let me do as well as I may. No man had laid hands on me, to whip me, for the last ten years, and I have long since come to the conclusion not to be whipped by any man living." Cook, finding by Randall's determined look and gestures, that he would resist, called three of the hands from their work, and commanded them to seize Randall, and tie him. The hands stood still;—they knew Randall—and they also knew him to be a powerful man, and were afraid to grapple with him. As soon as Cook had ordered the men to seize him, Randall turned to them, and said—"Boys, you all know me; you know that I can handle any three of you, and the man that lays hands on me shall die. This white man can't whip me himself, and therefore he has called you to help him." The overseer was unable to prevail upon them to seize and secure Randall, and finally ordered them all to go to their work together.

Nothing was said to Randall by the overseer for more than a week. One morning, however, while the hands were at work in the field, he came into it, accompanied by three friends of his, Thompson, Woodbridge and Jones. They came up to where Randall was at work, and Cook ordered him to leave his work, and go with them to the barn. He refused to go; whereupon he was attacked by the overseer and his companions, when he turned upon them, and laid them, one after another, prostrate on the ground. Woodbridge drew out his pistol, and fired at him, and brought him to the ground by a pistol ball. The others rushed upon him with their clubs, and beat him over the head and face, until they succeeded in tying him. He was then taken to the barn, and tied to a beam. Cook gave him over one hundred lashes with a heavy cowhide, had him washed with salt and water, and left him tied during the day. The next day he was untied, and taken to a blacksmith's shop, and had a ball and chain attached to his leg. He was compelled to labor in the field, and perform the same amount of work that the other hands did. When his master returned home, he was much pleased to find that Randall had been subdued in his absence.

CHAPTER II

Soon afterwards, my master removed to the city of St. Louis, and purchased a farm four miles from there, which he placed under the charge of an overseer by the name of Friend Haskell. He was a regular Yankee from New England. The Yankees are noted for making the most cruel overseers.

My mother was hired out in the city, and I was also hired out there to Major Freeland, who kept a public house. He was formerly from Virginia, and was a horse-racer, cock-fighter, gambler, and withal an inveterate drunkard. There were ten or twelve servants in the house, and when he was present, it was cut and slash—knock down and drag out. In his fits of anger, he would take up a chair, and throw it at a servant; and in his more rational moments, when he wished to chastise one, he would tie them up in the smoke-house, and whip them; after which, he would cause a fire to be made of tobacco stems, and smoke them. This he called *"Virginia play."*

I complained to my master of the treatment which I received from Major Freeland; but it made no difference. He cared nothing about it, so long as he received the money for my labor. After living with Major Freeland five or six months, I ran away, and went into the woods back of the city; and when night came on, I made my way to my master's farm, but was afraid to be seen, knowing that if Mr. Haskell, the overseer, should discover me, I should be again carried back to Major Freeland; so I kept in the woods. One day, while in the woods, I heard the barking and howling of dogs, and in a short time they came so near that I knew them to be the bloodhounds of Major Benjamin O'Fallon. He kept five or six, to hunt runaway slaves with.

As soon as I was convinced that it was them, I knew there was no chance of escape. I took refuge in the top of a tree, and the hounds were soon at its base, and there remained until the hunters came up in a half or three quarters of an hour afterwards. There were two men with the dogs, who, as soon as they came up, ordered me to descend. I came down, was tied, and taken to St. Louis jail. Major Freeland soon made his appearance, and took me out, and ordered me to follow him, which I did. After we returned home, I was tied up in the smoke-house, and was very severely whipped. After the major had flogged me to his satisfaction, he sent out his son Robert, a young man eighteen or twenty years of age, to see that I was well smoked. He made a fire of tobacco stems, which was soon set me to coughing and sneezing. This, Robert told me, was the way his father used to do to his slaves in Virginia. After giving me what they conceived to be a decent smoking, I was untied and again set to work.

Robert Freeland was a "chip of the old block." Though quite young, it was not unfrequently that he came home in a state of intoxication. He is now, I believe, a popular commander of a steamboat on the Mississippi river. Major Freeland soon after failed in business, and I was put on board the steamboat Missouri, which plied between St. Louis and Galena. The commander of the boat was William B. Culver. I remained on her during the sailing season, which was the most pleasant time for me that I had ever experienced. At the close of navigation I was hired to Mr. John Colburn, keeper of the Missouri Hotel. He was from one of the free states; but a more inveterate hater of the negro I do not believe ever walked God's green earth. This hotel was at that time one of the largest in the city, and there were employed in it twenty or thirty servants, mostly slaves.

Mr. Colburn was very abusive, not only to the servants, but to his wife also, who was an excellent woman, and one from whom I never knew a servant to receive a harsh word; but never did I know a kind one to a servant from her husband. Among the slaves employed in the hotel was one by the name of Aaron, who belonged to Mr. John F. Darby, a lawyer. Aaron was the knife-cleaner. One day, one of the knives was put on the table, not as clean as it might have been. Mr. Colburn, for this offence, tied Aaron up in the wood-house, and gave him over fifty lashes on the bare back with a cow-hide, after which, he made me wash him down with rum. This seemed to put him into more agony than the whipping. After being untied he went home to his master, and complained of the treatment which he had received. Mr. Darby would give no heed to anything he had to say, but sent him directly back. Colburn, learning that he had been to his master with complaints, tied him up again, and gave him a more severe whipping than before. The poor fellow's back was literally cut to pieces; so much so, that he was not able to work for ten or twelve days.

There was, also, among the servants, a girl whose master resided in the country. Her name was Patsey. Mr. Colburn tied her up one evening, and whipped her until several of the boarders came out and begged him to desist. The reason for whipping her was this. She was engaged to be married to a man belonging to Major William Christy, who resided four or five miles north of the city. Mr. Colburn had forbid her to see John Christy. The reason of this was said to be the regard which he himself had for Patsey. She went to meeting that evening, and John returned home with her. Mr. Colburn had intended to flog John, if he came within the inclosure; but John knew too well the temper of his rival, and kept at a safe distance:—so he took vengeance on the poor girl. If all the slave-drivers had been called together, I do not think a more cruel man than John Colburn—and he too a northern man—could have been found among them.

While living at the Missouri hotel, a circumstance occurred which caused me great unhappiness. My master sold my mother, and all her children, except myself. They were sold to different persons in the city of St. Louis.

CHAPTER III

I was soon after taken from Mr. Colburn's, and hired to Elijah P. Lovejoy,* who was at that time publisher and editor of the "St. Louis Times." My work, while with him, was mainly in the printing office, waiting on the hands, working the press, &c. Mr. Lovejoy was a very good man, and decidedly the best master that I had ever had. I am chiefly indebted to him, and to my employment in the printing office, for what little learning I obtained while in slavery.

Though slavery is thought, by some, to be mild in Missouri, when compared with the cotton, sugar and rice growing states, yet no part of our slaveholding country is more noted for the barbarity of its inhabitants than St. Louis. It was here that Col. Harney, a United States officer, whipped a slave woman to death. It was here that Francis McIntosh, a free colored

---

*In the memoir of Brown's life which was included with his novel *Clotel* he identified Lovejoy as the abolitionist editor who was murdered in Alton, Illinois in 1837 while defending his press against a mob. William Wells Brown, *Clotel, or the President's Daughter, a Narrative of Slave Life in the United States* (London, 1853), 4.

man from Pittsburg, was taken from the steamboat Flora and burned at the stake. During a residence of eight years in this city, numerous cases of extreme cruelty came under my own observation; to record them all would occupy more space than could possibly be allowed in this little volume. I shall, therefore, give but a few more in addition to what I have already related.

Capt. J. B. Brant, who resided near my master, had a slave named John. He was his body servant, carriage driver, &c. On one occasion, while driving his master through the city—the streets being very muddy, and the horses going at a rapid rate—some mud spattered upon a gentleman by the name of Robert More. More was determined to be revenged. Some three or four months after this occurrence, he purchased John, for the express purpose, as he said "to tame the d——d nigger." After the purchase he took him to a blacksmith's shop, and had a ball and chain fastened to his leg, and then put him to driving a yoke of oxen, and kept him at hard labor, until the iron around his leg was so worn into the flesh, that it was thought mortification would ensue. In addition to this, John told me that his master whipped him regularly three times a week for the first two months:—and all this to *"tame him."* A more noble looking man than he was not to be found in all St. Louis, before he fell into the hands of More; and a more degraded and spirit-crushed looking being was never seen on a southern plantation, after he had been subjected to this *"taming"* process for three months. The last time that I saw him, he had nearly lost the entire use of his limbs.

While living with Mr. Lovejoy, I was often sent on errands to the office of the "Missouri Republican," published by Mr. Edward Charles. Once, while returning to the office with type, I was attacked by several large boys, sons of slave-holders, who pelted me with snow-balls. Having the heavy form of type in my hands, I could not make my escape by running; so I laid down the type and gave them battle. They gathered around me, pelting me with stones and sticks, until they overpowered me, and would have captured me, if I had not resorted to my heels. Upon my retreat they took possession of the type; and what to do to regain it I could not devise. Knowing Mr. Lovejoy to be a very humane man, I went to the office and laid the case before him. He told me to remain in the office. He took one of the apprentices with him and went after the type, and soon returned with it; but on his return informed me that Samuel McKinney had told him he would whip me, because I had hurt his boy. Soon after, McKinney was seen making his way to the office by one of the printers, who informed me of the fact, and I made my escape through the back door.

McKinney not being able to find me on his arrival, left the office in a great rage, swearing that he would whip me to death. A few days after, as I was walking along Main street, he seized me by the collar, and struck me over the head five or six times with a large cane, which caused the blood to gush from my nose and ears in such a manner that my clothes were completely saturated with blood. After beating me to his satisfaction he let me go, and I returned to the office so weak from the loss of blood that Mr. Lovejoy sent me home to my master. It was five weeks before I was able to walk again. During this time it was necessary to have some one to supply my place at the office, and I lost the situation.

After my recovery, I was hired to Capt. Otis Reynolds, as a waiter on board the steamboat Enterprise, owned by Messrs. John and Edward Walsh, commission merchants at St. Louis. This boat was then running on the upper Mississippi. My employment on board was to wait on gentlemen, and the captain being a good man, the situation was a pleasant one to me;—but in passing from place to place, and seeing new faces every day, and knowing that they could go where they pleased, I soon became unhappy, and several times thought of leaving the boat at some landing-place, and trying to make my escape to Canada, which I had heard much about as a place where the slave might live, be free, and be protected.

But whenever such thoughts would come into my mind, my resolution would soon be shaken by the remembrance that my dear mother was a slave in St. Louis, and I could not bear the idea of leaving her in that condition. She had often taken me upon her knee, and told me how she had carried me upon her back to the field when I was an infant—how often she had been whipped for leaving her work to nurse me—and how happy I would appear when she would take me into her arms. When these thoughts came over me, I would resolve never to leave the land of slavery without my mother. I thought that to leave her in slavery, after she had undergone and suffered so much for me, would be proving recreant to the duty which I owed to her. Besides this, I had three brothers and a sister there— two of my brothers having died.

My mother, my brothers Joseph and Millford, and my sister Elizabeth, belonged to Mr. Isaac Mansfield, formerly from one of the free states, (Massachusetts, I believe). He was a tinner by trade, and carried on a large manufacturing establishment. Of all my relatives, mother was first, and sister next. One evening, while visiting them, I made some allusion to a proposed journey to Canada, and sister took her seat by my side, and taking my hand in hers, said, with tears in her eyes—

"Brother, you are not going to leave mother and your dear sister here without a friend, are you?"

I looked into her face, as the tears coursed swiftly down her cheeks, and bursting into tears myself, said—

"No, I will never desert you and mother!"

She clasped my hand in hers, and said—

"Brother, you have often declared that you would not end your days in slavery. I see no possible way in which you can escape with us; and now, brother, you are on a steamboat where there is some chance for you to escape to a land of liberty. I beseech you not to let us hinder you. If we cannot get our liberty, we do not wish to be the means of keeping you from a land of freedom."

I could restrain my feelings no longer, and an outburst of my own feelings caused her to cease speaking upon that subject. In opposition to their wishes, I pledged myself not to leave them in the hand of the oppressor. I took leave of them, and returned to the boat, and laid down in my bunk; but "sleep departed from mine eyes, and slumber from mine eyelids."

A few weeks after, on our downward passage, the boat took on board, at Hannibal, a drove of slaves, bound for the New Orleans market. They numbered from fifty to sixty, consisting of men and women from eighteen to forty years of age. A drove of slaves on a southern steamboat, bound for the cotton or sugar regions, is an occurrence so common, that no one, not even the passengers, appear to notice it, though they clank their chains at every step. There was, however, one in this gang that attracted the attention of the passengers and crew. It was a beautiful girl, apparently about twenty years of age, perfectly white, with straight light hair and blue eyes. But it was not the whiteness of her skin that created such sensation among those who gazed upon her—it was her almost unparalleled beauty. She had been on the boat but a short time, before the attention of all the passengers, including the ladies, had been called to her, and the common topic of conversation was about the beautiful slave-girl. She was not in chains. The man who claimed this article of human merchandise was a Mr. Walker—a well known slave-trader, residing in St. Louis. There was a general anxiety among the passengers and crew to learn the history of the girl. Her master kept close by her side, and it would have been considered impudent for any of the passengers to have spoken to her, and the crew were not allowed to have any conversation with them. When we reached St. Louis, the slaves were removed to a boat bound for New Orleans, and the history of the beautiful slave-girl remained a mystery.

I remained on the boat during the season, and it was not an unfrequent occurrence to have on board gangs of slaves on their way to the cotton, sugar and rice plantations of the south.

Toward the latter part of the summer Captain Reynolds left the boat, and I was sent home. I was then placed on the farm, under Mr. Haskell, the overseer. As I had been some time out of the field, and not accustomed to work in the burning sun, it was very hard; but I was compelled to keep up with the best of the hands.

I found a great difference between the work in the steamboat cabin and that in a corn-field.

My master, who was then living in the city, soon after removed to the farm, when I was taken out of the field to work in the house as a waiter. Though his wife was very peevish, and hard to please, I much preferred to be under her control than the overseer's. They brought with them Mr. Sloane, a Presbyterian minister; Miss Martha Tulley, a niece of theirs from Kentucky; and their nephew William. The latter had been in the family a number of years, but the others were all newcomers.

Mr. Sloane was a young minister, who had been at the south but a short time, and it seemed as if his whole aim was to please the slaveholders, especially my master and mistress. He was intending to make a visit during the winter, and he not only tried to please them, but I think he succeeded admirably. When they wanted singing, he sung; when they wanted praying, he prayed; when they wanted a story told, he told a story. Instead of his teaching my master theology, my master taught theology to him. While I was with Captain Reynolds my master "got religion," and new laws were made on the plantation. Formerly we had the privilege of hunting, fishing, making splint brooms, baskets, &c., on Sunday; but this was all stopped. Every Sunday we were all compelled to attend meeting. Master was so religious that he induced some others to join him in hiring a preacher to preach to the slaves.

CHAPTER IV

My master had family worship, night and morning. At night the slaves were called in to attend; but in the mornings they had to be at their work, and master did all the praying. My master and mistress were great lovers of mint julep, and every morning, a pitcher-full was made, of which they all partook freely, not excepting little master William. After drinking freely all around, they would have family worship, and then breakfast. I cannot say but I loved the julep as well as any of them, and during prayer was always careful to seat myself close to the table where it stood, so as to help myself when they were all busily engaged in their devotions. By the time prayer was over, I was about as happy as any of them. A sad accident happened one morning. In helping myself, and at the same time keeping an eye on my old mistress, I accidentally let the pitcher fall upon the floor, breaking it in pieces, and spilling the contents. This was a bad affair for me; for as soon as prayer was over, I was taken and severely chastised.

My master's family consisted of himself, his wife, and their nephew, William Moore. He was taken into the family when only a few weeks of age. His name being that of my own, mine was changed for the purpose of giving precedence to his, though I was his senior by ten or twelve years. The plantation being four miles from the city, I had to drive the family to church. I always dreaded the approach of the Sabbath; for, during service, I was obliged to stand by the horses in the hot, broiling sun, or in the rain, just as it happened.

One Sabbath, as we were driving past the house of D. D. Page, a gentleman who owned a large baking establishment, as I was sitting upon the box of the carriage, which was very much elevated, I saw Mr. Page pursuing a slave around the yard with a long whip, cutting him at every jump. The man soon escaped from the yard, and was followed by Mr. Page. They came running past us, and the slave, perceiving that he would be overtaken, stopped suddenly, and Page stumbled over him, and falling on the stone pavement, fractured one of his legs, which crippled him for life. The same gentleman, but a short time previous, tied up a woman of his, by the name of Delphia, and whipped her nearly to death; yet he was a deacon in the Baptist church, in good and regular standing. Poor Delphia! I was well acquainted with her, and called to see her while upon her sick bed; and I shall never forget her appearance. She was a member of the same church with her master.

Soon after this, I was hired out to Mr. Walker, the same man whom I have mentioned as having carried a gang of slaves down the river on the steamboat Enterprise. Seeing me in the capacity of a steward on the boat, and thinking that I would make a good hand to take care of slaves, he determined to have me for that purpose; and finding that my master would not sell me, he hired me for the term of one year.

When I learned the fact of my having been hired to a negro speculator, or a "soul driver," as they are generally called among slaves, no one can tell my emotions. Mr. Walker had offered a high price for me, as I afterwards learned, but I suppose my master was restrained from selling me by the fact that I was a near relative of his. On entering the service of Mr. Walker, I found that my opportunity of getting to a land of liberty was gone, at least for the time being. He had a gang of slaves in readiness to start for New Orleans, and in a few days we were on our journey. I am at a loss for language to express my feelings on that occasion. Although my master had told me that he had not sold me, and Mr. Walker had told me that he had not purchased me, I did not believe them; and not until I had been to New Orleans, and was on my return, did I believe that I was not sold.

There was on the boat a large room on the lower deck, in which the slaves were kept, men and women, promiscuously—all chained two and two, and a strict watch kept that they did not get loose; for cases have occurred in which slaves have got off their chains, and made their escape at landing-places, while the boats were taking in wood;—and with all our care, we lost one woman who had been taken from her husband and children, and having no desire to live without them, in the agony of her soul jumped overboard, and drowned herself. She was not chained.

It was almost impossible to keep that part of the boat clean.

On landing at Natchez, the slaves were all carried to the slave-pen, and there kept one week, during which time several of them were sold. Mr. Walker fed his slaves well. We took on board at St. Louis several hundred pounds of bacon (smoked meat) and corn-meal, and his slaves were better fed than slaves generally were in Natchez, so far as my observation extended.

At the end of a week, we left for New Orleans, the place of our final destination, which we reached in two days. Here the slaves were placed in a negro-pen, where those who wished to purchase could call and examine them. The negro-pen is a small yard, surrounded by buildings, from fifteen to twenty feet wide, with the exception of a large gate with iron bars. The slaves are kept in the building during the night, and turned out into the yard during the day. After the best of the stock was sold at private sale at the pen, the balance were taken to the Exchange Coffee-House Auction Rooms, kept by Isaac L. McCoy, and sold at public auction. After the sale of this lot of slaves, we left New Orleans for St. Louis.

CHAPTER V

On our arrival at St. Louis I went to Dr. Young, and told him that I did not wish to live with Mr. Walker any longer. I was heart-sick at seeing my fellow-creatures bought and sold. But the Dr. had hired me for the year, and stay I must. Mr. Walker again commenced purchasing another gang of slaves. He bought a man of Colonel John O'Fallon, who resided in the suburbs of the city. This man had a wife and three children. As soon as the purchase was made, he was put in jail for safe keeping, until we should be ready to start for New Orleans. His wife visited him while there, several times, and several times when she went for that purpose was refused admittance.

In the course of eight or nine weeks Mr. Walker had his cargo of human flesh made up. There was in this lot a number of old men and women, some of them with gray locks. We left St. Louis in the steamboat Carlton, Captain Swan, bound for New Orleans. On our way down, and before we reached Rodney, the place where we made our first stop, I had to prepare the old slaves for market. I was ordered to have the old men's whiskers shaved off, and the grey hairs plucked out where they were not too numerous, in which case he had a preparation of blacking to color it, and with a blacking brush we would put it on. This was new business to me, and was performed in a room where the passengers could not see us. These slaves were also taught how old they were by Mr. Walker, and after going through the blacking process they looked ten or fifteen years younger; and I am sure that some of those who purchased slaves of Mr. Walker were dreadfully cheated, especially in the ages of the slaves which they bought.

We landed at Rodney, and the slaves were driven to the pen in the back part of the village. Several were sold at this place, during our stay of four or five days, when we proceeded to Natchez. There we landed at night, and the gang were put in the warehouse until morning, when they were driven to the pen. As soon as the slaves are put in these pens, swarms of planters may be seen in and about them. They knew when Walker was expected, as he always had the time advertised beforehand when he would be in Rodney, Natchez, and New Orleans. These were the principal places where he offered his slaves for sale.

When at Natchez the second time, I saw a slave very cruelly whipped. He belonged to a Mr. Broadwell, merchant who kept a store on the wharf. The slave's name was Lewis. I had known him several years, as he was formerly from St. Louis. We were expecting a steamboat down the river, in which we were to take passage for New Orleans. Mr. Walker sent me to the landing to watch for the boat, ordering me to inform him on its arrival. While there I went into the store to see Lewis. I saw a slave in the store, and asked him where Lewis was. Said he, "They have got Lewis hanging between the heavens and the earth." I asked him what he meant by that. He told me to go into the warehouse and see. I went in, and found Lewis there. He was tied up to a beam, with his toes just touching the floor. As there was no one in the warehouse but himself, I inquired the reason of his being in that situation. He said Mr. Broadwell had sold his wife to a planter six miles from the city, and that he had been to visit her—that he went in the night, expecting to return before daylight, and went without his master's permission. The patrol had taken him up before he reached his wife. He was put in jail, and his master had to pay for his catching and keeping, and that was what he was tied up for.

Just as he finished his story, Mr. Broadwell came in, and inquired what I was doing there. I knew not what to say, and while I was thinking what reply to make he struck me over the head with the cowhide, the end of which struck me over my right eye, sinking deep into the flesh, leaving a scar which I carry to this day. Before I visited Lewis he had received fifty lashes. Mr. Broadwell gave him fifty lashes more after I came out, as I was afterwards informed by Lewis himself.

The next day we proceeded to New Orleans, and put the gang in the same negro-pen which we occupied before. In a short time the planters came flocking to the pen to purchase slaves. Before the slaves were exhibited for sale, they were dressed and driven out into the yard. Some were set to dancing, some to jumping, some to singing, and some to playing cards. This was done to make them appear cheerful and happy. My business was to see that they were placed in those situations before the arrival of the purchasers, and I have often set them to dancing when their cheeks were wet with tears. As slaves were in good demand at that time, they were all soon disposed of, and we again set out for St. Louis.

On our arrival, Mr. Walker purchased a farm five or six miles from the city. He had no family, but made a housekeeper of one of his female slaves. Poor Cynthia! I knew her well. She was a quadroon, and one of the most beautiful women I ever saw. She was a native of St. Louis, and bore an irreproachable character for virtue and propriety of conduct. Mr. Walker bought her for the New Orleans market, and took her down with him on one of the trips that I made with him. Never shall I forget the circumstances of that voyage! On the first night that we were on board the steamboat, he directed me to put her into a state-room he had provided for her, apart from the other slaves. I had seen too much of the workings of slavery not to know what this meant. I accordingly watched him into the state-room, and listened to hear what passed between them. I heard him make his base offers, and her reject them. He told her that if she would accept his vile proposals, he would take her back with him to St. Louis, and establish her as his housekeeper on his farm. But if she persisted in rejecting them, he would sell her as a field hand on the worst plantation on the river. Neither threats nor bribes prevailed, however, and he retired, disappointed of his prey.

The next morning poor Cynthia told me what had passed, and bewailed her sad fate with floods of tears. I comforted and encouraged her all I could; but I foresaw but too well what the result must be. Without entering into any further particulars, suffice it to say that Walker performed his part of the contract at that time. He took her back to St. Louis, established her as his mistress and housekeeper at his farm, and before I left, he had two children by her. But, mark the end! Since I have been at the North, I have been credibly informed that Walker has been married, and, as a previous measure, sold Cynthia and her four children (she having had two more since I came away) into hopeless bondage![3]

He soon commenced purchasing to make up the third gang. We took steamboat, and went to Jefferson City, a town on the Missouri river. Here we landed, and took stage for the interior of the state. He bought a number of slaves as he passed the different farms and villages. After getting twenty-two or twenty-three men and women, we arrived at St. Charles, a village on the banks of the Missouri. Here he purchased a woman who had a child in her arms, appearing to be four or five weeks old.

We had been travelling by land for some days, and were in hopes to have found a boat at this place for St. Louis, but were disappointed. As no boat was expected for some days, we started for St. Louis by land. Mr. Walker had purchased two horses. He rode one, and I the other. The slaves were chained together, and we took up our line of march, Mr. Walker taking the lead, and I bringing up the rear. Though the distance was not more than twenty miles, we did not reach it the first day. The road was worse than any that I have ever travelled.

Soon after we left St. Charles the young child grew very cross, and kept up a noise during the greater part of the day. Mr. Walker complained of its crying several times, and told the mother to stop the child's d— —d noise, or he would. The woman tried to keep the child from crying, but could not. We put up at night with an acquaintance of Mr. Walker, and in the morning, just as we were about to start, the child again commenced crying. Walker stepped up to her, and told her to give the child to him. The mother tremblingly obeyed. He took the child by one arm, as you would a cat by the leg, walked into the house, and said to the lady,

"Madam, I will make you a present of this little nigger; it keeps such a noise that I can't bear it."

"Thank you, sir," said the lady.

The mother, as soon as she saw that her child was to be left, ran up to Mr. Walker, and falling upon her knees, begged him to let her have her child; she clung around his legs, and cried, "Oh, my child! my child! master, do let me have my child! oh, do, do, do! I will stop its crying if you will only let me have it again." When I saw this woman crying for her child so piteously, a shudder—a feeling akin to horror—shot through my frame. I have often since in imagination heard her crying for her child:—

"O, master, let me stay to catch
  My baby's sobbing breath,
His little glassy eye to watch,
  And smooth his limbs in death,

And cover him with grass and leaf,
  Beneath the large oak tree:
It is not sullenness, but grief—
  O, master, pity me!

The morn was chill—I spoke no word,
  But feared my babe might die,
And heard all day, or thought I heard,
  My little baby cry.

At noon, oh, how I ran and took
  My baby to my breast!
I lingered—and the long lash broke
  My sleeping infant's rest.

I worked till night—till darkest night,
  In torture and disgrace;
Went home and watched till morning light,
  To see my baby's face.

Then give me one little hour—
  O! do not lash me so!

One little hour—one little hour—
　　And gratefully I'll go."

Mr. Walker commanded her to return into the ranks with the other slaves. Women who had children were not chained, but those that had none were. As soon as her child was disposed of she was chained in the gang.

The following song I have often heard the slaves sing, when about to be carried to the far south. It is said to have been composed by a slave.

"See these poor souls from Africa
Transported to America;
We are stolen, and sold to Georgia—
Will you go along with me?
We are stolen, and sold to Georgia—
Come sound the jubilee!

See wives and husbands sold apart,
Their children's screams will break my heart;—
There's a better day a coming—
Will you go along with me?
There's a better day a coming,
Go sound the jubilee!

O, gracious Lord! when shall it be,
That we poor souls shall all be free?
Lord, break them slavery powers—
Will you go along with me?
Lord, break them slavery powers,
Go sound the jubilee!

Dear Lord, dear Lord, when slavery 'll cease,
Then we poor souls will have our peace;—
There's a better day a coming—
Will you go along with me?
There's a better day a coming,
Go sound the jubilee!"

We finally arrived at Mr. Walker's farm. He had a house built during our absence to put slaves in. It was a kind of domestic jail. The slaves were put in the jail at night, and worked on the farm during the day. They were kept here until the gang was completed, when we again started for New Orleans, on board the steamboat North America, Capt. Alexander Scott. We had a large number of slaves in this gang. One, by the name of Joe, Mr. Walker was training up to take my place, as my time was nearly out, and glad was I. We made our first stop at Vicksburg, where we remained one week and sold several slaves.

Mr. Walker, though not a good master, had not flogged a slave since I had been with him, though he had threatened me. The slaves were kept in the pen, and he always put up at the best hotel, and kept his wines in his room, for the accommodation of those who called to negotiate with him for the purchase of slaves. One day, while we were at Vicksburg, several gentlemen came to see him for that purpose, and as usual the wine was called for. I took the tray and started around with it, and having accidentally filled some of the glasses too full, the gentlemen spilled the wine on their clothes as they went to drink. Mr. Walker apologized to them for my carelessness, but looked at me as though he would see me again on this subject.

After the gentlemen had left the room, he asked me what I meant by my carelessness, and said that he would attend to me. The next morning he gave me a note to carry to the jailer, and a dollar in money to give to him. I suspected that all was not right, so I went down near the landing, where I met with a sailor, and, walking up to him, asked him if he would be so kind as to read the note for me. He read it over, and then looked at me. I asked him to tell me what was in it. Said he,

"They are going to give you hell."

"Why?" said I.

He said, "This is a note to have you whipped, and says that you have a dollar to pay for it."

He handed me back the note, and off I started. I knew not what to do, but was determined not to be whipped. I went up to the jail—took a look at it, and walked off again. As Mr. Walker was acquainted with the jailer, I feared that I should be found out if I did not go, and be treated in consequence of it still worse.

While I was meditating on the subject, I saw a colored man about my size walk up, and the thought struck me in a moment to send him with my note. I walked up to him, and asked him who he belonged to. He said he was a free man, and had been in the city but a short time. I told him I had a note to go into the jail, and get a trunk to carry to one of the steamboats; but was so busily engaged that I could not do it, although I had a dollar to pay for it. He asked me if I would not give him the job. I handed him the note and the dollar, and off he started for the jail.

I watched to see that he went in, and as soon as I saw the door close behind him, I walked around the corner, and took my station, intending to see how my friend looked when he came out. I had been there but a short time, when a colored man came around the corner, and said to another colored man with whom he was acquainted—

"They are giving a nigger scissors in the jail."

"What for?" said the other. The man continued.

"A nigger came into the jail, and asked for the jailer. The jailer came out, and he handed him a note, and said he wanted to get a trunk. The jailor told him to go with him, and he would give him the trunk. So he took him into the room, and told the nigger to give up the dollar. He said a man had given him the dollar to pay for getting the trunk. But that lie would not answer. So they made him strip himself, and then they tied him down, and are now whipping him."

I stood by all the while listening to their talk, and soon found out that the person alluded to was my customer. I went into the street opposite the jail, and concealed myself in such a manner that I could not be seen by any one coming out. I had been there but a short time, when the young man made his appearance, and looked around for me. I, unobserved, came forth from my hiding place, behind a pile of brick, and he pretty soon saw me, and came up to me complaining bitterly, saying that I had played a trick upon him. I denied any knowledge of what the note contained, and asked him what they had done to him. He told me in substance what I heard the man tell who had come out of the jail.

"Yes," he said he, "they whipped me and took my dollar, and gave me this note."

He showed me the note which the jailer had given him, telling him to give it to his master. I told him I would give him fifty cents for it—that being all the money I had. He gave it to me and took his money. He had received twenty lashes on his bare back, with the negro-whip.

I took the note and started for the hotel where I had left Mr. Walker. Upon reaching the hotel, I handed it to a stranger whom I had not seen before, and requested him to read it to me. As near as I can recollect, it was as follows:—

"Dear Sir:—By your direction, I have given your boy twenty lashes. He is a very saucy boy, and tried to make me believe that he did not belong to you, and I put it on to him well for lying to me.
                    "I remain
                              "Your obedient servant."

It is true that in most of the slave-holding cities, when a gentleman wishes his servants whipped, he can send him to the jail and have it done. Before I went in where Mr. Walker was, I wet my cheeks a little, as though I had been crying. He looked at me, and inquired what was the matter. I told that I had never had such a whipping in my life, and handed him the note. He looked at it and laughed;—"And so you told him that you did not belong to me?" "Yes, sir," said I. "I did not know that there was any harm in that." He told me I must behave myself, if I did not want to be whipped again.

This incident shows how it is that slavery makes its victims lying and mean; for which vices it afterwards reproaches them, and uses them as arguments to prove that they deserve no better fate. Had I entertained the same views of right and wrong which I now do, I am sure I should never have practised the deception upon that poor fellow which I did. I know of no act committed by me while in slavery which I have regretted more than that; and I heartily desire that it may be at some time or other in my power to make him amends for his vicarious sufferings in my behalf.

CHAPTER VI

In a few days we reached New Orleans, and arriving there in the night, remained on board until morning. While at New Orleans this time, I saw a slave killed; an account of which has been published by Theodore D. Weld, in his book entitled "Slavery as it is."* The circumstances were as follows. In the evening, between seven and eight o'clock, a slave came running down the levee, followed by several men and boys. The whites were crying out, "Stop that nigger! stop that nigger!" while the poor panting slave, in almost breathless accents, was repeating, "I did not steal the meat—I did not steal the meat." The poor man at last took refuge in the river. The whites who were in pursuit of him, run on board of one of the boats to see if they could discover him. They finally espied him under the bow of the steamboat Trenton. They got a pike-pole, and tried to drive him from his hiding place. When they would strike at him he would dive under the water. The water was so cold, that it soon became evident that he must come out or be drowned.

While they were trying to drive him from under the bow of the boat or drown him, he would in broken and imploring accents say, "I did not steal the meat; I did not steal the meat. My master lives up the river. I want to

---

*Theodore D. Weld, *Slavery As It Is: Testimony of a Thousand Witnesses* (New York, 1839) included numerous clippings of incidents involving slaves from various southern newspapers.

see my master. I did not steal the meat. Do let me go home to master."
After punching him, and striking him over the head for some time, he at
last sunk in the water, to rise no more alive.

On the end of the pike-pole with which they were striking him was a
hook, which caught in his clothing, and they hauled him up on the bow of
the boat. Some said he was dead; others said he was *"playing possum;"*
while others kicked him to make him get up; but it was of no use—he was
dead.

As soon as they became satisfied of this, they commenced leaving, one
after another. One of the hands on the boat informed the captain that they
had killed the man, and that the dead body was lying on the deck. The
captain came on deck, and said to those who were remaining, "You have
killed this nigger; now take him off of my boat." The captain's name was
Hart. The dead body was dragged on shore and left there. I went on board
of the boat where our gang of slaves were, and during the whole night my
mind was occupied with what I had seen. Early in the morning I went on
shore to see if the dead body remained there. I found it in the same
position that it was left the night before. I watched to see what they would
do with it. It was left there until between eight and nine o'clock, when a
cart, which takes up the trash out of the streets, came along, and the body
was thrown in, and in a few minutes more was covered over with dirt which
they were removing from the streets. During the whole time, I did not see
more than six or seven persons around it, who, from their manner, evidently regarded it as no uncommon occurrence.

During our stay in the city I met with a young white man with whom I
was well acquainted in St. Louis. He had been sold into slavery, under the
following circumstances. His father was a drunkard, and very poor, with a
family of five or six children. The father died, and left the mother to take
care of and provide for the children as best she might. The eldest was a
boy, named Burrill, about thirteen years of age, who did chores in a store
kept by Mr. Riley, to assist his mother in procuring a living for the family.
After working with him two years, Mr. Riley took him to New Orleans to
wait on him while in that city on a visit, and when he returned to St. Louis,
he told the mother of the boy that he had died with the yellow fever.
Nothing more was heard from him, no one supposing him to be alive. I was
much astonished when Burrill told me his story. Though I sympathized
wth him I could not assist him. We were both slaves. He was poor,
uneducated, and without friends; and, if living, is, I presume, still held as a
slave.[4]

After selling out his cargo of human flesh, we returned to St. Louis, and
my time was up with Mr. Walker. I had served him one year, and it was the
longest year I ever lived.

CHAPTER VII

I was sent home, and was glad enough to leave the service of one who was tearing the husband from the wife, the child from the mother, and the sister from the brother—but a trial more severe and heart-rending than any which I had yet met with awaited me. My dear sister had been sold to a man who was going to Natchez, and was lying in jail awaiting the hour of his departure. She had expressed her determination to die, rather than go to the far south, and she was put in jail for safekeeping. I went to the jail the same day that I arrived, but as the jailer was not in I could not see her.

I went home to my master, in the country, and the first day after my return he came where I was at work, and spoke to me very politely. I knew from his appearance that something was the matter. After talking to me about my several journeys to New Orleans with Mr. Walker, he told me that he was hard pressed for money, and as he had sold my mother and all her children except me, he thought it would be better to sell me than any other one, and that as I had been used to living in the city, he thought it probable that I would prefer it to country life. I raised up my head, and looked him full in the face. When my eyes caught his he immediately looked to the ground. After a short pause, I said,

"Master, mother has often told me that you are a near relative of mine, and I have often heard you admit the fact; and after you have hired me out, and received, as I once heard you say, nine hundred dollars for my services—after receiving this large sum, will you sell me to be carried to New Orleans or some other place?"

"No," said he, "I do not intend to sell you to a negro trader. If I had wished to have done that, I might have sold you to Mr. Walker for a large sum, but I would not sell you to a negro trader. You may go to the city, and find you a good master."

"But," said I, "I cannot find a good master in the whole city of St. Louis."

49

"Why?" said he.

"Because there are no good masters in the state."

"Do you not call me a good master?"

"If you were you would not sell me."

"Now I will give you one week to find a master in, and surely you can do it in that time."

The price set by my evangelical master upon my soul and body was the trifling sum of five hundred dollars. I tried to enter into some arrangement by which I might purchase my freedom; but he would enter into no such arrangement.

I set out for the city with the understanding that I was to return in a week with some one to become my new master. Soon after reaching the city, I went to the jail, to learn if I could once more see my sister; but could not gain admission. I then went to mother, and learned from her that the owner of my sister intended to start for Natchez in a few days.

I went to the jail again the next day, and Mr. Simonds, the keeper, allowed me to see my sister for the last time. I cannot give a just description of the scene at that parting interview. Never, never can be erased from my heart the occurrences of that day! When I entered the room where she was, she was seated in one corner, alone. There were four other women in the same room, belonging to the same man. He had purchased them, he said, for his own use. She was seated with her face towards the door where I entered, yet she did not look up until I walked up to her. As soon as she observed me she sprung up, threw her arms around my neck, leaned her head upon my breast, and without uttering a word, burst into tears. As soon as she recovered herself sufficiently to speak, she advised me to take mother, and try to get out of slavery. She said there was no hope for herself—that she must live and die a slave. After giving her some advice, and taking from my finger a ring and placing it upon hers, I bade her farewell forever, and returned to my mother, and then and there made up my mind to leave for Canada as soon as possible.

I had been in the city nearly two days, and as I was to be absent only a week, I thought best to get on my journey as soon as possible. In conversing with mother, I found her unwilling to make the attempt to reach a land of liberty, but she counselled me to get my liberty if I could. She said, as all her children were in slavery, she did not wish to leave them. I could not bear the idea of leaving her among those pirates, when there was a prospect of being able to get away from them. After much persuasion I succeeded in inducing her to make the attempt to get away.

The time fixed for our departure was the next night. I had with me a little money that I had received, from time to time, from gentlemen for whom I had done errands. I took my scanty means and purchased some dried beef, crackers and cheese, which I carried to mother, who had provided herself with a bag to carry it in. I occasionally thought of my old master, and of my mission to the city to find a new one. I waited with the most intense anxiety for the appointed time to leave the land of slavery, in search of a land of liberty.

The time at length arrived, and we left the city just as the clock struck nine. We proceeded to the upper part of the city, where I had been two or three times during the day, and selected a skiff to carry us across the river. The boat was not mine, nor did I know to whom it did belong; neither did I care. The boat was fastened with a small pole, which, with the aid of a rail, I soon loosened from its moorings. After hunting round and finding a board to use as an oar, I turned to the city, and bidding it a long farewell, pushed off my boat. The current running very swift, we had not reached the middle of the stream before we were directly opposite the city.

We were soon upon the Illinois shore, and, leaping from the boat, turned It adrift, and the last I saw of it it was going down the river at good speed. We took the main road to Alton, and passed through just at daylight, when we made for the woods, where we remained during the day. Our reason for going into the woods was, that we expected that Mr. Mansfield (the man who owned my mother) would start in pursuit of her as soon as he discovered that she was missing. He also knew that I had been in the city looking for a new master, and we thought probably he would go out to my master's to see if he could find my mother, and in so doing, Dr. Young might be led to suspect that I had gone to Canada to find a purchaser.

We remained in the woods during the day, and as soon as darkness overshadowed the earth, we started again on our gloomy way, having no guide but the NORTH STAR. We continued to travel by night, and secrete ourselves in the woods by day; and every night, before emerging from our hidingplace, we would anxiously look for our friend and leader—the NORTH STAR. And in the language of Pierpont* we might have exclaimed,

> "Star of the North! while blazing day
> Pours round me its full tide of light,
> And hides thy pale but faithful ray,
> I, too, lie hid, and long for night.
> For night;—I dare not walk at noon,

---

*John Pierpont (1785–1866) was a clergyman, reformer and abolitionist poet.

Nor dare I trust the faithless moon,
Nor faithless man, whose burning lust
For gold hath riveted my chain;
No other leader can I trust
But thee, of even the starry train;
For, all the host around thee burning,
Like faithless man, keep turning, turning.

In the dark top of southern pines
I nestled, when the driver's horn
Called to the field, in lengthening lines,
My fellows, at the break of morn.
And there I lay, till thy sweet face
Looked in upon my 'hiding place,'
Star of the North!
Thy light, that no poor slave deceiveth,
Shall set me free."

CHAPTER VIII

As we travelled towards a land of liberty, my heart would at times leap for joy. At other times, being, as I was, almost constantly on my feet, I felt as though I could travel no further. But when I thought of slavery, with its democratic whips—its republican chains—its evangelical blood-hounds, and its religious slave-holders—when I thought of all this paraphernalia of American democracy and religion behind me, and the prospect of liberty before me, I was encouraged to press forward, my heart was strengthened, and I forgot that I was tired or hungry.

On the eighth day of our journey, we had a very heavy rain, and in a few hours after it commenced we had not a dry thread upon our bodies. This made our journey still more unpleasant. On the tenth day, we found ourselves entirely destitute of provisions, and how to obtain any we could not tell. We finally resolved to stop at some farmhouse, and try to get something to eat. We had no sooner determined to do this, than we went to a house, and asked them for some food. We were treated with great kindness, and they not only gave us something to eat, but gave us provisions to carry with us. They advised us to travel by day and lie by at night. Finding ourselves about one hundred and fifty miles from St. Louis, we concluded that it would be safe to travel by daylight, and did not leave the house until the next morning. We travelled on that day through a thickly settled country, and through one small village. Though we were fleeing from a land of oppression, our hearts were still there. My dear sister and two beloved brothers were behind us, and the idea of giving them up, and leaving them forever, made us feel sad. But with all this depression of heart, the thought that I should one day be free, and call my body my own, buoyed me up, and made my heart leap for joy. I had just been telling my mother how I should try to get employment as soon as we reached Canada, and how I intended to purchase us a little farm, and how I would earn money enough to buy sister and brothers, and how happy we would be in our FREE HOME—when three men came up on horseback, and ordered us to stop.

I turned to the one who appeared to be the principal man, and asked him what he wanted. He said he had a warrant to take us up. The three immediately dismounted, and one took from his pocket a handbill, advertising us as runaways, and offering a reward of two hundred dollars for our apprehension and delivery in the city of St. Louis. The advertisement had been put out by Isaac Mansfield and John Young.

While they were reading the advertisement, mother looked me in the face, and burst into tears. A cold chill ran over me, and such a sensation I never experienced before, and I hope never to again. They took out a rope and tied me, and we were taken back about six miles, to the house of the individual who appeared to be the leader. We reached there about seven o'clock in the evening, had supper, and were separated for the night. Two men remained in the room during the night. Before the family retired to rest, they were all called together to attend prayers. The man who but a few hours before had bound my hands together with a strong cord, read a chapter from the Bible, and then offered up prayer, just as though God had sanctioned the act he had just committed upon a poor, panting, fugitive slave.

The next morning a blacksmith came in, and put a pair of handcuffs on me, and we started on our journey back to the land of whips, chains and Bibles. Mother was not tied, but was closely watched at night. We were carried back in a wagon, and after four days' travel, we came in sight of St. Louis. I cannot describe my feelings upon approaching the city.

As we were crossing the ferry, Mr. Wiggins, the owner of the ferry, came up to me, and inquired what I had been doing that I was in chains. He had not heard that I had run away. In a few minutes we were on the Missouri side, and were taken directly to the jail. On the way thither, I saw several of my friends, who gave me a nod of recognition as I passed them. After reaching the jail, we were locked up in different apartments.

CHAPTER IX

I had been in jail but a short time when I heard that my master was sick, and nothing brought more joy to my heart than that intelligence. I prayed fervently for him—not for his recovery, but for his death. I knew he would be exasperated at having to pay for my apprehension, and knowing his cruelty, I feared him. While in jail, I learned that my sister Elizabeth, who was in prison when we left the city, had been carried off four days before our arrival.

I had been in jail but a few hours when three negro-traders, learning that I was secured thus for running away, came to my prison-house and looked at me, expecting that I would be offered for sale. Mr. Mansfield, the man who owned mother, came into the jail as soon as Mr. Jones, the man who arrested us, informed him that he had brought her back. He told her that he would not whip her, but would sell her to a negro-trader, or take her to New Orleans himself. After being in jail about one week, master sent a man to take me out of jail, and send me home. I was taken out and carried home, and the old man was well enough to sit up. He had me brought into the room where he was, and as I entered, he asked me where I had been? I told him I had acted according to his orders. He had told me to look for a master, and I had been to look for one. He answered that he did not tell me to go to Canada to look for a master. I told him that as I had served him faithfully, and had been the means of putting a number of hundreds of dollars into his pocket, I thought I had a right to my liberty. He said he had promised my father that I should not be sold to supply the New Orleans market, or he would sell me to a negro-trader.

I was ordered to go into the field to work, and was closely watched by the overseer during the day, and locked up at night. The overseer gave me a severe whipping on the second day that I was in the field. I had been at home but a short time, when master was able to ride to the city; and on his return he informed me that he had sold me to Samuel Willi, a merchant tailor. I knew Mr. Willi. I had lived with him three or four months some years before, when he hired me of my master.

Mr. Willi was not considered by his servants as a very bad man, nor was he the best of masters. I went to my new home, and found my new mistress very glad to see me. Mr. Willi owned two servants before he purchased me—Robert and Charlotte. Robert was an excellent white-washer, and hired his time from his master, paying him one dollar per day, besides taking care of himself. He was known in the city by the name of Bob Music. Charlotte was an old woman, who attended to the cooking, washing, &c. Mr. Willi was not a wealthy man, and did not feel able to keep many servants around his house; so he soon decided to hire me out, and as I had been accustomed to service in steamboats, he gave me the privilege of finding such employment.

I soon secured a situation on board the steamer Otto, Capt. J. B. Hill, which sailed from St. Louis to Independence, Missouri. My former master, Dr. Young, did not let Mr. Willi know that I had run away, or he would not have permitted me to go on board a steamboat. The boat was not quite ready to commence running, and therefore I had to remain with Mr. Willi. But during this time, I had to undergo a trial for which I was entirely unprepared. My mother, who had been in jail since her return until the present time, was now about being carried to New Orleans, to die on a cotton, sugar, or rice plantation!

I had been several times to the jail, but could obtain no interview with her. I ascertained, however, the time the boat in which she was to embark would sail, and as I had not seen mother since her being thrown into prison, I felt anxious for the hour of sailing to come. At last, the day arrived when I was to see her for the first time after our painful separation, and, for aught that I knew, for the last time in this world!

At about ten o'clock in the morning I went on board of the boat, and found her there in company with fifty or sixty other slaves. She was chained to another woman. On seeing me, she immediately dropped her head upon her heaving bosom. She moved not, neither did she weep. Her emotions were too deep for tears. I approached, begging her forgiveness, for I thought myself to blame for her sad condition; for if I had not persuaded her to accompany me, she would not have been in chains.

She finally raised her head, looked me in the face, (and such a look none but an angel can give!) and said, *"My dear son, you are not to blame for my being here. You have done nothing more nor less than your duty. Do not, I pray you, weep for me. I cannot last long upon a cotton plantation. I feel that my heavenly Master will soon call me home, and then I shall be out of the hands of the slave-holders!"*

I could bear no more—my heart struggled to free itself from the human form. In a moment she saw Mr. Mansfield coming toward that part of the boat, and she whispered into my ear, *"My child, we must soon part to meet no more this side of the grave. You have ever said that you would not die a slave; that you would be a freeman. Now try to get your liberty! You wil soon have no one to look after but yourself!"* and just as she whispered the last sentence into my ear, Mansfield came up to me, and with an oath, said, "Leave here this instant; you have been the means of my losing one hundred dollars to get this wench back"—at the same time kicking me with a heavy pair of boots. As I left her, she gave one shriek, saying, "God be with you!" It was the last time that I saw her, and the last word I heard her utter.

I walked on shore. The bell was tolling. The boat was about to start. I stood with a heavy heart, waiting to see her leave the wharf. As I thought of my mother, I could but feel that I had lost

> "— — the glory of my life,
> My blessing and my pride!
> I half forgot the name of slave,
> When she was by my side."

The love of liberty that had been burning in my bosom had well-nigh gone out. I felt as though I was ready to die. The boat moved gently from the wharf, and while she glided down the river, I realized that my mother was indeed

> "Gone—gone—sold and gone,
> To the rice swamp, dank and lone!"

After the boat was out of sight I returned home; but my thoughts were so absorbed in what I had witnessed, that I knew not what I was about half of the time. Night came, but it brought no sleep to my eyes.

In a few days, the boat upon which I was to work being ready, I went on board to commence. This employment suited me better than living in the city, and I remained until the close of navigation; though it proved anything but pleasant. The captain was a drunken, profligate, hard-hearted creature, not knowing how to treat himself, or any other person.

The boat, on its second trip, brought down Mr. Walker, the man of whom I have spoken in a previous chapter, as hiring my time. He had between one and two hundred slaves, chained and manacled. Among them was a man that formerly belonged to my old master's brother, Aaron Young. His name was Solomon. He was a preacher, and belonged to the same church with his master. I was glad to see the old man. He wept like a child when he told me how he had been sold from his wife and children.

The boat carried down, while I remained on board, four or five gangs of slaves. Missouri, though a comparatively new state, is very much engaged in raising slaves to supply the southern market. In a former chapter, I have mentioned that I was once in the employ of a slave-trader, or driver, as he is called at the south. For fear that some may think that I have misrepresented a slave-driver, I will here give an extract from a paper published in a slave-holding state, Tennessee, called the "Millennial Trumpeter."

"Droves of negroes, chained together in dozens and scores, and handcuffed, have been driven through our country in numbers far surpassing any previous year, and these vile slave-drivers and dealers are swarming like buzzards around a carrion. Through this country, you cannot pass a few miles in the great roads without having every feeling of humanity insulted and lacerated by this spectacle, nor can you go into any county or any neighborhood, scarely, without seeing or hearing of some of these despicable creatures, called negro-drivers.

"Who is a negro-driver? One whose eyes dwell with delight on lacerated bodies of helpless men, women and children; whose soul feels diabolical raptures at the chains, and hand-cuffs, and cart-whips, for inflicting tortures on weeping mothers torn from helpless babes, and on husbands and wives torn asunder forever!"

Dark and revolting as is the picture here drawn, it is from the pen of one living in the midst of slavery. But though these men may cant about negro-drivers, and tell what despicable creatures they are, who is it, I ask, that supplies them with the human beings that they are tearing asunder? I answer, as far as I have any knowledge of the state where I came from, that those who raise slaves for the market are to be found among all classes, from Thomas H. Benton down to the lowest political demogogue who may be able to purchase a woman for the purpose of raising stock, and from the doctor of divinity down to the most humble lay member of the church.

It was not uncommon in St. Louis to pass by an auction-stand, and behold a woman upon the auction-block, and hear the seller crying out, *"How much is offered for this woman? She is a good cook, good washer, a good obedient servant. She has got religion!"* Why should this man tell the purchasers that she has religion? I answer, because in Missouri, and as far as I have any knowledge of slavery in the other states, the religious teaching consists in teaching the slave that he must never strike a white man; that God made him for a slave; and that, when whipped, he must not find fault—for the Bible says, "He that knoweth his master's will and doeth it not, shall be beaten with many stripes!" And slave-holders find such religion very profitable to them.

After leaving the steamer Otto, I resided at home, in Mr. Willi's family, and again began to lay my plans for making my escape from slavery. The anxiety to be a freeman would not let me rest day or night. I would think of the northern cities that I had heard so much about;—of Canada, where so many of my acquaintances had found a refuge. I would dream at night that I was in Canada, a freeman, and on waking in the morning, weep to find myself so sadly mistaken.

> "I would think of Victoria's domain
>   And in a moment I seemed to be there!
> But the fear of being taken again,
>   Soon hurried me back to despair."

Mr. Willi treated me better than Dr. Young ever had; but instead of making me contented and happy, it only rendered me the more miserable, for it enabled me better to appreciate liberty. Mr. Willi was a man who loved money as most men do, and without looking for an opportunity to sell me, he found one in the offer of Captain Enoch Price, a steamboat owner and commission merchant, living in the city of St. Louis. Captain Price tendered seven hundred dollars, which was two hundred more than Mr. Willi had paid. He therefore thought best to accept the offer. I was wanted for a carriage driver, and Mrs. Price was very much pleased with the captain's bargain. His family consisted besides of one child. He had three servants besides myself—one man and two women.

Mrs. Price was very proud of her servants, always keeping them well dressed, and as soon as I had been purchased, she resolved to have a new carriage. And soon one was procured, and all preparations were made for a turn-out in grand style, I being the driver.

One of the female servants was a girl some eighteen or twenty years of age, named Maria. Mrs. Price was very soon determined to have us united, if she could so arrange matters. She would often urge upon me the necessity of having a wife, saying that it would be so pleasant for me to take one in the same family! But getting married, while in slavery, was the last of my thoughts; and had I been ever so inclined, I should not have married Maria, as my love had already gone in another quarter. Mrs. Price soon found out that her efforts at this match-making between Maria and myself would not prove successful. She also discovered (or thought she had) that I was rather partial to a girl named Eliza, who was owned by Dr. Mills. This induced her at once to endeavor the purchase of Eliza, so great was her desire to get me a wife!

Before making the attempt, however, she deemed it best to talk to me a little upon the subject of love, courtship, and marriage. Accordingly, one afternoon she called me into her room—telling me to take a chair and sit down. I did so, thinking it rather strange, for servants are not very often asked thus to sit down in the same room with the master or mistress. She said that she had found out that I did not care enough about Maria to marry her. I told her that was true. She then asked me if there was not a girl in the city that I loved. Well, now, this was coming into too close quarters with me! People, generally, don't like to tell their love stories to everybody that may think fit to ask about them, and it was so with me. But, after blushing a while and recovering myself, I told her that I did not want a wife. She then asked me if I did not think something of Eliza. I told her that I did. She then said that if I wished to marry Eliza, she would purchase her if she could.

I gave but little encouragement to this proposition, as I was determined to make another trial to get my liberty, and I knew that if I should have a wife, I should not be wiling to leave her behind; and if I should attempt to bring her with me, the chances would be difficult for success. However, Eliza was purchased, and brought into the family.

CHAPTER X

But the more I thought of the trap laid by Mrs. Price to make me satisfied with my new home, by getting me a wife, the more I determined never to marry any woman on earth until I should get my liberty. But this secret I was compelled to keep to myself, which placed me in a very critical position. I must keep upon good terms with Mrs. Price and Eliza. I therefore promised Mrs. Price that I would marry Eliza; but said that I was not then ready. And I had to keep upon good terms with Eliza, for fear that Mrs. Price would find out that I did not intend to get married.

I have here spoken of marriage, and it is very common among slaves themselves to talk of it. And it is common for slaves to be married; or at least to have the marriage ceremony performed. But there is no such thing as slaves being lawfully married. There has never yet a case occurred where a slave has been tried for bigamy. The man may have as many women as he wishes, and the women as many men; and the law takes no cognizance of such acts among slaves. And in fact some masters, when they have sold the husband from the wife, compel her to take another.

There lived opposite Captain Price's, Doctor Farrar, well known in St. Louis. He sold a man named Ben, to one of the traders. He also owned Ben's wife, and in a few days he compelled Sally (that was her name) to marry Peter, another man belonging to him. I asked Sally "why she married Peter so soon after Ben was sold." She said, "because master made her do it."

Mr. John Calvert, who resided near our place, had a woman named Lavinia. She was quite young, and a man to whom she was about to be married was sold, and carried into the country near St. Charles, about twenty miles from St. Louis. Mr. Calvert wanted her to get a husband; but she had resolved not to marry any other man, and she refused. Mr. Calvert whipped her in such a manner that it was thought she would die. Some of the citizens had him arrested, but it was soon hushed up. And that was the last of it. The woman did not die, but it would have been the same if she had.

Captain Price purchased me in the month of October, and I remained with him until December, when the family made a voyage to New Orleans, in a boat owned by himself, and named the "Chester." I served on board as one of the stewards. On arriving at New Orleans, about the middle of the month, the boat took in freight for Cincinnati; and it was decided that the family should go up the river in her, and what was of more interest to me, I was to accompany them.

The long looked for opportunity to make my escape from slavery was near at hand.

Captain Price had some fears as to the propriety of taking me near a free state, or a place where it was likely I could run away, with a prospect of liberty. He asked me if I had ever been in a free state. "Oh yes," said I, "I have been in Ohio; my master carried me into that state once, but I never liked a free state."

It was soon decided that it would be safe to take me with them, and what made it more safe, Eliza was on the boat with us, and Mrs. Price, to try me, asked if I thought as much as ever of Eliza. I told her that Eliza was very dear to me indeed, and that nothing but death should part us. It was the same as if we were married. This had the desired effect. The boat left New Orleans, and proceeded up the river.

I had at different times obtained little sums of money, which I had reserved for a "rainy day." I procured some cotton cloth, and made me a bag to carry provisions in. The trials of the past were all lost in hopes for the future. The love of liberty, that had been burning in my bosom for years, and had been well-nigh extinguished, was now resuscitated. At night, when all around was peaceful, I would walk the decks, meditating upon my happy prospects.

I should have stated, that, before leaving St. Louis, I went to an old man named Frank, a slave, owned by a Mr. Sarpee. This old man was very distinguished (not only among the slave population, but also the whites) as a fortune-teller. He was about seventy years of age, something over six feet high, and very slender. Indeed, he was so small around his body, that it looked as though it was not strong enough to hold up his head.

Uncle Frank was a very great favorite with the young ladies, who would go to him in great numbers to get their fortunes told. And it was generally believed that he could really penetrate into the mysteries of futurity. Whether true or not, he had the *name,* and that is about half of what one needs in this gullible age. I found Uncle Frank seated in the chimney corner, about ten o'clock at night. As soon as I entered, the old man left his seat. I watched his movement as well as I could by the dim light of the fire. He soon lit a lamp, and coming up, looked me full in the face, saying, "Well, my son, you have come to get uncle to tell your fortune, have you?" "Yes," said I. But how the old man should know what I came for, I could not tell. However, I paid the fee of twenty-five cents, and he commenced by looking into a gourd, filled with water. Whether the old man was a prophet, or the son of a prophet, I cannot say; but there is one thing certain, many of his predictions were verified.

I am no believer in soothsaying; yet I am sometimes at a loss to know how Uncle Frank could tell so accurately what would occur in the future. Among the many things he told was one which was enough to pay me for all the trouble of hunting him up. It was that I *should be free!* He further said, that in trying to get my liberty I would meet with many severe trials. I thought to myself any fool could tell me that!

The first place in which we landed in a free state was Cairo, a small village at the mouth of the Ohio river. We remained here but a few hours, when we proceeded to Louisville. After unloading some of the cargo, the boat started on her upward trip. The next day was the first of January. I had looked forward to New Year's day as the commencement of a new era in the history of my life. I had decided upon leaving the peculiar institution that day.

During the last night that I served in slavery I did not close my eyes a single moment. When not thinking of the future, my mind dwelt on the past. The love of a dear mother, a dear sister, and three dear brothers, yet living, caused me to shed many tears. If I could only have been assured of their being dead, I should have felt satisifed; but I imagined I saw my dear mother in the cotton-field, followed by a merciless taskmaster, and no one to speak a consoling word to her! I beheld my dear sister in the hands of a slave-driver, and compelled to submit to his cruelty! None but one placed in such a situation can for a moment imagine the intense agony to which these reflections subjected me. At last the time for action arrived. The boat landed at a point which appeared to me the place of all others to start from. I found that it would be impossible to carry anything with me but what was upon my person. I had some provisions, and a single suit of clothes, about half worn. When the boat was discharging her cargo, and the passengers engaged carrying their baggage on and off shore, I improved the opportunity to convey myself with my little effects on land. Taking up a trunk, I went up the wharf, and was soon out of the crowd. I made directly for the woods, where I remained until night, knowing well that I could not travel, even in the state of Ohio, during the day, without danger of being arrested.

CHAPTER XI

At last the time for action arrived. The boat landed at a point which appeared to me the place of all others to start from. I found that it would be impossible to carry anything with me but what was upon my person. I had some provisions, and a single suit of clothes, about half worn. When the boat was discharging her cargo, and the passengers engaged carrying their baggage on and off shore, I improved the opportunity to convey myself with my little effects on land. Taking up a trunk, I went up the wharf, and was soon out of the crowd. I made directly for the woods, where I remained until night, knowing well that I could not travel, even in the state of Ohio, during the day, without danger of being arrested.

I had long since made up my mind that I would not trust myself in the hands of any man, white or colored. The slave is brought up to look upon every white man as an enemy to him and his race; and twenty-one years in slavery had taught me that there were traitors, even among colored people. After dark, I emerged from the woods into a narrow path, which led me into the main travelled road. But I knew not which way to go. I did not know north from south, east from west. I looked in vain for the North Star; a heavy cloud hid it from my view. I walked up and down the road until near midnight, when the clouds disappeared, and I welcomed the sight of my friend—truly the slave's friend—the North Star!

As soon as I saw it, I knew my course, and before daylight I travelled twenty or twenty-five miles. It being in the winter, I suffered intensely from the cold; being without an overcoat, and my other clothes rather thin for the season. I was provided with a tinder-box, so that I could make up a fire when necessary. And but for this, I should certainly have frozen to death; for I was determined not to go to any house for shelter. I knew of a man belonging to Gen. Ashly, of St. Louis, who had run away near Cincinnati, on the way to Washington, but had been caught and carried back into slavery; and I felt that a similar fate awaited me, should I be seen by any one. I travelled at night, and lay by during the day.

On the fourth day my provisions gave out, and then what to do I could not tell. Have something to eat I must; but how to get it was the question! On the first night after my food was gone, I went to a barn on the road-side and there found some ears of corn. I took ten or twelve of them, and kept on my journey. During the next day, while in the woods, I roasted my corn and feasted upon it, thanking God that I was so well provided for.

My escape to a land of freedom now appeared certain, and the prospects of the future occupied a great part of my thoughts. What should be my occupation, was a subject of much anxiety to me; and the next thing what should be my name? I have before stated that my old master, Dr. Young, had no children of his own, but had with him a nephew, the son of his brother, Benjamin Young. When this boy was brought to Dr. Young, his name being William, the same as mine, my mother was ordered to change mine to something else. This, at the time, I thought to be one of the most cruel acts that could be committed upon my rights; and I received several very severe whippings for telling people that my name was William, after orders were given to change it. Though young, I was old enough to place a high appreciation upon my name. It was decided, however, to call me "Sandford," and this name I was known by, not only upon my master's plantation, but up to the time that I made my escape. I was sold under the name of Sandford.

But as soon as the subject came to my mind, I resolved on adopting my old name of William, and let Sandford go by the board, for I always hated it. Not because there was anything peculiar in the name; but because it had been forced upon me. it is sometimes common, at the south, for slaves to take the name of their masters. Some have a legitimate right to do so.

But I always detested the idea of being called by the name of either of my masters. And as for my father, I would rather have adopted the name of "Friday," and been known as the servant of some Robinson Crusoe, than to have taken his name. So I was not only hunting for my liberty, but also hunting for a name; though I regarded the latter as of little consequence, if I could but gain the former. Travelling along the road, I would sometimes speak to myself, sounding my name over, by way of getting used to it, before I should arrive among civilized human beings. On the fifth or six day, it rained very fast, and froze about as fast as it fell, so that my clothes were one glare of ice. I travelled on at night until I became so chilled and benumbed—the wind blowing into my face—that I found it impossible to go any further, and accordingly took shelter in a barn, where I was obliged to walk about to keep from freezing.

I have ever looked upon that night as the most eventful part of my escape from slavery. Nothing but the providence of God, and that old barn, saved me from freezing to death. I received a very severe cold, which settled upon my lungs, and from time to time my feet had been frostbitten, so that it was with difficulty I could walk. In this situation I travelled two days, when I found that I must seek shelter somewhere, or die.

The thought of death was nothing frightful to me, compared with that of being caught, and again carried back into slavery. Nothing but the prospect of enjoying liberty could have induced me to undergo such trials, for

> "Behind I left the whips and chains,
> Before me were sweet Freedom's plains!"

This, and this alone, cheered me onward. But I at last resolved to seek protection from the inclemency of the weather, and therefore I secured myself behind some logs and brush, intending to wait there until some one should pass by; for I thought it probable that I might see some colored person, or, if not, some one who was not a slave-holder; for I had an idea that I should know a slave-holder as far as I could see him.

The first person that passed was a man in a buggy-wagon. He looked too genteel for me to hail him. Very soon another passed by on horseback. I attempted to speak to him, but fear made my voice fail me. As he passed, I left my hidingplace and was approaching the road, when I observed an old man walking towards me, leading a white horse. He had on a broad-brimmed hat and a very long coat, and was evidently walking for exercise. As soon as I saw him, and observed his dress, I thought to myself, "You are the man that I have been looking for!" Nor was I mistaken. He was the very man!

On approaching me, he asked me, "if I was not a slave." I looked at him some time, and then asked him "if he knew of any one who would help me, as I was sick." He answered that he would; but again asked, if I was not a slave. I told him I was. He then said that I was in a very pro-slavery neighborhood, and if I would wait until he went home, he would get a covered wagon for me. I promised to remain. He mounted his horse, and was soon out of sight.

After he was gone, I meditated whether to wait or not; being apprehensive that he had gone for some one to arrest me. But I finally concluded to remain until he should return; removing some few rods to watch his movements. After a suspense of an hour and a half or more, he returned with a two-horse covered wagon, such as are usually seen under the shed of a Quaker meetinghouse on Sundays and Thursdays; for the old man proved to be a Quaker of the George Fox stamp.[5]

He took me to his house, but it was some time before I could be induced to enter it; not until the old lady came out, did I venture into the house. I thought I saw something in the old lady's cap that told me I was not only safe, welcome, in her house. I was not, however, prepared to receive their hospitalities. The only fault I found with them was their being too kind. I had never had a white man treat me as an equal, and the idea of a white lady waiting on me at the table was still worse! Though the table was loaded with the good things of this life, I could not eat. I thought if I could only be allowed the privilege of eating in the kitchen I should be more than satisfied!

Finding that I could not eat, the old lady, who was a "Thompsonian,"* made me a cup of "composition," or "number six;" but it was so strong and hot, that I called it *"number seven!"*[6] However, I soon found myself at home in this family. On different occasions, when telling these facts, I have been asked how I felt upon finding myself regarded as a man by a white family; especially just having run away from one. I cannot say that I have ever answered the question yet.

The fact that I was in all probability a freeman, sounded in my ears like a charm. I am satisfied that none but a slave could place such an appreciation upon liberty as I did at that time. I wanted to see mother and sister, that I might tell them "I was free!" I wanted to see my fellow-slaves in St. Louis, and let them know that the chains were no longer upon my limbs. I wanted to see Captain Price, and let him learn from my own lips that I was no more a chattel, but a man! I was anxious, too, thus to inform Mrs. Price

---

*A system of medicine named for Samuel Thomson (1769–1843) who advocated the exclusive use of vegetable drugs in treating disease. See Francis R. Packard, *History of Medicine in the United States* (2 vols., New York and London, 1963), II:1233–1239.

that she must get another coachman. And I wanted to see Eliza more than I did either Mr. or Mrs. Price!

The fact that I was a freeman—could walk, talk, eat and sleep, as a man, and no one to stand over me with the blood-clotted cow-hide—all this made me feel that I was not myself.

The kind friend that had taken me in was named Wells Brown.* He was a devoted friend of the slave; but was very old, and not in the enjoyment of good health. After being by the fire awhile, I found that my feet had been very much frozen. I was seized with a fever, which threatened to confine me to my bed. But my Thompsonian friends soon raised me, treating me as kindly as if I had been one of their own children. I remained with them twelve or fifteen days, during which time they made me some clothing, and the old gentleman purchased me a pair of boots.

I found that I was about fifty or sixty miles from Dayton, in the State of Ohio, and between one and two hundred miles from Cleaveland, on Lake Erie, a place I was desirous of reaching on my way to Canada. This I know will sound strangely to the ears of people in foreign lands, but it is nevertheless true. An American citizen was fleeing from a democratic, republican, Christian government, to receive protection under the monarchy of Great Britain.[7] While the people of the United States boast of their freedom, they at the same time keep three millions of their own citizens in chains; and while I am seated here in sight of Bunker Hill Monument, writing this narrative, I am a slave, and no law, not even in Massachusetts, can protect me from the hands of the slave-holder!

Before leaving this good Quaker friend, he inquired what my name was besides William. I told him that I had no other name. "Well," said he, "thee must have another name. Since thee has got out of slavery, thee has become a man, and men always have two names."

I told him that he was the first man to extend the hand of friendship to me, and I would give him the privilege of naming me.

"If I name thee," said he, "I shall call thee Wells Brown, after myself."

"But," said I, "I am not willing to lose my name of William. As it was taken from me once against my will, I am not willing to part with it again upon any terms.

"Then," said he, "I will call thee William Wells Brown."

"So be it," said I; and I have been known by that name ever since I left the house of my first white friend, Wells Brown.

---

*A search for more information about Wells Brown by Professor W. Edward Farrison yielded no results. See W. Edward Farrison, "A Flight Across Ohio: The Escape of William Wells Brown From Slavery," *Ohio State Archaeological and Historical Quarterly*, 61:280 (July, 1952).

After giving me some little change, I again started for Canada. In four days I reached a public house, and went in to warm myself. I there learned that some fugitive slaves had just passed through the place. The men in the bar-room were talking about it, and I thought that it must have been myself they referred to, and I was therefore afraid to start, fearing they would seize me; but I finally mustered courage enough, and took my leave. As soon as I was out of sight, I went into the woods, and remained there until night, when I again regained the road, and travelled on until next day.

Not having had any food for nearly two days, I was faint with hunger, and was in a dilemma what to do, as the little cash supplied me by my adopted father, and which had contributed to my comfort, was now all gone. I however concluded to go to a farm-house, and ask for something to eat. On approaching the door of the first one presenting itself, I knocked, and was soon met by a man who asked me what I wanted. I told him that I would like something to eat. He asked me where I was from, and where I was going. I replied that I had come some way, and was going to Cleaveland.

After hesitating a moment or two, he told me that he could give me nothing to eat, adding, "that if I would work, I could get something to eat."

I felt bad, being thus refused something to sustain nature, but did not dare tell him that I was a slave.

Just as I was leaving the door, with a heavy heart, a woman, who proved to be the wife of this gentleman, came to the door, and asked her husband what I wanted. He did not seem inclined to inform her. She therefore asked me herself. I told her that I had asked for something to eat. After a few other questions, she told me to come in, and that she would give me something to eat.

I walked up to the door, but the husband remained in the passage, as if unwilling to let me enter.

She asked him two or three times to get out of the way, and let me in. But as he did not move, she pushed him on one side, bidding me walk in! I was never before so glad to see a woman push a man aside! Ever since that act, I have been in favor of "woman's rights!"[8]

After giving me as much food as I could eat, she presented me with ten cents, all the money then at her disposal, accompanied with a note to a friend, a few miles further on the road. Thanking this angel of mercy from an overflowing heart, I pushed on my way, and in three days arrived at Cleaveland, Ohio.

Being an entire stranger in this place, it was difficult for me to find where to stop. I had no money, and the lake being frozen, I saw that I must remain until the opening of the navigation, or go to Canada by way of Buffalo. But believing myself to be somewhat out of danger, I secured an engagement at the Mansion House, as a table waiter, in payment for my board. The proprietor, however, whose name was E. M. Segur, in a short time, hired me for twelve dollars a month; on which terms I remained until spring, when I found good employment on board a lake steamboat.

I purchased some books, and at leisure moments perused them with considerable advantage to myself. While at Cleaveland, I saw, for the first time, an anti-slavery newspaper. It was the *"Genius of Universal Emancipation,"* published by Benjamin Lundy; and though I had no home, I subscribed for the paper. It was my great desire, being out of slavery myself, to do what I could for the emancipation of my brethren yet in chains, and while on Lake Erie, I found many opportunities of "helping their cause along."

It is well known that a great number of fugitives make their escape to Canada, by way of Cleaveland; and while on the lakes, I always made arrangement to carry them on the boat to Buffalo or Detroit, and thus effect their escape to the "promised land." The friends of the slave, knowing that I would transport them without charge, never failed to have a delegation when the boat arrived at Cleaveland. I have sometimes had four or five on board at one time.

In the year 1842, I conveyed, from the first of May to the first of December, sixty-nine fugitives over Lake Erie to Canada. In 1843, I visited Malden, in Upper Canada, and counted seventeen in that small village, whom I had assisted in reaching Canada. Soon after coming north I subscribed for the Liberator, edited by that champion of freedom, William Lloyd Garrison. I had heard nothing of the anti-slavery movement while in slavery, and as soon as I found that my enslaved countrymen had friends who were laboring for their liberation, I felt anxious to join them, and give what aid I could to the cause.

I early embraced the temperance cause, and found that a temperance reformation was needed among my colored brethren. In company with a few friends, I commenced a temperance reformation among the colored people in the city of Buffalo, and labored three years, in which time a society was built up, numbering over five hundred out of a population of less than seven hundred.

In the autumn, 1843, impressed with the importance of spreading anti-slavery truth, as a means to bring about the abolition of slavery, I commenced lecturing as an agent of the western New York Anti-Slavery Society, and have ever since devoted my time to the cause of my enslaved countrymen.

ENDNOTES

1. This locution refers to *white* abolitionists. It raises the issue of point of view, and evidences the problems free Negroes had with the tendency of their white comrades-in-arms to patronize them and to speak on their behalf. Note that farther along on this page Hathaway refers to "our cause" as being greatly aided by the testimony of fugitive slaves. Only recently has the ideological and programmatic significance of the different points of view of whites and blacks in the anti-slavery movement been fully unpacked. The basic texts are Benjamin Quarles, *Black Abolitionists* (New York: Oxford University Press, 1969) and Jane H. Pease and William H. Pease, *They Who Would Be Free: Blacks' Search for Freedom, 1830–1861* (New York: Atheneum, 1974), pp. 3–16 and *passim*.

2. These sentences identify Joseph C. Hathaway, president of the Western New York Anti-Slavery Society, as a Garrisonian. The followers of William Lloyd Garrison believed that the Constitution was a pro-slavery document and that the nation's churches prostituted themselves by countenancing an inter-sectional alliance of the "lords of the loom" and the "lords of the lash." The Garrisonian motto was "no union with slaveholders."

3. The callousness of slave-driver James Walker in selling his own mistress and children is atypical. This particular sort of inhumanity was not common. In fact, Wilberforce College was established in Ohio before the Civil War as an institution to which wealthy southern slave masters interested in the welfare of their mulatto offspring could send them to be educated.

4. There is no way to confirm this story. If true, its credibility rests on the fact that the young man was sold as a slave in New Orleans, a market in which many light-skinned slaves—particularly females—changed hands. That is, he was not sold into slavery *as* a white man.

5. George Fox founded the Society of Friends in England in 1650. The phrasing "a Quaker of the George Fox stamp" highlights Wells Brown's fidelity to fundamental Quaker principles, principles which, as early as 1758, led the Philadelphia Yearly Meeting to pledge to rid the Society of Friends of slave-holding. Both as an organized body and individually, Quakers were consistently in the vanguard of the fight

against the peculiar institution. The definitive study is still Thomas E. Drake, *Quakers and Slavery in America* (New Haven: Yale University Press, 1950).

6. Thomsonians, or followers of the preventive medical doctrines of Dr. Samuel Thomson (1769–1843), believed in steam baths, herbal elixirs and other natural remedies.

7. By the mid-nineteenth century, Great Britain was a friend of the slave, both in jurisprudence and in imperial policy. In Somerset v. Stewart (1772), in determining that a sojourn in England rendered a slave free, the chief justice of the King's Bench ruled that slavery is "so odious that nothing can be suffered to support it but positive law." Subsequently, on August 12, 1833 Parliament passed an act—to take effect August 1, 1834—ending slavery throughout the British empire.

8. This humorous remark alludes to the historical connection between the abolitionist movement and the birth of the movement for women's rights in the United States in the 1840s. As ecumenical radicals, the Garrisonians of the American Anti-Slavery Society were more inclined than their more pragmatic and politically astute fellows in the American and Foreign Anti-Slavery Society to embrace the cause of women's rights—being at once less fearful that it would subvert the abolitionist agenda, and more inclined to act on principle, whatever the consequences.

William Wells Brown

Fredrick Douglass

William and Ellen Craft

Session of the Paris Peace Congress, 1849

The American Fugitive in Europe.
Sketches of Places and People Abroad

by
William Wells Brown

with
A Memoir of The Author

PREFACE
TO THE ENGLISH EDITION

While I feel conscious that most of the contents of these Letters will be interesting chiefly to American readers, yet I may indulge the hope that the fact of their being the first production of a Fugitive Slave as a history of travels may carry with them novelty enough to secure for them, to some extent, the attention of the reading public of Great Britain. Most of the letters were written for the private perusal of a few personal friends in America, some were contributed to *Frederick Douglass' Paper,* a journal published in the United States. In a printed circular sent some weeks since to some of my friends, asking subscriptions to this volume, I stated the reasons for its publication: these need not be repeated here. To those who so promptly and kindly responded to that appeal, I tender my most sincere thanks. It is with no little diffidence that I lay these letters before the public; for I am not blind to the fact that they must contain many errors; and to those who shall find fault with them on that account, it may not be too much for me to ask them kindly to remember that the author was a slave in one of the Southern States of America until he had attained the age of twenty years; and that the education he has acquired was by his own exertions, he never having had a day's schooling in his life.

W. WELLS BROWN.

22 Cecil Street, Strand,
London

NOTE TO THE AMERICAN EDITION

During my sojourn abroad I found it advantageous to my purse to publish a book of travels, which I did under the title of "Three Years in Europe, or Places I have seen and People I have met." The work was reviewed by the ablest journals in Great Britain, and from their favorable criticisms I have been induced to offer it to the American public, with a dozen or more additional chapters.

W. W. B.

Boston, November, 1854.

CONTENTS

MEMOIR OF THE AUTHOR

"Shall tongues be mute when deeds are wrought
Which well might shame extremest Hell?
Shall freemen lack the indignant thought?
Shall mercy's bosom cease to swell?
Shall Honor bleed?—shall Truth succumb?
Shall pen, and press, and *soul* be dumb?"—*Whittier.*

William Wells Brown, the subject of this narrative, was born a slave in Lexington, Kentucky, not far from the residence of the late Hon. Henry Clay. His mother was the slave of Dr. John Young. His father was a slaveholder, and, besides being a near relation of his master, was connected with the Wickliffe family, one of the oldest, wealthiest, and most aristocratic of the Kentucky planters. Dr. Young was the owner of forty or fifty slaves, whose chief employment was in cultivating tobacco, hemp, corn, and flax. The doctor removed from Lexington, when William was five or six years old, to the State of Missouri, and commenced farming in a beautiful and fertile valley, within a mile of the Missouri river.

Here the slaves were put to work under a harsh and cruel overseer, named Cook. A finer situation for a farm could not have been selected in the state. With climate favorable to agriculture, and soil rich, the products came in abundance. At an early age William was separated from his mother, she being worked in the field, and he as a servant in his master's medical department. When about ten years of age, the young slave's feelings were much hurt at hearing the cries of his mother while being flogged by the negro-driver for being a few minutes behind the other hands in reaching the field. He heard her cry, "O, pray! O, pray! O, pray!" These are the words which slaves generally utter when imploring mercy at the hands of their oppressors. The son heard it, though he was some way off. He heard the crack of the whip, and the groans of his poor mother. The cold chill ran over him, and he wept aloud; but he was a slave like his mother, and could render her no assistance. He was taught by the most bitter experience, that nothing could be more heart-rending than to see a dear and beloved mother or sister tortured by unfeeling men, and to hear her cries, and not to be able to render the least aid. When William was twelve years of age, his master left his farm and took up his residence near St. Louis. The doctor having more hands than he wanted for his own use, William was let out to a Mr. Freeland, an innkeeper. Here the young slave found himself in the hands of a most cruel and heartless master. Freeland was one of the real chivalry of the South; besides being himself a slaveholder, he was a horse-racer, cock-fighter, gambler, and, to crown the whole, an inveterate drunkard. What else but bad treatment could be expected from such a character? After enduring the tyrannical and inhuman usage of this man for five or six months, William resolved to stand it no longer, and therefore ran away, like other slaves who leave their masters, owing to severe treatment; and not knowing where to flee, the young fugitive went into the forest, a few miles from St. Louis. He had been in the woods but a short time, when he heard the barking and howling of dogs, and was soon satisfied that he was pursued by the negro-dogs; and, aware of their ferocious nature, the fugitive climbed a tree, to save himself from being torn to pieces. The hounds were soon at the trunk of the tree, and remained there, howling and barking, until those in whose charge they were came up. The slave was ordered down, tied, and taken home. Immediately on his arrival there, he was, as he expected, tied up in the smoke-house, and whipped till Freeland was satisfied, and then smoked with tobacco-stems. This the slaveholder called *"Virginia play."* After being well whipped and smoked, he was again set to work. William remained with this monster a few months longer, and was then let out to Elijah P. Lovejoy, who years after became the editor of an abolition newspaper, and was murdered at Alton, Illinois, by a mob of slaveholders from the adjoining State of Missouri. The system of letting out slaves is one among the worst of the evils of slavery. The man who hires a slave looks upon him in the same light as does the man who hires a horse for a limited period; he feels no interest in him, only to get the worth of his money. Not so with the man who owns the slave; he regards him as so much property, of which care should be taken. After being let out to a steamer as an under-steward, William was hired by James Walker, a slave-trader. Here the subject of our memoir was made superintendent of the gangs of slaves that were taken to the New Orleans market. In this capacity, William had opportunities, far greater than most slaves, of acquiring knowledge of the different phases of the *"peculiar institution."* Walker was a negro speculator, who was amassing a fortune by trading in the bones, blood and nerves, of God's children. The thought of such a traffic causes us to exclaim with the poet,

> "——Is there not some chosen curse,
> Some hidden thunder in the stores of heaven,
> Red with uncommon wrath, to blast the man
> Who gains his fortune from the blood of souls?"

Between fifty and sixty slaves were chained together, put on board a steamboat bound for New Orleans, and started on the voyage. New and strange scenes began to inspire the young slave with the hope of escaping to a land of freedom. There was in the boat a large room on the lower deck in which the slaves were kept, men and women promiscuously, all chained two and two together, not even leaving the poor slaves the privileges of choosing their partners. A strict watch was kept over them, so that they had no chance of escape. Cases had occurred in which slaves had got off their chains and made their escape at the landing-places, while the boat stopped to take in wood. But, with all their care, they lost one woman who had been taken from her husband and children, and, having no desire to live without them, in the agony of her soul jumped overboard and drowned herself. Her sorrows were greater than she could bear; slavery and its cruel inflictions had broken her heart. She, like William, sighed for freedom, but not the freedom which even British soil confers and inspires, but freedom from torturing pangs, and overwhelming grief.

At the end of the week they arrived at New Orleans, the place of their destination. Here the slaves were placed in a negro-pen, where those who wished to purchase could call and examine them. The negro-pen is a small yard surrounded by buildings, from fifteen to twenty feet wide, with the exception of a large gate with iron bars. The slaves are kept in the buildings during the night, and turned into the pen during the day. After the best of the gang were sold off, the balance was taken to the Exchange Coffee-house auction-rooms, and sold at public auction. After the sale of the last slave, William and Mr. Walker left New Orleans for St. Louis.

After they had been at St. Louis a few weeks, another cargo of human flesh was made up. There were amongst the lot several old men and women, some of whom had gray locks. On their way down to New Orleans William had to prepare the old slaves for market. He was ordered to shave off the old men's whiskers, and to pluck out the gray hairs where they were not too numerous; where they were, he colored them with a preparation of blacking with a blacking-brush. After having gone through the blacking process, they looked ten or fifteen years younger. William, though not well skilled in the use of scissors and razor, performed the office of the barber tolerably. After the sale of this gang of negroes they returned to St. Louis, and a second cargo was made up. In this lot was a woman who had a child at the breast, yet was compelled to travel through the interior of the country on foot with the other slaves. In a published memoir of his life, William says, "The child cried during the most of the day which displeased Mr. Walker, and he told the mother that if her child did not stop crying he would stop its mouth. After a long and weary journey under a burning sun, we put up for the night at a country inn. The following morning, just as they were about to start, the child again commenced crying. Walker stepped up to her and told her to give the child to him. The mother tremblingly obeyed. He took the child by one arm, as any one would a cat by the leg, and walked into the house where they had been staying, and said to the lady, 'Madam, I will make you a present of this little nigger; it keeps making such a noise that I can't bear it.' 'Thank you, sir,' said the lady. The mother, as soon as she saw that the child was to be left, ran up to Mr. Walker, and, falling on her knees, begged of him, in an agony of despair, to let her have her child. She clung round his legs so closely that for some time he could not kick her off; and she cried, 'O my child, my child! Master, do let me have my dear, dear child! O! do, do! I will stop its crying, and love you forever, if you will only let me have my child again.' But her prayers were not heeded; they passed on, and the mother was separated from her child forever.

"After the woman's child had been given away, Mr. Walker rudely commanded her to retire into the ranks with the other slaves. Women who had children were not chained, but those who had none were. As soon as her child was taken she was chained to the gang."

Nothing was more grievous to the sensitive feelings of William than seeing the separation of families by the slave-trader: husbands taken from their wives, and mothers from their children, without the least appearance of feeling on the part of those who separated them. While at New Orleans, on one occasion, William saw a slave murdered. The circumstances were as follows: In the evening, between seven and eight o'clock, a slave came running down the levee, followed by several men and boys. The whites were crying out, "Stop that nigger! stop that nigger!" while the poor panting slave, in almost breathless accents, was repeating, "I did not steal the meat—I did not steal the meat!" The poor man at last took refuge in the river. The whites who were in pursuit of him ran on board of one of the boats to see if they could discover him. They finally espied him under the bow of the steamboat "Trenton." They got a pike-pole, and tried to drive him from his hiding-place. When they struck at him, he would dive under the water. The water was so cold that it soon became evident that he must come out or be drowned.

While they were trying to drive him from under the boat or drown him, he, in broken and imploring accents, said, "I did not steal the meat! I did not steal the meat! My master lives up the river. I want to see my master, I did not steal the meat! Do let me go home to master!" After punching and striking him over the head for some time, he at last sunk in the water, to rise no more alive.

On the end of the pike-pole with which they had been striking him was a hook, which caught in his clothing, and they hauled him up on the bow of the boat. Some said he was dead; others said he was "playing 'possum," while others kicked him to make him get up; but it was of no use—he was dead.

As soon as they became satisfied of this, they commenced leaving, one after another. One of the hands on the boat informed the captain that they had killed the man, and that the dead body was lying on the deck. The captain, whose name was Hart, came on deck, and said to those who were remaining, "You have killed this nigger; now take him off my boat." The dead body was dragged on shore and left there. William went on board of the boat where the gang of slaves were, and during the whole night his mind was occupied with what he had seen. Early in the morning he went on shore to see if the dead body remained there. He found it in the same position that it was left the night before. He watched to see what they would do with it. It was left there until between eight and nine o'clock, when a cart, which took up the trash from the streets, came along, and the body was thrown in, and in a few minutes more was covered over with dirt, which they were removing from the streets.

At the expiration of the period of his hiring with Walker, William returned to his master, rejoiced to have escaped an employment as much against his own feelings as it was repugnant to human nature. But this joy was of short duration. The doctor wanted money, and resolved to sell William's sister and two brothers. The mother had been previously sold to a gentleman residing in the city of St. Louis. William's master now informed him that he intended to sell him, and, as he was his own nephew, he gave him the privilege of finding some one to purchase him, who would treat him better than if he was sold on the auction-block. William tried to make some arrangement by which he could purchase his own freedom, but the old doctor would hear nothing of the kind. If there is one thing more revolting in the trade of human flesh than another, it is the selling of one's own blood relations.

He accordingly set out for the city in search of a new master. When he arrived there, he proceeded to the jail with the hope of seeing his sister, but was again disappointed. On the following morning he made another attempt, and was allowed to see her once, for the last time. When he entered the room where she was seated in one corner, alone and disconsolate, there were four other women in the room belonging to the same man, who were bought, the jailer said, for the master's own use.

William's sister was seated with her face towards the door when he entered, but her gaze was transfixed on nothingness, and she did not look up when he walked up to her; but as soon as she observed him she sprang up, threw her arms around his neck, leaned her head upon his breast, and, without uttering a word, in silent, indescribable sorrow, burst into tears. She remained so for some minutes, but when she recovered herself sufficiently to speak she urged him to take his mother immediately, and try to get to the land of freedom. She said there was no hope for herself; she must live and die a slave. After giving her some advice, and taking a ring from his finger, he bade her farewell forever. Reader, did ever a fair sister of thine go down to the grave prematurely? If so, perchance thou hast drank deeply from the cup of sorrow. But how infinitely better is it for a sister to "go into the silent land" with her honor untarnished, but with bright hopes, than for her to be sold to sensual slaveholders!

William had been in the city now two days, and, as he was to be absent for only a week, it was well that he should make the best use of his time, if he intended to escape. In conversing with his mother, he found her unwilling to make the attempt to reach the land of liberty, but she advised him by all means to get there himself, if he possibly could. She said, as all her children were in slavery, she did not wish to leave them; but he loved his mother so intensely, that he could not think of leaving without her. He consequently used all his simple eloquence to induce her to fly with him, and, at last, he prevailed. They consequently fixed upon the next night as the time for their departure. The time at length arrived, and they left the city just as the clock struck nine. Having found a boat, they crossed the river in it. Whose boat it was he did not know; neither did he care. When it had served his purpose, he turned it adrift, and when he saw it last it was going at a good speed down the river. After walking in the main road as fast as they could all night when the morning came they made for the woods, and remained there during the day; but when night came again, they proceeded on their journey, with nothing but the North Star to guide them. They continued to travel by night, and to bury themselves in the silent solitudes of the forest by day. Hunger and fatigue could not stop them, for the prospect of freedom at the end of the journey nerved them up. The very thought of leaving slavery, with its democratic whips, republican chains, and bloodhounds, caused the hearts of the weary fugitives to leap with joy. After travelling ten nights, and hiding in the woods during the day for fear of being arrested and taken back, they thought they might with safety go the rest of their way by daylight. In nearly all the free states there are men who make a business of catching runaway slaves and returning them to their owners for the reward that may be offered; some of those were on the alert for William and his mother, for they had already seen the runaways advertised in the St. Louis newspapers.

All at once they heard the click of a horse's hoof, and looking back saw three men on horseback galloping towards them. They soon came up, and demanded them to stop. The three men dismounted, arrested them on a warrant, and showed them a handbill, offering two hundred dollars for their apprehension and delivery to Dr. Young and Isaac Mansfield, in St. Louis.

While they were reading the handbill, William's mother looked him in the face and burst into tears. "A cold chill ran over me," says he, "and such a sensation I never experienced before, and I trust I never shall again." They took out a rope and tied him, and they were taken back to the house of the individual who appeared to be the leader. They then had something given them to eat, and were separated. Each of them was watched over by two men during the night. The religious characteristic of the American slaveholder soon manifested itself, as, before the family retired to rest, they were all called together to attend prayers; and the very man who, but a few hours before, had arrested poor, panting, fugitive slaves, now read a chapter from the Bible, and offered a prayer to God; as if that benignant and omnipotent One consecrated the infernal act he had just committed.

The next morning they were chained and handcuffed, and started back to St. Louis. A journey of three days brought the fugitives again to the place they had left twelve days previously, with the hope that they would never return. They were put in prison to await the orders of their owners. When a slave attempts to escape and fails, he feels sure of either being severely punished, or sold to the negro-traders and taken to the far south, there to be worked up on a cotton, sugar or rice plantation. This William and his mother dreaded. While they were in suspense as to what would be their fate, news came to them that the mother had been sold to a slave-speculator. William was soon sold to a merchant residing in the city, and removed to his new owner's dwelling. In a few days the gang of slaves, of which William's mother was one, were taken on board a steamer, to be carried to the New Orleans market. The young slave obtained permission from his new owner to go and take a last farewell of his mother. He went to the boat, and found her there, chained to another woman, and the whole number of slaves, amounting to some fifty or sixty, chained in the same manner. As the son approached his mother she moved not, neither did she weep; her emotions were too deep for tears. William approached her, threw his arms around her neck, kissed her, fell upon his knees begging her forgiveness, for he thought he was to blame for her sad condition, and if he had not persuaded her to accompany him she might not have been in chains then.

She remained for some time apparently unimpressionable, tearless, sighless, but in the innermost depths of her heart moved mighty passions. William says, "She finally raised her head, looked me in the face,—and such a look none but an angel can give!—and said, 'My dear son, you are not to blame for my being here. You have done nothing more nor less than your duty. Do not, I pray you, weep for me; I cannot last long upon a cotton plantation. I feel that my heavenly Master will soon call me home, and then I shall be out of the hands of the slaveholders.' I could hear no more; my heart struggled to free itself from the human form. In a moment she saw Mr. Mansfield, her master, coming toward that part of the boat, and she whispered in my ear, 'My child, we must soon part to meet no more on this side of the grave. You have ever said that you would not die a slave; that you would be a freeman. Now try to get your liberty! You will soon have no one to look after but yourself!' and just as she whispered the last sentence into my ear, Mansfield came up to me, and, with an oath, said, 'Leave here this instant! you have been the means of my losing one hundred dollars to get this wench back,' at the same time kicking me with a heavy pair of boots. As I left her she gave one shriek, saying, 'God be with you!' It was the last time that I saw her, and the last word I heard her utter.

"I walked on shore. The bell was tolling. The boat was about to start. I stood with a heavy heart, waiting to see her leave the wharf. As I thought of my mother, I could but feel that I had lost

'The glory of my life,
    My blessing and my pride!
I half forgot the name of slave
    When she was by my side.'

"The love of liberty that had been burning in my bosom had well-nigh gone out. I felt as though I was ready to die. The boat moved gently from the wharf, and while she glided down the river I realized that my mother was indeed

'Gone—gone—sold and gone
To the rice-swamp, dank and lone.'

"After the boat was out of sight I returned home; but my thoughts were
so absorbed in what I had witnessed that I knew not what I was about.
Night came, but it brought no sleep to my eyes." When once the love of
freedom is born in the slave's mind, it always increases and brightens; and
William having heard so much about Canada, where a number of his
acquaintances had found a refuge and a home, he heartily desired to join
them. Building castles in the air in the day-time, incessantly thinking of
freedom, he would dream of the land of liberty, but on waking in the
morning would weep to find it but a dream.

"He would dream of Victoria's domain,
  And in a moment he seemed to be there;
But the fear of being taken again
  Soon hurried him back to despair."

Having been for some time employed as a servant in a hotel, and being
of a very active turn, William's new owner resolved to let him out on board
a steamboat. Consequently the young slave was hired out to the steamer
St. Louis, and soon after sold to Captain Enoch Price, the owner of that
boat. Here he was destined to remain but a short period, as Mrs. Price
wanted a carriage-driver, and had set her heart upon William for that
purpose.

Scarcely three months had elapsed from the time that William became
the property of Captain Price, ere that gentleman's family took a pleasure-
trip to New Orleans, and William accompanied them. From New Orleans
the family proceeded to Louisville. The hope of escape again dawned
upon the slave's mind, and the trials of the past were lost in hopes for the
future. The love of liberty, which had been burning in his bosom for years,
and which, at times, had been well-nigh extinguished, was now resuscitated. Hopes nurtured in childhood, and strengthened as manhood
dawned, now spread their sails to the gales of his imagination. At night,
when all around was peaceful, and in the mystic presence of the everlast-
ing starlight, he would walk the steamer's decks, meditating on his happy
prospects, and summoning up gloomy reminiscences of the dear hearts he
was leaving behind him. When not thinking of the future his mind would
dwell on the past. The love of a dear mother, a dear and affectionate sister,
and three brothers yet living, caused him to shed many tears. If he could
only be assured of their being dead, he would have been comparatively
happy; but he saw, in imagination, his mother in the cotton-field, followed

by a monster task-master, and no one to speak a consoling word to her. He beheld his sister in the hands of the slave-driver, compelled to submit to his cruelty, or, what was unutterably worse, his lust; but still he was far away from them, and could not do anything for them if he remained in slavery; consequently he resolved, and consecrated the resolve with a prayer, that he would start on the first opportunity.

That opportunity soon presented itself. When the boat got to the wharf where it had to stay for some time, at the first convenient moment William made towards the woods, where he remained until night-time. He dared not walk during the day, even in the State of Ohio, he had seen so much of the perfidy of white men, and resolved, if possible, not to get into their hands. After darkness covered the world, he emerged from his hiding-place; but he did not know east from west, or north from south; clouds hid the North Star from his view. In this desolate condition he remained for some hours, when the clouds rolled away, and his friend, with its shining face,—the North Star,—welcomed his sight. True as the needle to the pole, he obeyed its attractive beauty, and walked on till daylight dawned.

It was winter-time; the day on which he started was the first of January, and, as it might be expected, it was intensely cold; he had no overcoat, no food, no friend, save the North Star, and the God which made it. How ardently must the love of freedom burn in the poor slave's bosom, when he will pass through so many difficulties, and even look death in the face, in winning his birthright freedom! But what crushed the poor slave's heart in his flight most was, not the want of food or clothing, but the thought that every white man was his deadly enemy. Even in the free States the prejudice against color is so strong, that there appears to exist a deadly antagonism between the white and colored races.

William in his flight carried a tinder-box with him, and when he got very cold he would gather together dry leaves and stubble and make a fire, or certainly he would have perished. He was determined to enter into no house, fearing that he might meet a betrayer.

It must have been a picture which would have inspired an artist, to see the fugitive roasting the ears of corn that he found or took from barns during the night, at solitary fires in the deep solitudes of woods.

The suffering of the fugitive was greatly increased by the cold, from the fact of his having just come from the warm climate of New Orleans. Slaves seldom have more than one name, and William was not an exception to this, and the fugitive began to think of an additional name. A heavy rain of three days, in which it froze as fast as it fell, and by which the poor fugitive was completely drenched, and still more chilled, added to the depression of his spirits already created by his weary journey. Nothing but the fire of hope burning within his breast could have sustained him under such overwhelming trials.

> "Behind he left the whip and chains;
> Before him were sweet Freedom's plains."

Through cold and hunger, William was now ill, and he could go no further. The poor fugitive resolved to seek protection, and accordingly hid himself in the woods near the road, until some one should pass. Soon a traveller came along, but the slave dared not speak. A few moments more and a second passed; the fugitive attempted to speak, but fear deprived him of voice. A third made his appearance. He wore a broad-brimmed hat and a long coat, and was evidently walking only for exercise. William scanned him well, and, though not much skilled in physiognomy, he concluded he was the man. William approached him, and asked him if he knew any one who would help him, as he was sick. The gentleman asked whether he was not a slave. The poor slave hesitated; but, on being told that he had nothing to fear, he answered "Yes." The gentleman told him he was in a pro-slavery neighborhood, but, if he would wait a little, he would go and get a covered wagon, and convey him to his house. After he had gone, the fugitive meditated whether he should stay or not, being apprehensive that the broad-brimmed gentleman had gone for some one to assist him: he however concluded to remain.

After waiting about an hour—an hour big with fate to him—he saw the covered-wagon making its appearance, and no one in it but the person he before accosted. Trembling with hope and fear, he entered the wagon, and was carried to the person's house. When he got there, he still halted between two opinions, whether he should enter or take to his heels; but he soon decided, after seeing the glowing face of the wife. He saw something in her that bid him welcome, something that told him he would not be betrayed.

He soon found that he was under the shed of a Quaker, and a Quaker of the George Fox stamp. He had heard of Quakers and their kindness; but was not prepared to meet with such hospitality as now greeted him. He saw nothing but kind looks, and heard nothing but tender words. He began to feel the pulsations of a new existence. White men always scorned him, but now a white benevolent woman felt glad to wait on him; it was a revolution in his experience. The table was loaded with good things, but he could not eat. If he were allowed the privilege of sitting in the kitchen, he thought he could do justice to the viands. The surprise being over, his appetite soon returned.

"I have frequently been asked," says William, "how I felt upon finding myself regarded as a man by a white family; especially having just run away from one. I cannot say that I have ever answered the question yet. The fact that I was, in all probability, a freeman, sounded in my ears like a charm. I am satisfied that none but a slave could place such an appreciation upon liberty as I did at that time. I wanted to see my mother and sister, that I might tell them that 'I was free!' I wanted to see my fellow-slaves in St. Louis, and let them know that the chains were no longer upon my limbs. I wanted to see Captain Price, and let him learn from my own lips that I was no more a chattel, but a MAN. I was anxious, too, thus to inform Mrs. Price that she must get another coachman, and I wanted to see Eliza more than I did Mr. Price or Mrs. Price. The fact that I was a freeman—could walk, talk, eat, and sleep as a man, and no one to stand over me with the blood-clotted cow-hide—all this made me feel that I was not myself."

The kind Quaker, who so hospitably entertained William, was called Wells Brown. He remained with him about a fortnight, during which time he was well fed and clothed. Before leaving, the Quaker asked him what was his name besides William. The fugitive told him he had no other. "Well," said he, "thee must have another name. Since thee has got out of slavery, thee has become a man, and men always have two names."

William told him that as he was the first man to extend the hand of friendship to him, he would give him the privilege of naming him.

"If I name thee," said he, "I shall call thee Wells Brown, like myself."

"But," said he, "I am not willing to lose my name of William. It was taken from me once against my will, and I am not willing to part with it on any terms."

"Then," said the benevolent man, "I will call thee William Wells Brown."

"So be it," said William Wells Brown, and he has been known by this name ever since.

After giving the newly-christened freeman "a name," the Quaker gave him something to aid him to get "a local habitation." So, after giving him some money, Brown again started for Canada. In four days he reached a public-house, and went in to warm himself. He soon found that he was not out of the reach of his enemies. While warming himself he heard some men in an adjoining bar-room talking about some runaway slaves. He thought it was time to be off, and suiting the action to the thought, he was soon in the woods out of sight. When night came, he returned to the road and walked on; and so, for two days and two nights, till he was faint and ready to perish of hunger.

In this condition he arrived in the town of Cleveland, Ohio, on the banks of Lake Erie, where he determined to remain until the spring of the year, and then to try and reach Canada. Here he was compelled to work merely for his food.

Having tasted the sweets of freedom himself, his great desire was to extend its blessing to his race, and in the language of the poet he would ask himself,

> "Is true freedom but to break
> Fetters for our own dear sake,
> And with leathern hearts forget
> That we owe mankind a debt?
>
> "No! true freedom is to share
> All the chains our brothers wear,
> And with heart and hand to be
> Earnest to make others free."

While acting as a servant to one of the steamers on Lake Erie, Brown often took fugitives from Cleveland and other ports to Buffalo, or Detroit, from either of which places they could cross to Canada in an hour. During the season of 1842, this fugitive slave conveyed no less than *sixty-nine* runaway slaves across Lake Erie, and placed them safe on the soil of Canada.

In proportion as his mind expanded under the more favorable circumstances in which he was placed, Brown became anxious, not merely for the redemption of his race from personal slavery, but for the moral and religious elevation of those who were free. Finding that habits of intoxication were too prevalent among his colored brethren, he, in conjunction with others, commenced a temperance reformation in their body. Such was the success of their efforts that, in three years, in the city of Buffalo alone a society of upwards of five hundred members was raised out of a colored population of less than seven hundred. Of that society Mr. Brown was thrice elected president.

In the spring of 1844 he became an agent of the Western New York Anti-Slavery Society, and afterwards spent some time in the service of the Massachusetts Society. In 1849 Mr. Brown embarked for Europe as a delegate to the Paris Peace Conference.

The reception of Mr. Brown at the Peace Congress, in Paris, was most flattering. He admirably maintained his reputation as a public speaker. His brief address upon that "war spirit of America, which holds in bondage nearly four millions of his brethren," produced a profound sensation. At its conclusion the speaker was warmly greeted by Victor Hugo, the Abbé Duguerry, Emile de Giradin, Richard Cobden, and every man of note in the assembly. At the soirée given by M. de Tocqueville, the Minister for Foreign Affairs, and the other fêtes given to the members of the Congress, Mr. Brown was received with marked attention.

Having finished his peace mission in France, he returned to England, where he was received with a hearty welcome by some of the most influential abolitionists of that country. Most of the fugitive slaves, and, in fact, nearly all of the colored men who have visited Great Britain from the United States, have come upon begging missions, either for some society or for themselves. Mr. Brown has been almost the only exception. With that independence of feeling which those who are acquainted with him know to be one of his chief characteristics, he determined to maintain himself and family by his own exertions,—by his literary labors, and the honorable profession of a public lecturer. From nearly all the cities and large provincial towns he received invitations to lecture or address public meetings. The mayors, or other citizens of note, presided over many of these meetings. At Newcastle-upon-Tyne a soirée was given him, and an address presented by the citizens. A large and influential meeting was held at Bolton, Lancashire, which was addressed by Mr. Brown, and at its close the ladies presented to him the following address:

"AN ADDRESS PRESENTED TO MR. WILLIAM WELLS BROWN, THE
FUGITIVE SLAVE FROM AMERICA, BY THE LADIES OF BOLTON, MARCH
22ND, 1850:

"DEAR FRIEND AND BROTHER: We cannot permit you to depart from among us without giving expression to the feelings which we entertain towards yourself personally, and to the sympathy which you have awakened in our breasts for the three millions of our sisters and brothers who still suffer and groan in the prison-house of American bondage. You came among us an entire stranger; we received you for the sake of your mission; and having heard the story of your personal wrongs, and gazed with horror on the atrocities of slavery as seen through the medium of your touching descriptions, we are resolved, henceforward, in reliance on divine assistance, to render what aid we can to the cause which you have so eloquently pleaded in our presence.

"We have no words to express our detestation of the crimes which, in the name of liberty, are committed in the country which gave you birth. Language fails to tell our deep abhorrence of the impiety of those who, in the still more sacred name of religion, rob immortal beings not only of an earthly citizenship, but do much to prevent them for obtaining a heavenly one; and, as mothers and daughters, we embrace this opportunity of giving utterance to our utmost indignation at the cruelties perpetrated upon our sex, by a people professedly acknowledging the equality of all mankind. Carry with you, on your return to the land of your nativity, this our solemn protest against the wicked institution which, like a dark and baleful cloud, hangs over it; and ask the unfeeling enslavers, as best you can, to open the prison-doors to them that are bound, and let the oppressed go free.

"Allow us to assure you that your brief sojourn in our town has been to ourselves, and to vast multitudes, of a character long to be remembered; and when you are far removed from us, and toiling, as we hope you many be long spared to do, in this righteous enterprise, it may be some solace to your mind to know that your name is cherished with affectionate regard, and that the blessing of the Most High is earnestly supplicated in behalf of yourself, your family, and the cause to which you have consecrated your distinguished talents."

A most respectable and enthusiastic public meeting was held at Sheffield to welcome Mr. Brown, and the next day he was invited to inspect several of the large establishments there. While going through the manufactory of Messrs. Broadhead and Atkin, silver and electro platers, &c., in Love-street, and whilst he was being shown through the works, a subscription was hastily set on foot on his behalf, by the workmen and women of the establishment, which was presented to Mr. Brown, in the counting-house, by a deputation of the subscribers. The spokesman (the designer to Messrs. Broadhead & Atkin), addressing Mr. Brown on behalf of the work-people, begged his acceptance of the present as a token of esteem, as well as an expression of their sympathy in the cause he advocates, namely, that of the American slave. Mr. Brown briefly thanked the parties for their spontaneous free-will offering, accompanied, as it was, by a generous expression of sympathy for his afflicted brethren and sisters in bondage.

Mr. Brown was in England five years, and during his sojourn there travelled above twenty-five thousand miles through Great Britain, addressed more than one thousand public meetings, lectured in twenty-three mechanics' and literary institutions, and gave his services to many of the benevolent and religious societies on the occasion of their anniversary meetings. After a lecture which he delivered before the Whittington Club, he received from the managers of that institution the following testimonial:

"WHITTINGTON CLUB AND METROPOLITAN ATHENÆUM,
189 STRAND, *June* 21, 1850.

"MY DEAR SIR: I have much pleasure in conveying to you the best thanks of the Managing Committee of this institution for the excellent lecture you gave here last evening, and also in presenting you in their names with an honorary membership of the club. It is hoped that you will often avail yourself of its privileges by coming amongst us. You will then see, by the cordial welcome of the members, that they protest against the odious distinctions made between man and man, and the abominable traffic of which you have been the victim.

"For my own part, I shall be happy to be serviceable to you in any way, and at all times be glad to place the advantages of the institution at your disposal.

"I am, my dear sir, yours, truly,

"WILLIAM STRUDWICKE, *Secretary.*

"Mr. W. WELLS BROWN."

———

The following lines were read at a soirèe given to Mr. Brown at Bristol, in 1850:

TO WILLIAM WELLS BROWN,
THE AMERICAN FUGITIVE SLAVE
By E. S. Mathews.

Brother, farewell to thee!
  His blessing on thee rest
Who hates all slavery
  And helps the poor oppressed.

Go forth with power to break
  The bitter, galling yoke;
Go forth 'mongst strong and weak,
  The aid of all invoke.

O, thou wilt have much woe,
  Tossed on a sea of strife,
Hunted by many a foe
  Eager to take thy life.

Perchance thou'lt have to brook
  The taunts of bond and free,
The cold, disdainful look
  of men—less men than thee.

We feel thy soul will rise
  Superior to it all;
For thou hast heard the cries,
  And drained the cup of gall.

Thine eyes have wept the tears
  Which tyrants taught to flow,

While craven scorn and sneers
    Fell with the shameful blow.

And now that thou art come
    To Freedom's blessed land,
Thou broodest on thy home
    And Slavery's hateful brand.

Thou thinkest thou canst hear
    Three million voices call;
They raise to thee their prayer,—
    Haste, help to break their thrall!

Say, wilt thou have, thy steps to guard,
    Some powerful spell or charm?
Then listen to thy sister's word,
    Nor fear thou hurt or harm.

When shines the North Star, cold and bright,
    Cheer thou thy heart, lift up thy head!
Feel, as thou look'st upon its light,
    That blessings on its beams are shed!
For rich, and poor, and bond, and free,
Will also gaze and pray for thee.

CHAPTER 1

"Adieu, adieu!—my native shore
   Fades o'er the waters blue;
The night-winds sigh, the breakers roar,
   And shrieks the wild sea-mew.
Yon sun that sets upon the sea
   We follow in his flight;
Farewell a while to him and thee!
   My native land, good-night!"

CHILDE HAROLD.

On the 18th July, I took passage in the steamship *Canada,* Captain Judkins, bound for Liverpool. The day was a warm one; so much so, that many persons on board, as well as on shore, stood with their umbrellas up, so intense was the heat of the sun. The ringing of the ship's bell was a signal for us to shake hands with our friends, which we did, and then stepped on the deck of the noble craft. The *Canada* quitted her moorings at half-past twelve, and we were soon in motion. As we were passing out of Boston Bay, I took my stand on the quarter-deck, to take a last farewell (at least for a time) of my native land. A visit to the Old World, up to that time, had seemed but a dream. As I looked back upon the receding land, recollections of the past rushed through my mind in quick succession. From the treatment that I had received from the Americans as a victim of slavery, and the knowledge that I was at that time liable to be seized and again reduced to whips and chains, I had supposed that I would leave the country without any regret; but in this I was mistaken, for when I saw the last thread of communication cut off between me and the land, and the dim shores dying away in the distance, I almost regretted that I was not on shore.

An anticipated trip to a foreign country appears pleasant when talking about it, especially when surrounded by friends whom we love; but when we have left them all behind, it does not seem so pleasant. Whatever may be the fault of the government under which we live, and no matter how oppressive her laws may appear, yet we leave our native land (if such it be) with feelings akin to sorrow. With the steamer's powerful engine at work, and with a fair wind, we were speedily on the bosom of the Atlantic, which was as calm and as smooth as our own Hudson in its calmest aspect. We had on board above one hundred passengers, forty of whom were the "Vienneise children"—a troop of dancers. The passengers represented several different nations, English, French, Spaniards, Africans, and Americans. One man, who had the longest mustache that mortal man was ever doomed to wear, especially attracted my attention. He appeared to belong to no country in particular, but was yet the busiest man on board. After viewing for some time the many strange faces around me, I descended to the cabin to look after my luggage, which had been put hurriedly on board. I hope that all who take a trip of so great a distance may be as fortunate as I was, in being supplied with books to read on the voyage. My friends had furnished me with literature, from "Macaulay's History of England" to "Jane Eyre," so that I did not want for books to occupy my time.

A pleasant passage of about thirty hours brought us to Halifax, at six o'clock in the evening. In company with my friend the President of the Oberlin Institute,[1] I took a stroll through the town; and from what little I saw of the people in the streets, I am sure that the taking of the temperance pledge would do them no injury. Our stay in Halifax was short. Having taken in a few sacks of coals, the mails, and a limited number of passengers, we were again out, and soon at sea.

As the steamer moved gently from the shore I felt like repeating those lines of a distinguished poet:

> "With thee, my bark, I'll swiftly go
>   Athwart the foaming brine;
> Nor care what land thou bear'st me to,
>   So not again to mine.
> Welcome, welcome, ye dark blue waves!
>   And when you fail my sight
> Welcome ye deserts and ye caves!
>   My native land, good-night!"

Nothing occurred during the passage to mar the pleasure which we anticipated from a voyage by sea in such fine weather. And, after a

splendid run of seven days more, I heard the welcome cry of "Land a-
head." It was early in the morning, and I was not yet out of bed; but I had
no wish to remain longer in my berth. Although the passage had been
unprecedently short, yet this news was hailed with joy by all on board.

For my own part, I was soon on deck. Away in the distance, and on our
larboard quarter, were the gray hills of old Ireland. Yes; we were in sight of
the land of Curran, Emmet and O'Connell.[2] While I rejoiced with the
other passengers at the sight of land, and the near approach to the end of
our voyage, I felt low-spirited, because it reminded me of the great distance
I was from home, and of dear ones left behind. But the experience of above
twenty years' travelling had prepared me to undergo what most persons
must, in visiting a strange country. This was the last day but one that we
were to be on board; and, as if moved by the sight of land, all seemed to be
gathering their different things together—brushing up their old clothes and
putting on their new ones, as if this would bring them any sooner to the
end of their journey.

The last night on board was the most pleasant, apparently, that we had
experienced; probably, because it was the last. The moon was in her
meridian splendor, pouring her broad light over the calm sea; while near to
us, on our starboard side, was a ship, with her snow-white sails spread
aloft, and stealing through the water like a thing of life. What can present a
more picturesque view than two vessels at sea on a moonlight night, and
within a few rods of each other? With a gentle breeze, and the powerful
engine at work, we seemed to be flying to the embrace of our British
neighbors.

The next morning I was up before the sun, and found that we were
within a few miles of Liverpool. The taking of a pilot on board at eleven
o'clock warned us to prepare to quit our ocean palace, and seek other
quarters. At a little past three o'clock, the ship cast anchor, and we were
all tumbled, bag and baggage, into a small steamer, and in a few moments
were at the door of the custom-house. The passage had only been nine
days and twenty-two hours, the quickest on record at that time, yet it was
long enough. I waited nearly three hours before my name was called, and
when it was I unlocked my trunks and handed them over to one of the
officers, whose dirty hands made no improvement on the work of the
laundress. First one article was taken out, and then another, till an *Iron
Collar* that had been worn by a female slave on the banks of the Mississippi was hauled out, and this democratic instrument of torture became
the centre of attraction; so much so, that instead of going on with the
examination, all hands stopped to look at the "Negro Collar."

Several of my countrymen who were standing by were not a little displeased at answers which I gave to questions on the subject of slavery; but they held their peace. The interest created by the appearance of the iron collar closed the examination of my luggage. As if afraid that they would find something more hideous, they put the custom-house mark on each piece, and passed them out, and I was soon comfortably installed at Brown's Temperance Hotel, Clayton-square.

No person of my complexion can visit this country without being struck with the marked difference between the English and the Americans. The prejudice which I have experienced on all and every occasion in the United States, and to some extent on board the *Canada,* vanished as soon as I set foot on the soil of Britain. In America I had been bought and sold as a slave in the Southern States. In the so-called Free States, I had been treated as one born to occupy an inferior position,—in steamers, compelled to take my fare on the deck; in hotels, to take my meals in the kitchen; in coaches, to ride on the outside; in railways, to ride in the "negro-car;" and in churches, to sit in the "negro-pew." But no sooner was I on British soil, than I was recognized as a man, and an equal. The very dogs in the streets appeared conscious of my manhood. Such is the difference, and such is the change that is brought about by a trip of nine days in an Atlantic steamer.

I was not more struck with the treatment of the people than with the appearance of the great seaport of the world. The gray stone piers and docks, the dark look of the magnificent warehouses, the substantial appearance of everything around, causes one to think himself in a new world instead of the old. Everything in Liverpool looks old, yet nothing is worn out. The beautiful villas on the opposite side of the river, in the vicinity of Birkenhead, together with the countless number of vessels in the river, and the great ships to be seen in the stream, give life and animation to the whole scene.

Everything in and about Liverpool seems to be built for the future as well as the present. We had time to examine but few of the public buildings, the first of which was the custom-house, an edifice that would be an ornament to any city in the world.

CHAPTER 2

"It seems as if every ship their sovereign knows,
    His awful summons they so soon obey;
So hear the scaly herds when Proteus blows,
    And so to pasture follow through the sea."

After remaining in Liverpool two days, I took passage in the little steamer *Adelaide* for Dublin. The wind being high on the night of our voyage, the vessel had scarcely got to sea ere we were driven to our berths; and, though the distance from Liverpool to Dublin is short, yet, strange to say, I witnessed more effects of the sea and rolling of the steamer upon the passengers, than was to be seen during the whole of our voyage from America. We reached Kingstown, five miles below Dublin, after a passage of nearly fifteen hours, and were soon seated on a car, and on our way to the city. While coming into the bay, one gets a fine view of Dublin and the surrounding country. Few sheets of water make a more beautiful appearance than Dublin Bay. We found it as still and smooth as a mirror, with a soft mist on its surface,—a strange contrast to the boisterous sea that we had left a moment before.

The curious phrases of the Irish sounded harshly upon my ear, probably because they were strange to me. I lost no time, on reaching the city, in seeking out some to whom I had letters of introduction, one of whom gave me an invitation to make his house my home during my stay,—an invitation which I did not think fit to decline.

Dublin, the metropolis of Ireland, is a city of above two hundred thousand inhabitants, and is considered by the people of Ireland to be the second city in the British empire. The Liffey, which falls into Dublin Bay a little below the custom-house, divides the town into two nearly equal

99

parts. The streets are—some of them—very fine, especially Sackville-street, in the centre of which stands a pillar erected to Nelson, England's most distinguished naval commander. The Bank of Ireland, to which I paid a visit, is a splendid building, and was formerly the Parliament House. This magnificent edifice fronts College Green, and near at hand stands a bronze statue of William III. The Bank and the Custom-House are two of the finest monuments of architecture in the city; the latter of which stands near the river Liffey, and its front makes an imposing appearance, extending three hundred and seventy-five feet. It is built of Portland stone, and is adorned with a beautiful portico in the centre, consisting of four Doric columns, supporting an enriched entablature, decorated with a group of figures in alto-relievo, representing Hibernia and Britannia presenting emblems of peace and liberty. A magnificent dome, supporting a cupola, on whose apex stands a colossal figure of Hope, rises nobly from the centre of the building to a height of one hundred and twenty-five feet. It is, withal, a fine specimen of what man can do.

From this noble edifice we bent our steps to another part of the city, and soon found ourselves in the vicinity of St. Patrick's, where we had a heart-sickening view of the poorest of the poor. All the recollections of poverty which I had ever beheld seemed to disappear in comparison with what was then before me. We passed a filthy and noisy market, where fruit and vegetable women were screaming and begging those passing by to purchase their commodities; while in and about the market-place were throngs of beggars fighting for rotten fruit, cabbage-stock, and even the very trimmings of vegetables. On the side-walks were great numbers hovering about the doors of the more wealthy, and following strangers, importuning them for "pence to buy bread." Sickly and emaciated looking creatures, half naked, were at our heels at every turn.

In our return home, we passed through a respectable-looking street, in which stands a small three-story brick building, that was pointed out to us as the birthplace of Thomas Moore, the poet. The following verse from one of his poems was continually in my mind while viewing this house:

> "Where is the slave so lowly,
> Condemned to chains unholy,
> Who, could be burst
> His bonds at first,
> Would pine beneath them slowly?"

The next day was the Sabbath, but it had more the appearance of a holiday than a day of rest. It had been announced the day before that the royal fleet was expected, and at an early hour on Sunday the entire town seemed to be on the move towards Kingstown, and as the family with whom I was staying followed the multitude, I was not inclined to remain behind, and so went with them. On reaching the station, we found it utterly impossible to get standing room in any of the trains, much less a seat, and therefore determined to reach Kingstown under the plea of a morning's walk; and in this we were not alone, for during the walk of five miles the road was filled with thousands of pedestrians, and a countless number of carriages, phaëtons, and vehicles of a more humble order.

We reached the lower town in time to get a good dinner, and rest ourselves before going to make further searches for her majesty's fleet. At a little past four o'clock, we observed the multitude going towards the pier, a number of whom were yelling, at the top of their voices, "It's coming, it's coming!" but on going to the quay we found that a false alarm had been given. However, we had been on the look-out but a short time, when a column of smoke, rising as it were, out of the sea, announced that the royal fleet was near at hand. The concourse in the vicinity of the pier was variously estimated at from eighty to one hundred thousand.

It was not long before the five steamers were entering the harbor, the one bearing her majesty leading the way. As each vessel had a number of distinguished persons on board, the people appeared to be at a loss to know which was the queen; and as each party made its appearance on the promenade deck, they were received with great enthusiasm, the party having the best-looking lady being received with the greatest applause. The Prince of Wales, and Prince Alfred, while crossing the deck were recognized, and greeted with three cheers; the former, taking off his hat and bowing to the people, showed that he had had some training as a public man, although not ten years of age. But not so with Prince Alfred; for, when his brother turned to him and asked him to take off his hat, and make a bow to the people, he shook his head, and said, "No." This was received with hearty laughter by those on board, and was responded to by the thousands on shore. But greater applause was yet in store for the young prince; for the captain of the steamer being near by, and seeing that the Prince of Wales could not prevail on his brother to take off his hat, stepped up to him and undertook to take it off for him, when, seemingly to the delight of all, the prince put both hands to his head, and held his hat fast. This was regarded as a sign of courage and future renown, and was received with the greatest enthusiasm, many crying out, "Good, good! he will make a brave king when his day comes."

After the greetings and applause had been wasted on many who had appeared on deck, all at once, as if by some magic power, we beheld a lady, rather small in stature, with auburn hair, attired in a plain dress, and wearing a sky-blue bonnet, standing on the larboard paddle-box, by the side of a tall, good-looking man, with a mustache. The thunders of applause that now rent the air, and cries of "The queen, the queen!" seemed to set at rest the question of which was her majesty. But a few moments were allowed to the people to look at the queen, before she again disappeared; and it was understood that she would not be seen again that evening. A rush was then made for the railway, to return to Dublin.

*   *   *   *   *   *

The seventh of August was a great day in Dublin. At an early hour the bells began their merry peals, and the people were soon seen in groups in the streets and public squares. The hour of ten was fixed for the procession to leave Kingstown, and it was expected to enter the city at eleven. The windows of the houses in the streets through which the royal train was to pass were at a premium, and seemed to find ready occupants.

Being invited the day previous to occupy part of a window in Sackville-street, I was stationed at my allotted place at an early hour, with an outstretched neck and open eyes. My own color differing from those about me, I attracted not a little attention from many; and often, when gazing down the street to see if the royal procession was in sight, would find myself eyed by all around. But neither while at the window or in the streets was I once insulted. This was so unlike the American prejudice, that it seemed strange to me. It was near twelve o'clock before the procession entered Sackville-street, and when it did all eyes seemed to beam with delight. The first carriage contained only her majesty and the Prince Consort; the second the royal children, and the third the lords in waiting. Fifteen carriages were used by those that made up the royal party. I had a full view of the queen and all who followed in the train. Her majesty—whether from actual love for her person, or the novelty of the occasion, I know not which—was received everywhere with the greatest enthusiasm. One thing, however, is certain, and that is, Queen Victoria is beloved by her subjects.

But the grant *fête* was reserved for the evening. Great preparations had been made to have a grand illumination on the occasion, and hints were thrown out that it would surpass anything ever witnessed in London. In this they were not far out of the way; for all who witnessed the scene admitted that it could scarcely have been surpassed. My own idea of an illumination, as I had seen it in the back-woods of my native land, dwindled into nothing when compared with this magnificent affair.

In company with a few friends, and a lady under my charge, I undertook to pass through Sackville and one or two other streets about eight o'clock in the evening, but we found it utterly impossible to proceed. Masses thronged the streets, and the wildest enthusiasm seemed to prevail. In our attempt to cross the bridge, we were wedged in and lost our companions; and on one occasion I was separated from the lady, and took shelter under a cart standing in the street. After being jammed and pulled about for nearly two hours, I returned to my lodgings, where I found part of my company, who had come in one after another. At eleven o'clock we had all assembled, and each told his adventures and "hair-breadth escapes;" and nearly every one had lost a pocket-handkerchief or something of the kind; my own was among the missing. However, I lost nothing; for a benevolent lady, who happened to be one of the company, presented me with one which was of far more value than the one I had lost.

Every one appeared to enjoy the holiday which the royal visit had caused. But the Irish are indeed a strange people. How varied their aspect, how contradictory their character! Ireland, the land of genius and degradation, of great resources and unparalleled poverty, noble deeds and the most revolting crimes, the land of distinguished poets, splendid orators, and the bravest of soldiers, the land of ignorance and beggary! Dublin is a splendid city, but its splendor is that of chiselled marble rather than real life. One cannot behold these architectural monuments without thinking of the great men that Ireland has produced. The names of Burke, Sheridan, Flood, Grattan, O'Connell and Shiel, have become as familiar to the Americans as household words. Burke is known as the statesman; Sheridan for his great speech on the trial of Warren Hastings; Grattan for his eloquence; O'Connell as the agitator, and Shiel as the accomplished orator.

But, of Ireland's sons, none stands higher in America than Thomas Moore, the poet. The vigor of his sarcasm, the glow of his enthusiasm, the coruscations of his fancy, and the flashing of his wit, seem to be as well understood in the New World as the Old; and the support which his pen has given to civil and religious liberty throughout the world entitles the Minstrel of Erin to this elevated position.

CHAPTER 3

"There is no other land like thee,
    No dearer shore;
Thou art the shelter of the free,—
The home, the port of Liberty."

After a pleasant sojourn of three weeks in Ireland, I took passage in one of the mail-steamers for Liverpool, and, arriving there, was soon on the road to the metropolis. The passage from Dublin to Liverpool was an agreeable one. The rough sea that we passed through on going to Ireland had given way to a dead calm; and our noble little steamer, on quitting the Dublin wharf, seemed to understand that she was to have it all her own way. During the first part of the evening, the boat appeared to feel her importance, and, darting through the water with majestic strides, she left behind her a dark cloud of smoke suspended in the air like a banner; while, far astern in the wake of the vessel, could be seen the rippled waves sparkling in the rays of the moon, giving strength and beauty to the splendor of the evening.

On reaching Liverpool, and partaking of a good breakfast, for which we paid double price, we proceeded to the railway station, and were soon going at a rate unknown to those accustomed to travel only on American railways. At a little past two o'clock in the afternoon we saw in the distance the outskirts of London. We could get but an indistinct view, which had the appearance of one architectural mass, extending all round to the horizon, and enveloped in a combination of fog and smoke; and towering above every other object to be seen was the dome of St. Paul's Cathedral.

A few moments more, and we were safely seated in a "Hansom's

Patent," and on our way to Hughes's—one of the politest men of the George Fox stamp we have ever met. Here we found forty or fifty persons, who, like ourselves, were bound for the Peace Congress.[3] The Sturges, the Wighams, the Richardsons, the Allens, the Thomases, and a host of others not less distinguished as friends of peace, were of the company—of many of whom I had heard, but none of whom I had ever seen; yet I was not an entire stranger to many, especially to the abolitionists. In company with a friend, I sallied forth after tea to take a view of the city. The evening was fine—the dense fog and smoke, having to some extent passed away, left the stars shining brightly, while the gas-light from the street-lamps and the brilliant shop-windows gave it the appearance of day-light in a new form. "What street is this?" we asked. "Cheapside," was the reply. The street was thronged, and everybody seemed to be going at a rapid rate, as if there was something of importance at the end of the journey. Flying vehicles of every description passing each other with a dangerous rapidity, men with lovely women at their sides, children running about as if they had lost their parents—all gave a brilliancy to the scene scarcely to be excelled. If one wished to get jammed and pushed about, he need go no further than Cheapside. But everything of the kind is done with a degree of propriety in London that would put the New Yorkers to blush. If you are run over in London, they "beg your pardon;" if they run over you in New York, you are "laughed at:" in London, if your hat is knocked off it is picked up and handed to you; if in New York, you must pick it up yourself. There is a lack of good manners among Americans that is scarcely known or understood in Europe. Our stay in the great metropolis gave us but little opportunity of seeing much of the place; for in twenty-four hours after our arrival we joined the rest of the delegates, and started on our visit to our Gallic neighbors.

We assembled at the London Bridge Railway Station, a few minutes past nine, to the number of six hundred. The day was fine, and every eye seemed to glow with enthusiasm. Besides the delegates, there were probably not less than six hundred more, who had come to see the company start. We took our seats, and appeared to be waiting for nothing but the iron-horse to be fastened to the train, when all at once we were informed that we must go to the booking-office and change our tickets. At this news every one appeared to be vexed. This caused great trouble; for, on returning to the train, many persons got into the wrong carriages; and several parties were separated from their friends, while not a few were calling out, at the top of their voices, "Where is my wife? Where is my husband? Where is my luggage? Who's got my boy? Is this the right train?" "What is that lady going to do with all these children?" asked the guard. "Is she a delegate? are all the children delegates?" In the carriage where I had taken my seat was a good-looking lady, who gave signs of being very much annoyed. "It is just so when I am going anywhere: I never saw the like in my life!" said she. "I really wish I was at home again."

An hour had now elapsed, and we were still at the station. However, we were soon on our way, and going at express speed. In passing through Kent we enjoyed the scenery exceedingly, as the weather was altogether in our favor; and the drapery which nature hung on the trees, in the part through which we passed, was in all its gayety. On our arrival at Folkstone, we found three steamers in readiness to convey the party to Boulogne. As soon as the train stopped, a general rush was made for the steamers, and in a very short time the one in which I had embarked was passing out of the harbor. The boat appeared to be conscious that we were going on a holy mission, and seemed to be proud of her load. There is nothing in this wide world so like a thing of life as a steamer, from the breathing of her steam and smoke, the energy of her motion, and the beauty of her shape; while the ease with which she is managed by the command of a single voice makes her appear as obedient as the horse is to the rein.

When we were about half way between the two great European powers, the officer began to gather the tickets. The first to whom he applied, and who handed out his "Excursion Ticket," was informed that we were all in the wrong boat. "Is this not one of the boats to take over the delegates?" asked a pretty little lady, with a whining voice. "No, madam," said the captain. "You must look to the committee for your pay," said one of the company to the captain. "I have nothing to do with committees," the captain replied. "Your fare, gentlemen, if you please."

Here the whole party were again thrown into confusion. "Do you hear that? We are in the wrong boat." "I knew it would be so," said the Rev. Dr. Ritchie, of Edinburgh. "It is indeed a pretty piece of work," said a plain-looking lady in a handsome bonnet. "When I go travelling again," said an elderly-looking gent, with an eye-glass to his face, "I will take the phaëton and old Dobbin." Every one seemed to lay the blame on the committee, and not, too, without some just grounds. However, Mr. Sturge, one of the committee, being in the boat with us, an arrangement was entered into by which we were not compelled to pay our fare the second time.

As we neared the French coast, the first object that attracted our attention was the Napoleon Pillar, on the top of which is a statue of the emperor in the imperial robes. We landed, partook of refreshment that had been prepared for us, and again repaired to the railway station. The arrangements for leaving Boulogne were no better than those at London. But after the delay of another hour we were again in motion.

It was a beautiful country through which we passed from Boulogne to Amiens. Straggling cottages which bespeak neatness and comfort abound on every side. The eye wanders over the diversified views with unabated pleasure, and rests in calm repose upon its superlative beauty. Indeed, the eye cannot but be gratified at viewing the entire country from the coast to the metropolis. Sparkling hamlets spring up, as the steam-horse speeds his way, at almost every point, showing the progress of civilization, and the refinement of the nineteenth century.

We arrived at Paris a few minutes past twelve o'clock at night, when, according to our tickets, we should have been there at nine. Elihu Burritt, who had been in Paris some days, and who had the arrangements there pretty much his own way, was at the station waiting the arrival of the train, and we had demonstrated to us the best evidence that he understood his business.[4] In no other place on the whole route had the affairs been so well managed; for we were seated in our respective carriages and our luggage placed on the top, and away we went to our hotels, without the least difficulty or inconvenience. The champion of an "Ocean Penny Postage" received, as he deserved, thanks from the whole company for his admirable management.

The silence of the night was only disturbed by the rolling of the wheels of the omnibus, as we passed through the dimly-lighted streets. Where, a few months before, was to be seen the flash from the cannon and the musket, and the hearing of the cries and groans behind the barricades, was now the stillness of death—nothing save here and there a *gens d'arme* was to be seen going his rounds in silence.

The omnibus set us down at the hotel Bedford, Rue de L'Card, where, although near one o'clock, we found a good supper waiting for us; and, as I was not devoid of an appetite, I did my share towards putting it out of the way.

The next morning I was up at an early hour, and out on the Boulevards to see what might be seen. As I was passing from the hotel to the Place de La Concord, all at once, and as if by some magic power, I found myself in front of the most splendid edifice imaginable, situated at the end of the Rue Nationale. Seeing a number of persons entering the church at that early hour, and recognizing among them my friend the President of the Oberlin (Ohio) Institute, and wishing not to stray too far from my hotel before breakfast, I followed the crowd and entered the building. The church itself consisted of a vast nave, interrupted by four pews on each side, fronted with lofty fluted Corinthian columns standing on pedestals, supporting colossal arches, bearing up cupolas pierced with skylights and adorned with compartments gorgeously gilt; their corners supported with saints and apostles in *alto relievo*. The walls of the church were lined with rich marble. The different paintings and figures gave the interior an imposing appearance. On inquiry, I found that I was in the Church of the Madeleine. It was near this spot that some of the most interesting scenes occurred during the Revolution of 1848, which dethroned Louis Philippe. Behind the Madeleine is a small but well-supplied market; and on an esplanade east of the edifice a flower-market is held on Tuesdays and Fridays.

At eleven o'clock the same day, the Peace Congress met in the Salle St. Cecile, Rue de la St. Lazare. The Parisians have no "Exeter Hall;" in fact, there is no private hall in the city of any size, save this, where such a meeting could be held. This hall had been fitted up for the occasion. The room is long, and at one end has a raised platform; and at the opposite end is a gallery, with seats raised one above another. On one side of the hall was a balcony with sofas, which were evidently the "reserved seats."

The hall was filled at an early hour with the delegates, their friends, and a good sprinkling of the French. Occasionally, small groups of gentlemen would make their appearance on the platform, until it soon appeared that there was little room left for others; and yet the officers of the Convention had not come in. The different countries were, many of them, represented here. England, France, Belgium, Germany, Switzerland, Greece, Spain, and the United States, had each their delegates. The assembly began to give signs of impatience, when very soon the train of officials made their appearance amid great applause. Victor Hugo led the way, followed by M. Duguerry, curé of the Madeleine, Elihu Burritt, and a host of others of less note. Victor Hugo took the chair as President of the Congress, supported by vice-presidents from several nations represented.[5] Mr. Richard, the secretary, read a dry report of the names of societies, committees, etc., which was deemed the opening of the Convention.

The president then arose, and delivered one of the most impressive and eloquent appeals in favor of peace that could possibly be imagined. The effect produced upon the minds of all present was such as to make the author of *"Notre Dame de Paris"* a great favorite with the Congress. An English gentleman near me said to his friend, "I can't understand a word of what he says, but is it not good?" Victor Hugo concluded his speech amid the greatest enthusiasm on the part of the French, which was followed by hurras in the old English style. The Convention was successively addressed by the President of the Brussels Peace Society; President Mahan, of the Oberlin (Ohio) Institute, U.S.; Henry Vincent; and Richard Cobden. The latter was not only the *lion* of the English delegation, but the great man of the Convention. When Mr. Cobden speaks there is no want of

hearers. The great power of this gentleman lies in his facts and his earnestness, for he cannot be called an eloquent speaker. Mr. Cobden addressed the Congress first in French, then in English; and, with the single
exception of Mr. Ewart, M. P., was the only one of the English delegation
that could speak to the French in their own language.[6]

The first day's proceedings were brought to a close at five o'clock, when
the numerous audience dispersed—the citizens to their homes, and the
delegates to see the sights.

I was not a little amused at an incident that occurred at the close of the
first session. On the passage from America, there were in the same
steamer with me several Americans, and among these three or four appeared to be much annoyed at the fact that I was a passenger, and enjoying
the company of white persons; and, although I was not only insulted, I
very often heard the remark, that "That nigger had better be on his
master's farm," and "What could the American Peace Society be thinking
about, to send a black man as a delegate to Paris?" Well, at the close of the
first sitting of the convention, and just as I was leaving Victor Hugo, to
whom I had been introduced by an M. P., I observed near me a gentleman
with his hat in hand, whom I recognized as one of the passengers who had
crossed the Atlantic with me in the *Canada,* and who appeared to be the
most horrified at having a negro for a fellow-passenger. This gentleman, as
I left M. Hugo, stepped up to me and said, "How do you do, Mr. Brown?"
"You have the advantage of me," said I. "O, don't you know me? I was a
fellow-passenger with you from America; I wish you would give me an
introduction to Victor Hugo and Mr. Cobden." I need not inform you that
I declined introducing this pro-slavery American to these distinguished
men. I only allude to this, to show what a change came over the dreams of
my white American brother by crossing the ocean. The man who would
not have been seen walking with me in the streets of New York, and who
would not have shaken hands with me with a pair of tongs while on the
passage from the United States, could come with hat in hand in Paris, and
say, "I was your fellow-passenger." From the Salle de St. Cecile, I visited
the Column Vendome, from the top of which I obtained a fine view of Paris
and its environs. This is the Bunker Hill Monument of Paris. On the top of
this pillar is a statue of the Emperor Napoleon, eleven feet high. The
monument is built with stone, and the outside covered with a metallic
composition, made of cannons, guns, spikes, and other warlike imple-
ments taken from the Russians and Austrians by Napoleon. Above twelve
hundred cannons were melted down to help to create this monument of
folly, to commemorate the success of the French arms in the German
campaign. The column is in imitation of the Trajan pillar at Rome, and is

twelve feet in diameter at the base. The door at the bottom of the pillar, and where we entered, was decorated above with crowns of oak, surmounted by eagles, each weighing five hundred pounds. The bas-relief of the shaft pursues a spiral direction to the top, and displays, in a chronological order, the principal actions of the French army, from the departure of the troops from Boulogne to the battle of Austerlitz. The figures are near three feet high, and their number said to be two thousand. This sumptuous monument stands on a plinth of polished granite, surmounted by an iron railing; and, from its size and position, has an imposing appearance when seen from any part of the city.

Everything here appears strange and peculiar—the people not less so than their speech. The horses, carriages, furniture, dress and manners, are in keeping with their language. The appearance of the laborers in caps, resembling night-caps, seemed particularly strange to me. The women without bonnets, and their caps turned the right side behind, had nothing of the look of our American women. The prettiest woman I ever saw was without a bonnet, walking on the Boulevards. While in Ireland, and during the few days I was in England, I was struck with the marked difference between the appearance of the women and those of my own country. The American women are too tall, too sallow, and too long-featured, to be called pretty. This is most probably owing to the fact that in America the people come to maturity earlier than in most other countries.

My first night in Paris was spent with interest. No place can present greater street attractions than the Boulevards of Paris. The countless number of cafés, with tables before the doors, and these surrounded by men with long moustaches, with ladies at their sides, whose very smiles give indication of happiness, together with the sound of music from the gardens in the rear, tell the stranger that he is in a different country from his own.

CHAPTER 4

"——A town of noble fame,
Where monuments are found in ancient guise,
Where kings and queens in pomp did long abide,
And where God pleased that good King Louis died."

After the Convention had finished its sittings yesterday, I accompanied Mrs. C—— and sisters to Versailles, where they are residing during the summer. It was really pleasing to see among the hundreds of strange faces in the Convention those distinguished friends of the slave from Boston.

Mrs. C——'s residence is directly in front of the great palace where so many kings have made their homes, the prince of whom was Louis XIV. The palace is now unoccupied. No ruler has dared to take up his residence here since Louis XVI and Marie Antoinette were driven from it by the mob from Paris on the eighth of October, 1789. The town looks like the wreck of what it once was. At the commencement of the first revolution, it contained one hundred thousand inhabitants; now it has only about thirty thousand. It seems to be going back to what it was in the time of Louis XIII, when, in 1624, he built a small brick chateau, and from it arose the magnificent palace which now stands here, and which attracts strangers to it from all parts of the world.

I arose this morning at an early hour, and took a walk through the grounds of the palace, and remained three hours among the fountains and statuary of this more than splendid place. At ten o'clock we again returned to Paris, to the Peace Congress.

The session was opened by a speech from M. Coquerel, the Protestant clergyman in Paris. His speech was received with much applause, and seemed to create great sensation in the Congress, especially at the close of

113

his remarks, when he was seized by the hand by the Abbé Duguerry, amid the most deafening and enthusiastic applause of the entire multitude. The meeting was then addressed in English by a short gentleman, of florid complexion. His words seemed to come without the least difficulty, and his gestures, though somewhat violent, were evidently studied; and the applause with which he was greeted by the English delegation showed that he was a man of no little distinction among them. His speech was one continuous flow of rapid, fervid eloquence, that seemed to fire every heart; and although I disliked his style, I was prepossessed in his favor. This was Henry Vincent, and his speech was in favor of disarmament.

Mr. Vincent was followed by M. Emile de Girardin, the editor of *La Presse,* in one of the most eloquent speeches that I ever heard; and his exclamation of "Soldiers of Peace" drew thunders of applause from his own countrymen. M. Girardin is not only the leader of the French press, but is a writer on politics of great distinction, and a leader of no inconsiderable party in the National Assembly; although still a young man, apparently not more than thirty-eight or forty years of age.

After a speech from Mr. Ewart, M. P., in French, and another from Mr. Cobden in the same language, the Convention was brought to a close for the day. I spent the morning yesterday in visiting some of the lions of the French capital, among which was the Louvre. The French government having kindly ordered that the members of the Peace Congress should be admitted free, and without ticket, to all the public works, I had nothing to do but present my card of membership, and was immediately admitted.

The first room I entered was nearly a quarter of a mile in length; is known as the "Long Gallery," and contains some of the finest paintings in the world. On entering this superb palace, my first impression was that all Christendom had been robbed, that the Louvre might make a splendid appearance. This is the Italian department, and one would suppose by its appearance that but few paintings had been left in Italy. The entrance end of the Louvre was for a long time in an unfinished state, but was afterwards completed by that master workman, the Emperor Napoleon. It was long thought that the building would crumble into decay, but the genius of the great Corsican rescued it from ruin.

During our walk through the Louvre, we saw some twenty or thirty artists copying paintings; some had their copies finished and were going out, other half done, while many had just commenced. I remained some minutes near a pretty French girl, who was copying a painting of a dog rescuing a child from a stream of water into which it had fallen.

I walked down one side of the hall and up the other, and was about leaving, when I was informed that this was only one room, and that a half-dozen more were at my service; but a clock on a neighboring church reminded me that I must quit the Louvre for the Salle de St. Cecile.

*　　　*　　　*　　　*　　　*　　　*

At the meeting of the third session of the Congress, the hall was filled at an early hour with rather a more fashionable-looking audience than on any former occasion, and all appeared anxious for its commencement, as it was understood to be the last day. After the reading of several letters from gentlemen, apologizing for their not being able to attend, the speech of Elihu Burritt was read by a son of M. Coquerel. I felt somewhat astonished that my countryman who was said to be master of fifty languages, had to get some one to read his speech in French.

The Abbé Duguerry now came forward amid great cheering, and said that "the eminent journalist, Girardin, and the great English logician, Mr. Cobden, had made it unnecessary for any further advocacy in that assembly of the peace cause; that if the principles laid down in the resolutions were carried out, the work would be done. He said that the question of general pacification was built on truth,—truth which emanated from God,—and it were as vain to undertake to prevent air from expanding as to check the progress of truth. It must and would prevail."

A pale, thin-faced gentleman next ascended the platform (or tribune, as it was called) amid shouts of applause from the English, and began his speech in rather a low tone, when compared with the sharp voice of Vincent, or the thunder of the Abbé Duguerry. An audience is not apt to be pleased or even contented with an inferior speaker, when surrounded by eloquent men, and I looked every moment for manifestations of disapprobation, as I felt certain that the English delegation had made a mistake in applauding this gentleman, who seemed to make such an unpromising beginning. But the speaker soon began to get warm on the subject, and even at times appeared as if he had spoken before. In a very short time, with the exception of his own voice, the stillness of death prevailed throughout the building, and the speaker delivered one of the most logical speeches made in the Congress, and despite of his thin, sallow look, interested me much more than any whom I had before heard. Towards the close of his remarks, he was several times interrupted by manifestations of approbation; and finally concluded amid great cheering. I inquired the gentleman's name, and was informed that it was Edward Miall, editor of the *Nonconformist*.

After speeches from several others, the great Peace Congress of 1849, which had brought men together from nearly all the governments of Europe, and many from America, was brought to a final close by a speech from the president, returning thanks for the honor that had been conferred upon him. He said: "My address shall be short, and yet I have to bid you adieu! How resolve to do so? Here, during three days, have questions of the deepest import been discussed, examined, probed to the bottom; and during these discussions counsels have been given to governments which they will do well to profit by. If these days' sittings are attended with no other result, they will be the means of sowing in the minds of those present germs of cordiality which must ripen into good fruit. England, France, Belgium, Europe and America, would all be drawn closer by these sittings. Yet the moment to part has arrived, but I can feel that we are strongly united in heart. But, before parting, I may congratulate you and myself on the result of our proceedings. We have been all joined together without distinction of country; we have all been united in one common feeling during our three days' communion. The good work cannot go back; it must advance, it must be accomplished. The course of the future may be judged of by the sound of the footsteps of the past. In the course of that day's discussion, a reminiscence had been handed up to one of the speakers, that this was the anniversary of the dreadful massacre of St. Bartholomew: the reverend gentleman who was speaking turned away from the thought of that sanguinary scene with pious horror, natural to his sacred calling. But I, who may boast of firmer nerve, I take up the remembrance. Yes, it was on this day, two hundred and seventy-seven years ago, that Paris was roused from slumber by the sound of that bell which bore the name of *cloche d'argent*. Massacre was on foot, seeking with keen eye for its victim; man was busy in slaying man. That slaughter was called forth by mingled passions of the worst description. Hatred of all kinds was there urging on the slayer,—hatred of a religious, a political, a personal character. And yet on the anniversary of that same day of horror, and in that very city whose blood was flowing like water, has God this day given a rendezvous to men of peace, whose wild tumult is transformed into order, and animosity into love. The stain of blood is blotted out, and in its place beams forth a ray of holy light. All distinctions are removed, and Papist and Huguenot meet together in friendly communion. (Loud cheers.) Who that thinks of these amazing changes can doubt of the progress that has been made? But whoever denies the force of progress must deny God, since progress is the boon of Providence, and emanated from the great Being above. I feel gratified for the change that has been effected, and pointing solemnly to the past, I say let this day be ever held memorable; let the twenty-fourth of August, 1572, be remembered only for the purpose of being compared with the twenty-fourth of August 1849; and when we think of the latter, and ponder over the high purpose to which it has been devoted,—the advocacy of the principles of peace,—let us not be so wanting in reliance on Providence as to doubt for one moment of the eventual success of our holy cause."

The most enthusiastic cheers followed this interesting speech. A vote of thanks to the government, and three times three cheers, with Mr. Cobden as "fugleman," ended the great Peace Congress of 1849.

Time for separating had arrived, yet all seemed unwilling to leave the place, where, for three days, men of all creeds and of no creed had met upon one common platform. In one sense the meeting was a glorious one, in another it was mere child's play; for the Congress had been restricted to the discussion of certain topics. They were permitted to dwell on the blessings of peace, but were not allowed to say anything about the very subjects above all others that should have been brought before the Congress. A French army had invaded Rome and put down the friends of political and religious freedom, yet not a word was said in reference to it. The fact is, the committee permitted the Congress to be *gagged* before it had met. They put padlocks upon their own mouths, and handed the keys to the government. And this was sorely felt by many of the speakers. Richard Cobden, who had thundered his anathemas against the corn-laws of his country, and against wars in every clime, had to sit quiet in his fetters. Henry Vincent, who can make a louder speech in favor of peace than almost any other man, and whose denunciations of "all war," have gained him no little celebrity with peace men, had to confine himself to the blessings of peace. O, how I wished for a Massachusetts atmosphere, a New England convention platform, with Wendell Phillips as the speaker, before that assembled multitude from all parts of the world!

But the Congress is over, and cannot now be made different; yet it is to be hoped that neither the London Peace Committee, nor any other men having the charge of getting up such another great meeting, will commit such an error again.

CHAPTER 5

"Man, on the dubious waves of error tossed,
His ship half foundered, and his compass lost,
Sees, far as human optics may command,
A sleeping fog, and fancies it dry land."

COWPER

The day after the close of the Congress, the delegates and their friends were invited to a soirée by M. de Tocqueville, Minister for Foreign Affairs,[7] to take place on the next evening (Saturday); and as my colored face and curly hair did not prevent my getting an invitation, I was present with the rest of my peace brethren.

Had I been in America, where color is considered a crime, I would not have been seen at such a gathering, unless as a servant. In company with several delegates, we left the Bedford Hotel for the mansion of the Minister of Foreign Affairs; and, on arriving, we found a file of soldiers drawn up before the gate. This did not seem much like peace: however, it was merely done in honor of the company. We entered the building through massive doors, and resigned ourselves into the hands of good-looking waiters in white wigs; and, after our names were duly announced, were passed from room to room, till I was presented to Madame de Tocqueville, who was standing near the centre of the large drawing-room, with a bouquet in her hand. I was about passing on, when the gentleman who introduced me intimated that I was an "American slave." At the announcement of this fact, the distinguished lady extended her hand and gave me a cordial welcome, at the same time saying, "I hope you feel yourself free in Paris." Having accepted an invitation to a seat by the lady's side, who seated herself on a sofa, I was soon what I most dislike, "the observed of all

119

observers." I recognized, among many of my own countrymen who were gazing at me, the American Consul, Mr. Walsh. My position did not improve his looks. The company present on this occasion were variously estimated at from one thousand to fifteen hundred. Among these were the ambassadors from the different countries represented at the French metropolis, and many of the *élite* of Paris. One could not but be interested with the difference in dress, looks and manners, of this assemblage of strangers, whose language was as different as their general appearance. Delight seemed to beam in every countenance, as the living stream floated from one room to another. The house and gardens were illuminated in the most gorgeous manner. Red, yellow, blue, green, and many other colored lamps, suspended from the branches of the trees in the gardens, gave life and animation to the whole scene out of doors. The soirée passed off satisfactorily to all parties; and by twelve o'clock I was again at my hotel.

Through the politeness of the government the members of the Congress have not only had the pleasure of seeing all the public works free, and without special ticket, but the palaces of Versailles and St. Cloud, together with their splendid grounds, have been thrown open, and the water-works set to playing in both places. This mark of respect for the peace movement is commendable in the French; and were I not such a strenuous friend of free speech, this act would cause me to overlook the padlocks that the government put upon our lips in the Congress.

Two long trains left Paris at nine o'clock for Versailles; and at each of the stations the company were loudly cheered by the people who had assembled to see them pass. At Versailles we found thousands at the station, who gave us a most enthusiastic welcome. We were blessed with a goodly number of the fair sex, who always give life and vigor to such scenes. The train had scarcely stopped, ere the great throng were wending their ways in different directions,—some to the cafés to get what an early start prevented their getting before leaving Paris, and others to see the soldiers who were on review. But most bent their steps towards the great palace.

At eleven o'clock we were summoned to the *déjeuner* which had been prepared by the English delegates in honor of their American friends. About six hundred sat down at the tables. Breakfast being ended, Mr. Cobden was called to the chair, and several speeches were made. Many who had not an opportunity to speak at the Congress thought this a good chance; and the written addresses which had been studied during the passage from America, with the hope that they would immortalize their authors before the Congress, were produced at the breakfast-table. But speech-making was not the order of the day. Too many thundering addresses had been delivered in the Salle de St. Cecile to allow the company to sit and hear dryly written and worse delivered speeches in the Teniscourt.

There was no limited time given to the speakers, yet no one had been on his feet five minutes before the cry was heard from all parts of the house, "Time, time!" One American was hissed down; another took his seat with a red face; and a third opened his bundle of paper, looked around at the audience, made a bow, and took his seat amid great applause. Yet some speeches were made, and to good effect; the best of which was by Elihu Burritt, who was followed by the Rev. James Freeman Clarke. I regretted very much that the latter did not deliver his address before the Congress, for he is a man of no inconsiderable talent, and an acknowledged friend of the slave.

The cry of "The water-works are playing!" "The water is on!" broke up the meeting, without even a vote of thanks to the chairman; and the whole party were soon revelling among the fountains and statues of Louis XIV. Description would fail to give a just idea of the grandeur and beauty of this splendid place. I do not think that anything can surpass the fountain of Neptune, which stands near the Grand Trianon. One may easily get lost in wandering through the grounds of Versailles, but he will always be in sight of some lifelike statue. These monuments, erected to gratify the fancy of a licentious king, make their appearance at every turn. Two lions, the one overturning a wild boar, the other a wolf, both the production of Fillen, pointed out to us the fountain of Diana. But I will not attempt to describe to you any of the very beautiful sculptured gods and goddesses here.

With a single friend I paid a visit to the two Trianons. The larger was, we were told, just as King Louis Philippe left it. One room was splendidly fitted up for the reception of Her Majesty Queen Victoria, who, it appeared, had promised a visit to the French court; but the French monarch ran away from his throne before the time arrived. The Grand Trianon is not larger than many noblemen's seats that may be seen in a day's ride through any part of the British empire. The building has only a ground floor, but its proportions are very elegant.

We next paid our respects to the Little Trianon. This appears to be the most republican of any of the French palaces. I inspected this little palace with much interest, not more for its beauty than because of its having been the favorite residence of that purest of princesses, and most affectionate of mothers, Marie Antoinette. The grounds and building may be said to be only a palace in miniature, and this makes it a still more lovely spot. The building consists of a square pavilion two stories high, and separated entirely from the accessory buildings, which are on the left, and among them a pretty chapel. But a wish to be with the multitude, who were roving among the fountains, cut short my visit to the Trianons.

The day was very fine, and the whole party seemed to enjoy it. It was said that there were more than one hundred thousand persons at Versailles during the day. The company appeared to lose themselves with the pleasure of walking among the trees, flower-beds, fountains, and statues. I met more than one wife seeking a lost husband, and *vice versa*. Many persons were separated from their friends, and did not meet them again till at the hotels in Paris. In the train returning to Paris, an old gentleman who was seated near me said, "I would rest contented if I thought I should ever see my wife again!"

At four o'clock we were *en route* to St. Cloud, the much-loved and favorite residence of the Emperor Napoleon. It seemed that all Paris had come out to St. Cloud to see how the English and Americans would enjoy the playing of the water-works. Many kings and rulers of the French have made St. Cloud their residence, but none have impressed their image so indelibly upon it as Napoleon. It was here he was first elevated to power, and here Josephine spent her most happy hours.

The apartments where Napoleon was married to Marie Louise, the private rooms of Josephine and Marie Antoinette, were all in turn shown to us. While standing on the balcony looking at Paris one cannot wonder that the emperor should have selected this place as his residence, for a more lovely spot cannot be found than St. Cloud.

The palace is on the side of a hill, two leagues from Paris, and so situated that it looks down upon the French capital. Standing, as we did, viewing Paris from St. Cloud, and the setting sun reflecting upon the domes, spires, and towers of the city of fashion, made us feel that this was the place from which the monarch should watch his subjects. From the hour of arrival at St. Cloud till near eight o'clock, we were either inspecting the splendid palace, or roaming the grounds and gardens, whose beautiful walks and sweet flowers made it appear a very paradise on earth.

At eight o'clock the water-works were put in motion, and the variegated lamps, with their many devices, displaying flowers, stars and wheels, all with a brilliancy that can scarcely be described, seemed to throw everything in the shade we had seen at Versailles. At nine o'clock the train was announced, and after a good deal of jamming and pushing about, we were again on the way to Paris.

CHAPTER 6

"There was not, on that day, a speck to stain
The azure heavens; the blessed sun alone,
In unapproachable divinity,
Careered rejoicing in the field of light."

SOUTHEY.

The sun had just appeared from behind a cloud and was setting, and its reflection upon the domes and spires of the great buildings in Paris made everything appear lovely and sublime, as the train, with almost lightning speed, was bringing me from the French metropolis. I gazed with eager eyes to catch a farewell glance of the tops of the regal palaces through which I had passed during a stay of fifteen days in the French capital.

A pleasant ride of four hours brought us to Boulogne, where we rested for the night. The next morning I was up at an early hour, and out viewing the town. Boulogne could present but little attraction after a fortnight spent in seeing the lions of Paris. A return to the hotel, and breakfast over, we stepped on board the steamer, and were soon crossing the channel. Two hours more, and I was safely seated in a railway carriage, *en route* to the English metropolis. We reached London at mid-day, where I was soon comfortably lodged as 22 Cecil-street, Strand. As it was three o'clock, I lost no time in seeking out a dining saloon, which I had no difficulty in finding in the Strand. It being the first house of the kind I had entered in London, I was not a little annoyed at the politeness of the waiter. The first salutation I had, after seating myself in one of the stalls, was "Ox tail, sir; gravy soup; carrot soup, sir; roast beef; roast pork; boiled beef; roast lamb; boiled leg of mutton, sir, with caper sauce; jugged hare, sir; boiled

123

knuckle of veal and bacon; roast turkey and oyster sauce; sucking pig, sir; curried chicken; harrico mutton, sir." These, and many other dishes, which I have forgotten, were called over with a rapidity that would have done credit to one of our Yankee pedlers in crying his wares in a New England village. I was so completely taken by surprise, that I asked for a "bill of fare," and told him to leave me. No city in the world furnishes a cheaper, better, and quicker meal for the weary traveller than a London eating-house.

*   *   *   *   *   *

A few days after my arrival in London, I received an invitation from John Lee, Esq., LL.D., whom I had met at the Peace Congress in Paris, to pay him a visit at his seat, near Aylesbury; and as the time was "fixed" by the doctor, I took the train on the appointed day, on my way to Hartwell House.

I had heard much of the aristocracy of England, and must confess that I was not a little prejudiced against them. On a bright sunshiny day, between the hours of twelve and two, I found myself seated in a carriage, my back turned upon Aylesbury, the vehicle whirling rapidly over the smooth macadamised road, and I on my first visit to an English gentleman. Twenty minutes' ride, and a turn to the right, and we were amid the fine old trees of Hartwell Park; one having suspended from its branches the national banners of several different countries, among them the "Stars and Stripes." I felt glad that my own country's flag had a place there, although Campbell's lines—

> "United States, your banner wears
>   Two emblems,—one of fame;
> Alas! the other that it bears
>   Reminds us of your shame!
> The white man's liberty in types
>   Stands blazoned by your stars;
> But what's the meaning of your stripes?—
>   They mean your Negro-scars"—

were at the time continually running through my mind. Arrived at the door, and we received what every one does who visits Dr. Lee—a hearty welcome. I was immediately shown into a room with a lofty ceiling, hung round with fine specimens of the Italian masters, and told that this was my apartment. Hartwell House stands in an extensive park, shaded with trees that made me think of the oaks and elms in an American forest, and many of whose limbs had been trimmed and nursed with the best of care. This was for several years the residence of John Hampden the patriot, and more recently that of Louis XVIII, during his exile in this country. The house is built on a very extensive scale, and is ornamented in the interior with carvings of wood of many of the kings and princes of bygone centuries. A room some sixty feet by twenty-five contains a variety of articles that the doctor has collected together—the whole forming a museum that would be considered a sight in the Western States of America.

The morning after my arrival at Hartwell I was up at an early hour—in fact, before any of the servants—wandering about through the vast halls, and trying to find my way out; in which I eventually succeeded, but not, however, without aid. It had rained the previous night, and the sun was peeping through a misty cloud as I strolled through the park, listening to the sweet voices of the birds that were fluttering in the tops of the trees, and trimming their wings for a morning flight. The silence of the night had not yet been broken by the voice of man; and I wandered about the vast park unannoyed, except by the dew from the grass that wet my slippers. Not far from the house I came abruptly upon a beautiful little pond of water, where the gold-fish were flouncing about, and the gentle ripples glittering in the sunshine looked like so many silver minnows playing on the surface.

While strolling about with pleasure, and only regretting that my dear daughters were not with me to enjoy the morning's walk, I saw the gardener on his way to the garden. I followed him, and was soon feasting my eyes upon the richest specimens of garden scenery. There were the peaches hanging upon the trees that were fastened to the wall; vegetables, fruit and flowers, were there in all their bloom and beauty; and even the variegated geranium of a warmer clime was there in its hot-house home, and seemed to have forgotten that it was in a different country from its own. Dr. Lee shows great taste in the management of his garden. I have seldom seen a more splendid variety of fruits and flowers in the Southern States of America than I saw at Hartwell House.

I should, however, state that I was not the only guest at Hartwell during my stay. Dr. Lee had invited several others of the American delegation to the Peace Congress, and two or three of the French delegates, who were on a visit to England, were enjoying the doctor's hospitality. Dr. Lee is a stanch friend of Temperance, as well as of the cause of universal freedom. Every year he treats his tenantry to a dinner, and I need not add that these are always conducted on the principle of total abstinence.

During the second day we visited several of the cottages of the work-people, and in these I took no little interest. The people of the United States know nothing of the real condition of the laboring classes of

England. The peasants of Great Britain are always spoken of as belonging to the soil. I was taught in America that the English laborer was no better off than the slave upon a Carolina rice-field. I had seen the slaves in Missouri huddled together, three, four, and even five families in a single room, not more than fifteen by twenty-five feet square, and I expected to see the same in England. But in this I was disappointed. After visiting a new house that the doctor was building, he took us into one of the cottages that stood near the road, and gave us an opportunity of seeing, for the first time, an English peasant's cot. We entered a low, whitewashed room, with a stone floor that showed an admirable degree of cleanness. Before us was a row of shelves filled with earthen dishes and pewter spoons, glittering as if they had just come from under the hand of a woman of taste. A "Cobden loaf" of bread, that had just been left by the baker's boy, lay upon an oaken table which had been much worn away with the scrubbing-brush; while just above lay the old family Bible, that had been handed down from father to son, until its possession was considered of almost as great value as its contents. A half-open door, leading into another room, showed us a clean bed; the whole presenting as fine a picture of neatness, order and comfort, as the most fastidious taste could wish to see. No occupant was present, and therefore I inspected everything with a greater degree of freedom. "In front of the cottage was a small grass-plot, with here and there a bed of flowers, cheated out of its share of sunshine by the tall holly that had been planted near it." As I looked upon the home of the laborer, my thoughts were with my enslaved countrymen. What a difference, thought I, there is between the tillers of the soil in England and America! There could not be a more complete refutation of the assertion that the English laborer is no better off than the American slave, then the scenes that were then before me. I called the attention of one of my American friends to a beautiful rose near the door of the cot, and said to him, "The law that will protect that flower will also guard and protect the hand that planted it." He knew that I had drank deep of the cup of slavery, was aware of what I meant, and merely nodded his head in reply. I never experienced hospitality more genuine, and yet more unpretending, than was meted out to me while at Hartwell. And the favorable impression made on my own mind by the distinguished proprietor of Hartwell Park was nearly as indelible as my humble name that the doctor had engraven in a brick, in a vault beneath the Observatory in Hartwell House. On my return to London I accepted an invitation to join a party on a visit to Windsor Castle; and, taking the train at the Waterloo Bridge Station, we were soon passing through a pleasant part of the country. Arrived at the castle, we committed ourselves into the hands of the servants, and were introduced into Her Majesty's

State Apartments, Audience Chamber, Vandyck Room, Waterloo Chambers, Gold Pantry, and many others whose names I have forgotten. In wandering about the different apartments I lost my company, and in trying to find them passed through a room in which hung a magnificent portrait of Charles I., by Vandyck. The hum and noise of my companions had ceased, and I had the scene and silence to myself. I looked in vain for the king's evil genius (Cromwell), but he was not in the same room. The pencil of Sir Peter Lely has left a splendid full-length likeness of James II. George IV is suspended from a peg in the wall, looking as if it was fresh from the hands of Sir Thomas Lawrence, its admirable painter. I was now in St. George's Hall, and I gazed upward to view the beautiful figures on the ceiling until my neck was nearly out of joint. Leaving this room, I inspected with interest the ancient *keep* of the castle. In past centuries this part of the palace was used as a prison. Here James the First of Scotland was detained a prisoner for eighteen years. I viewed the window through which the young prince had often looked to catch a glimpse of the young and beautiful Lady Jane, daughter of the Earl of Somerset, with whom he was enamored.

From the top of the Round Tower I had a fine view of the surrounding country. Stoke Park, once the residence of that great friend of humanity and civilization, William Penn, was among the scenes that I beheld with pleasure from Windsor Castle. Four years ago, when in the city of Philadelphia, and hunting up the places associated with the name of this distinguished man, and more recently when walking over the farm once occupied by him, examining the old malt-house which is now left standing, because of the veneration with which the name of the man who built it is held, I had no idea that I should ever see the dwelling which he had occupied in the Old World. Stoke Park is about four miles from Windsor, and is now owned by the Right Hon. Henry Labouchere.

The castle, standing as it does on an eminence, and surrounded by a beautiful valley covered with splendid villas, has a most magnificent appearance. It rears its massive towers and irregular walls over and above every other object. How full this old palace is of material for thought! How one could ramble here alone, or with one or two congenial companions, and enjoy a recapitulation of its history! But an engagement to be at Croydon in the evening cut short my stay at Windsor, and compelled me to return to town in advance of my party.

*   *   *   *   *   *

Having met with John Moreland, Esq., at Paris, he gave me an invitation to visit Croydon, and deliver a lecture on American Slavery; and last evening, at eight o'clock, I found myself in a fine old building in the town, and facing the first English audience that I had seen in the sea-girt isle. It was my first welcome in England. The assembly was an enthusiastic one, and made still more so by the appearance of George Thompson, Esq., M. P.,[8] upon the platform. It is not my intention to give accounts of my lectures or meetings in these pages. I therefore merely say that I left Croydon with a good impression of the English, and Heath Lodge with a feeling that its occupant was one of the most benevolent of men.

The same party with whom I visited Windsor being supplied with a card of admission to the Bank of England, I accepted an invitation to be one of the company. We entered the vast building at a little past twelve o'clock. The sun threw into the large halls a brilliancy that seemed to light up the countenances of the almost countless number of clerks, who were at their desks, or serving persons at the counters. As nearly all my countrymen who visit London pay their respects to this noted institution, I shall sum up my visit to it by saying that is surpassed my highest idea of a bank. But a stroll through this monster building of gold and silver brought to my mind an incident with which I was connected a year after my escape from slavery.

In the autumn of 1835, having been cheated out of the previous summer's earnings by the captain of the steamer in which I had been employed running away with the money, I was, like the rest of the men, left without any means of support during the winter, and therefore had to seek employment in the neighboring towns. I went to the town of Monroe, in the State of Michigan, and while going through the principal street looking for work, I passed the door of the only barber in the town, whose shop appeared to be filled with persons waiting to be shaved. As there was but one man at work, and as I had, while employed in the steamer, occasionally shaved a gentleman who could not perform that office himself, it occurred to me that I might get employment here as a journeyman barber. I therefore made immediate application for work, but the barber told me he did not need a hand. But I was not to be put off so easily, and, after making several offers to work cheap, I frankly told him that if he would not employ me I would get a room near to him, and set up an opposition establishment. This threat, however, made no impression on the barber; and, as I was leaving, one of the men who were waiting to be shaved said, "If you want a room in which to commence business, I have one on the opposite side of the street." This man followed me out; we went over, and I looked at the room. He strongly urged me to set up, at the same time promising to give me his influence. I took the room, purchased an old table, two chairs, got a pole with a red stripe painted around it, and the next day opened, with a sign over the door, "Fashionable Hair-dresser from New York, Emperor of the West." I need not add that my enterprise was very annoying to the "shop over the way,"—especially my sign, which happened to be the most expensive part of the concern. Of course, I had to tell all who came in that my neighbor on the opposite side did not keep clean towels, that his razors were dull, and, above all, he had never been to New York to see the fashions. Neither had I. In a few weeks I had the entire business of the town, to the great discomfiture of the other barber.

At this time, money matters in the Western States were in a sad condition. Any person who could raise a small amount of money was permitted to establish a bank, and allowed to issue notes for four times the sum raised. This being the case, many persons borrowed money merely long enough to exhibit to the bank inspectors, and the borrowed money was returned, and the bank left without a dollar in its vaults, if, indeed, it had a vault about its premises. The result was, that banks were started all over the Western States, and the country flooded with worthless paper. These were known as the "Wild-cat Banks." Silver coin being very scarce, and the banks not being allowed to issue notes for a smaller amount than one dollar, several persons put out notes from six to seventy-five cents in value; these were called "Shinplasters." The Shinplaster was in the shape of a promissory note, made payable on demand. I have often seen persons with large rolls of these bills, the whole not amounting to more than five dollars. Some weeks after I had commenced business on my "own hook," I was one evening very much crowded with customers; and, while they were talking over the events of the day, one of them said to me, "Emperor, you seem to be doing a thriving business. You should do as other business men, issue your Shinplasters." This, of course, as it was intended, created a laugh; but with me it was no laughing matter, for from that moment I began to think seriously of becoming a banker. I accordingly went a few days after to a printer, and he, wishing to get the job of printing, urged me to put out my notes, and showed me some specimens of engravings that he had just received from Detroit. My head being already filled with the idea of a bank, I needed but little persuasion to set the thing finally afloat. Before I left the printer the notes were partly in type, and I studying how I should keep the public from counterfeiting them. The next day my Shinplasters were handed to me, the whole amount being twenty dollars, and, after being duly signed, were ready for circulation. At first my notes did not take well; they were too new, and viewed with a suspicious eye. But through the assistance of my customers, and a good deal of exertion on my own part, my bills were soon in circulation; and nearly all the money received in return for my notes was spent in fitting up and decorating my shop.

Few bankers get through this world without their difficulties, and I was not to be an exception. A short time after my money had been out, a party of young men, either wishing to pull down my vanity, or to try the soundness of my bank, determined to give it "a run." After collecting together a number of my bills, they came one at a time to demand other money for them, and I, not being aware of what was going on, was taken by surprise. One day, as I was sitting at my table, strapping some new razors I had just got with the avails of my "Shinplasters," one of the men entered and said "Emperor, you will oblige me if you will give me some other money for these notes of yours." I immediately cashed the notes with the most worthless of the Wild-cat money that I had on hand, but which was a lawful tender. The young man had scarcely left, when a second appeared, with a similar amount, and demanded payment. These were cashed, and soon a third came with his roll of notes. I paid these with an air of triumph, although I had but half a dollar left. I began now to think seriously what I should do, or how to act, provided another demand should be made. While I was thus engaged in thought, I saw the fourth man crossing the street, with a handful of notes, evidently my "Shinplasters." I instantaneously shut the door, and, looking out of the window, said, "I have closed business for the day; come to-morrow, and I will see you." In looking across the street, I saw my rival standing in his shop-door, grinning and clapping his hands at my apparent downfall. I was completely "done *Brown*" for the day. However, I was not to be "used up" in this way; so I escaped by the back door, and went in search of my friend who had first suggested to me the idea of issuing notes. I found him, told him of the difficulty I was in, and wished him to point out a way by which I might extricate myself. He laughed heartily, and then said, "You must act as all bankers do in this part of the country." In inquired how they did, and he said, "When your notes are brought to you, you must redeem them, and then send them out and get other money for them, and with the latter you can keep cashing your own Shinplasters." This was indeed a new idea to me. I immediately commenced putting in circulation the notes which I had just redeemed, and my efforts were crowned with so much success that, before I slept that night, my "Shinplasters" were again in circulation, and my bank once more on a sound basis.

As I saw the clerks shoveling out the yellow coin upon the counters of the Bank of England, and men coming in and going out with weighty bags of the precious metal in their hands or on the shoulders, I could not but think of the great contrast between the monster institution within whose walls I was then standing and the Wild-cat banks of America!

CHAPTER 7

"We might as soon describe a dream
As tell where falls each golden beam;
As soon might reckon up the sand,
Sweet Weston! on thy sea-beat strand,
As count each beauty there."

MISS MITFORD.

I have devoted the past ten days to sight-seeing in the metropolis, the first two of which were spent in the British Museum. After procuring a guide-book at the door as I entered, I seated myself on the first seat that caught my eye, arranged as well as I could in my mind the different rooms, and then commenced in good earnest. The first part I visited was the gallery of antiquities, through to the north gallery, and thence to the Lycian room. This place is filled with tombs, bas-reliefs, statues, and other productions of the same art. Venus, seated, and smelling a lotus-flower which she held in her hand, and attended by three Graces, put a stop to the rapid strides that I was making through this part of the hall. This is really one of the most precious productions of the art that I have ever seen. Many of the figures in this room are very much mutilated; yet one can linger here for hours with interest. A good number of the statues are of uncertain date; they are of great value as works of art, and more so as a means of enlightening much that has been obscure with respect to Lycia, an ancient and celebrated country of Asia Minor.

In passing through the eastern zoological gallery, I was surrounded on every side by an army of portraits suspended upon the walls; and among these was the Protector. The people of one century kicks his bones through the streets of London, another puts his portrait in the British

Museum, and a future generation may possibly give him a place in Westminster Abbey. Such is the uncertainty of the human character. Yesterday, a common soldier; to-day, the ruler of an empire; tomorrow, suspended upon the gallows. In an adjoining room I saw a portrait of Baxter, which gives one a pretty good idea of the great nonconformist. In the same room hung a splendid modern portrait, without any intimation in the guide-book of who it represented, or when it was painted. It was so much like one whom I had seen, and on whom my affections were placed in my younger days, that I obtained a seat from an adjoining room and rested myself before it. After sitting half an hour or more, I wandered to another part of the building, but only to return again to my "first love," where I remained till the throng had disappeared, one after another, and the officer reminded me that it was time to close.

It was eight o'clock before I reached my lodgings. Although fatigued by the day's exertions, I again resumed the reading of Roscoe's "Leo X.," and had nearly finished seventy-three pages, when the clock on St. Martin's Church apprised me that it was two. He who escapes from slavery at the age of twenty years, without any education, as did the writer of this, must read when others are asleep, if he would catch up with the rest of the world. "To be wise," says Pope, "is but to know how little can be known." The true searcher after truth and knowledge is always like a child; although gaining strength from year to year, he still "learns to labor and to wait." The field of labor is ever expanding before him, reminding him that he has yet more to learn; teaching him that he is nothing more than a child in knowledge, and inviting him onward with a thousand varied charms. The son may take possession of the father's goods at his death, but he cannot inherit with the property the father's cultivated mind. He may put on the father's old coat, but that is all; the immortal mind of the first wearer has gone to the tomb. Property may be bequeathed, but knowledge cannot. Then let him who would be useful in his day and generation be up and doing. Like the Chinese student who learned perseverance from the woman whom he saw trying to rub a crow-bar into a needle, so should we take the experience of the past to lighten our feet through the paths of the future.

The next morning, at ten, I was again at the door of the great building; was soon within its walls seeing what time would not allow of the previous day. I spent some hours in looking through glass cases, viewing specimens of minerals such as can scarcely be found in any place out of the British Museum. During this day I did not fail to visit the great library. It is a spacious room, surrounded with large glass cases filled with volumes whose very look tells you that they are of age. Around, under the cornice, were arranged a number of old, black-looking portraits, in all probability the authors of some of the works in the glass cases beneath. About the room were placed long tables, with stands for reading and writing, and around these were a number of men busily engaged in looking over some chosen author. Old men with gray hairs, young men with moustaches, some in cloth, others in fustian,—indicating that men of different rank can meet here. Not a single word was spoken during my stay; all appearing to enjoy the silence that reigned throughout the great room. This is indeed a retreat from the world. No one inquires who the man is that is at his side, and each pursues in silence his own researches. The racing of pens over the sheets of paper was all that disturbed the stillness of the occasion.

From the library I strolled to other rooms, and feasted my eyes on what I had never before seen. He who goes over this immense building cannot do so without a feeling of admiration for the men whose energy has brought together this vast and wonderful collections of things, the like of which cannot be found in any other museum in the world. The reflection of the setting sun against a mirror in one of the rooms told me that night was approaching, and I had but a moment in which to take another look at the portrait that I had seen on the previous day, and them bade adieu to the museum.

Having published the narrative of my life and escape from slavery, and put it into the booksellers' hands, and seeing a prospect of a fair sale, I ventured to take from my purse the last sovereign to make up a small sum to remit to the United States, for the support of my daughters, who are at school there.[9] Before doing this, however, I had made arrangements to attend a public meeting in the city of Worcester, at which the mayor was to preside. Being informed by the friends of the slave there that I would in all probability sell a number of copies of my book, and being told that Worcester was only ten miles from London, I felt safe in parting with all but a few shillings, feeling sure that my purse would soon be again replenished. But you may guess my surprise, when I learned that Worcester was above a hundred miles from London, and that I had not retained money enough to defray my expenses to the place. In my haste and wish to make up the ten pounds to send to my children, I had forgotten that the payment for my lodgings would be demanded before I should leave town. Saturday morning came; I paid my lodging-bill, and had three shillings and fourpence left; and out of this sum I was to get three dinners, as I was only served with breakfast and tea at my lodgings.

Nowhere in the British empire do the people witness as dark days as in London. It was on Monday morning, in the fore part of October, as the clock on St. Martin's Church was striking ten, that I left my lodgings, and turned into the Strand. The street-lamps were yet burning, and the shops were all lighted, as if day had not made its appearance. This great thoroughfare, as usual at this time of the day, was thronged with business men going their way, and women sauntering about for pleasure or for the want of something better to do. I passed down the Strand to Charing Cross, and looked in vain to see the majestic statue of Nelson upon the top of the great shaft. The clock on St. Martin's Church struck eleven, but my sight could not penetrate through the dark veil that hung between its face and me. In fact, day had been completely turned into night; and the brilliant lights from the shop-windows almost persuaded me that another day had not appeared. A London fog cannot be described. To be appreciated, it must be seen, or, rather, felt, for it is altogether impossible to be clear and lucid on such a subject. It is the only thing which gives you an idea of what Milton meant when he talked of darkness visible. There is a kind of light, to be sure; but it only serves as a medium for a series of optical illusions; and, for all useful purposes of vision, the deepest darkness that ever fell from the heavens is infinitely preferable. A man perceives a coach a dozen yards off, and a single stride brings him among the horses' feet; he sees a gas-light faintly glimmering (as he thinks) at a distance, but scarcely has he advanced a step or two towards it, when he becomes convinced of its actual station by finding his head rattling against the post; and as for attempting, if you get once mystified, to distinguish one street from another, it is ridiculous to think of such a thing.

Turning, I retraced my steps, and was soon passing through the massive gates of Temple Bar, wending my way to the city, when a beggar-boy at my heels accosted me for a half-penny to buy bread. I had scarcely served the boy, when I observed near by, and standing close to a lamp-post, a colored man, and from his general appearance I was satisfied that he was an American. He eyed me attentively as I passed him, and seemed anxious to speak. When I had got some distance from him I looked back, and his eyes were still upon me. No longer able to resist the temptation to speak with him, I returned, and commencing conversation with him, learned a little of his history, which was as follows: He had, he said, escaped from slavery in Maryland, and reached New York; but not feeling himself secure there, he had, through the kindness of the captain of an English ship, made his way to Liverpool; and not being able to get employment there, he had come up to London. Here he had met with no better success, and having been employed in the growing of tobacco, and being unaccustomed to any other work, he could not get labor in England. I told him he had better try to get to the West Indies; but he informed me that he had not a single penny, and that he had had nothing to eat that day.

By this man's story I was moved to tears, and going to a neighboring shop, I took from my purse my last shilling, changed it, and gave this poor brother fugitive one half. The poor man burst into tears as I placed the sixpence in his hand, and said, "You are the first friend I have met in London." I bade him farewell, and left him with a feeling of regret that I could not place him beyond the reach of want. I went on my way to the city, and while going through Cheapside a streak of light appeared in the east, that reminded me that it was not night. In vain I wandered from street to street, with the hope that I might meet some one who would lend me money enough to get to Worcester. Hungry and fatigued I was returning to my lodgings, when the great clock of St. Paul's Church, under whose shadow I was then passing, struck four. A stroll through Fleet-street and the Strand, and I was again pacing my room. On my return, I found a letter from Worcester had arrived in my absence; informing me that a party of gentlemen would meet me the next day on my reaching that place, and saying," Bring plenty of books, as you will doubtless sell a large number." The last sixpence had been spent for postage-stamps, in order to send off some letters to other places, and I could not even stamp a letter in answer to the one last from Worcester. The only vestige of money about me was a smooth farthing that a little girl had given to me at the meeting at Croydon, saying, "This is for the slaves." I was three thousand miles from home, with but a single farthing in my pocket! Where on earth is a man without money more destitute? The cold hills of the Arctic regions have not a more inhospitable appearance than London to the stranger with an empty pocket. But whilst I felt depressed at being in such a sad condition, I was conscious that I had done right in remitting the last ten pounds to America. It was for the support of those whom God had committed to my care, and whom I love as I can no others. I had no friend in London to whom I could apply for temporary aid. My friend, Mr. T——, was out of town, and I did not know his address.

The dark day was rapidly passing away,—the clock in the hall had struck six. I had given up all hopes of reaching Worcester the next day, and had just rung the bell for the servant to bring me some tea, when a gentle tap at the door was heard; the servant entered, and informed me that a gentleman below was wishing to see me. I bade her fetch a light and ask him up. The stranger was my young friend, Frederick Stevenson, son of the excellent minister of the Borough-Road Chapel. I had lectured in this chapel a few days previous; and this young gentleman, with more than ordinary zeal and enthusiasm for the cause of bleeding humanity, and respect for me, had gone amongst his father's congregation and sold a number of copies of my book, and had come to bring me the money. I wiped the silent tear from my eyes as the young man placed the thirteen half-crowns in my hand. I did not let him know under what obligation I was to him for his disinterested act of kindness. He does not know to this day what aid he has rendered to a stranger in a strange land, and I feel that I am but discharging in a trifling degree my debt of gratitude to this young gentleman, in acknowledging my obligation to him. As the man who called for bread and cheese, when feeling in his pocket for the last threepence to pay for it, found a sovereign that he was not aware he possessed, countermanded the order for the lunch, and bade them bring him the best dinner they could get; so I told the servant, when she brought the tea, that I had changed my mind, and should go out to dine. With the means in my pocket of reaching Worcester the next day, I sat down to dinner at the Adelphi, with a good cut of roast beef before me, and felt myself once more at home. Thus ended a dark day in London.

CHAPTER 8

To give implicit credence to each tale
  Of monkish legends,—relics to order,
To think God honored by the cowl or veil,
  Regardless who, or what, the emblem wore,
Indeed is mockery, mummery, nothing more:
  But if cold Scepticism usurp the place
That Superstition held in days of yore,
  We may not be in much more hopeful case
Than if we still implored the Virgin Mary's grace.

BARTON

Some days since, I left the metropolis to fulfil a few engagements to visit provincial towns; and after a ride of nearly eight hours, we were in sight of the ancient city of York. It was night, the moon was in her zenith, and there seemed nothing between her and the earth but glittering cold. The moon, the stars, and the innumerable gas-lights, gave the city a panoramic appearance. Like a mountain starting out of a plain, there stood the cathedral in its glory, looking down upon the surrounding buildings, with all the appearance of a Gulliver standing over the Lilliputians. Night gave us no opportunity to view the minster. However, we were up the next morning before the sun, and walking round the cathedral with a degree of curiosity seldom excited within us. It is thought that a building of the same dimensions would take fifty years to complete it at the present time, even with all the improvements of the nineteenth century, and would cost no less than the enormous sum of two millions of pounds sterling. From what I had heard of this famous cathedral, my expectations were raised to the highest point; but it surpassed all the idea that I had formed of it. On entering the building, we lost all thought of the external appearance by the matchless beauty of the interior. The echo produced by the tread of our feet upon the floor as we entered, resounding through the aisles, seemed to say, "Put off your shoes, for the place whereon you tread is holy ground." We stood with hat in hand, and gazed with wonder and astonishment down the incomparable vista of more than five hundred feet. The organ, which stands near the centre of the building, is said to be one of the finest in the world. A wall, in front of which is a screen of the most gorgeous and florid architecture, and executed in solid stone, separates the nave from the service choir. The beautiful workmanship of this makes it appear so perfect, as almost to produce the belief that it is tracery-work of wood. We ascended the rough stone steps through a winding stair to the turrets, where we had such a view of the surrounding country as can be obtained from no other place. On the top of the centre and highest turret is a grotesque figure of a fiddler; rather a strange-looking object, we thought, to occupy the most elevated pinnacle on the house of God. All dwellings in the neighborhood appear like so many dwarfs crouching at the feet of the minster; while its own vastness and beauty impress the observer with feelings of awe and sublimity. As we stood upon the top of this stupendous mountain of ecclesiastical architecture, and surveyed the picturesque hills and valleys around, imagination recalled the tumult of the sanguinary battles fought in sight of the edifice. The rebellion of Octavius near three thousand years ago, his defeat and flight to the Scots, his return and triumph over the Romans, and being crowned king of all Britain; the assassination of Oswald, King of the Northumbrians; the flaying alive of Osbert; the crowning of Richard III.; the siege by William the Conqueror; the siege by Cromwell, and the pomp and splendor with which the different monarchs had been received in York, all appeared to be vividly before me. While we were thus calling to our aid our knowledge of history, a sweet peal from the lungs of the ponderous organ below cut short our stay among the turrets, and we descended to have our organ of tune gratified, as well as to finish the inspection of the interior.

I have heard the sublime melodies of Handel, Haydn and Mozart, performed by the most skilful musicians; I have listened with delight and awe to the soul-moving compositions of those masters, as they have been changed in the most magnificent churches; but never did I hear such music, and played upon such an instrument, as that sent forth by the great organ in the Cathedral of York. The verger took much delight in showing us the horn that was once mounted with gold, but is now garnished with brass. We viewed the monuments and tombs of the departed, and then spent an hour before the great north window. The design on the painted glass, which tradition states was given to the church by five virgin sisters, is the finest thing of the kind in Great Britain. I felt a relief on once more coming into the open air, and again beholding Nature's own sunlight. The splendid ruin of St. Mary's Abbey, with its eight beautiful light Gothic windows, next attracted our attention. A visit to the castle finished our stay in York; and as we were leaving the old city we almost imagined that we heard the chiming of the bells for the celebration of the first Christian Sabbath, with Prince Arthur as the presiding genius.

*   *   *   *   *   *

England stands preeminently the first government in the world for freedom of speech and of the press. Not even in our own beloved America can the man who feels himself oppressed speak as he can in Great Britain. In some parts of England, however, the freedom of thought is tolerated to a greater extent than in others; and of the places favorable to reforms of all kinds, calculated to elevate and benefit mankind, Newcastle-on-Tyne doubtless takes the lead. Surrounded by innumerable coalmines, it furnishes employment for a large laboring population, many of whom take a deep interest in the passing events of the day, and, consequently, are a reading class. The public debater or speaker, no matter what may be his subject, who fails to get an audience in other towns, is sure of a gathering in the Music Hall, or Lecture Room, in Newcastle.

Here I first had an opportunity of coming in contact with a portion of the laboring people of Britain. I have addressed large and influential meetings in Newcastle and the neighboring towns, and the more I see and learn of the condition of the working-classes of England, the more I am satisfied of the utter fallacy of the statements often made that their condition approximates to that of the slaves of America. Whatever may be the disadvantages that the British peasant labors under, he is free; and if he is not satisfied with his employer, he can make choice of another. He also has the right to educate his children; and he is the equal of the most wealthy person before an English court of justice. But how is it with the American slave? He has no right to himself; no right to protect his wife, his child, or his own person. He is nothing more than a living tool. Beyond his field or workshop he knows nothing. There is no amount of ignorance he is not capable of. He has not the least idea of the face of this earth, nor of the history or constitution of the country in which he dwells. To him the literature, science and art, the progressive history and the accumulated discoveries of by-gone ages, are as if they had never been. The past is to him as yesterday, and the future scarcely more than to-morrow. Ancestral monuments he has none; written documents, fraught with cogitations of other

times, he has none; and any instrumentality calculated to awaken and
expound the intellectual activity and comprehension of a present or approaching generation, he has none. His condition is that of the leopard of
his own native Africa. It lives, it propagates its kind; but never does it
indicate a movement towards that all but angelic intelligence of man. The
slave eats, drinks and sleeps, all for the benefit of the man who claims his
body as his property. Before the tribunals of his country he has no voice.
He has no higher appeal than the mere will of his owner. He knows
nothing of the inspired Apostles through their writings. He has no Sabbath, no church, no Bible, no means of grace,—and yet we are told that he
is as well off as the laboring classes of England. It is not enough that the
people of my country should point to their Declaration of Independence,
which declares that "all men are created equal." It is not enough that they
should laud to the skies a constitution containing boasting declarations in
favor of freedom. It is not enough that they should extol the genius of
Washington, the patriotism of Henry, or the enthusiasm of Otis. The time
has come when nations are judged by the acts of the present, instead of the
past. And so it must be with America. In no place in the United Kingdom
has the American slave warmer friends than in Newcastle.

*   *   *   *   *   *

I am now in Sheffield, and have just returned from a visit to James
Montgomery, the poet. In company with James Wall, Esq., I proceeded to
the Mount, the residence of Mr. Montgomery; and our names being sent
in, we were soon in the presence of the "Christian poet." He held in his
left hand the *Eclectic Review* for the month, and with the right gave me a
hearty shake, and bade me "Welcome to Old England." He was anything
but like the portraits I had seen of him, and the man I had in my mind's
eye. I had just been reading his "Pelican Island," and I eyed the poet with
no little interest. He is under the middle size; his forehead high and well
formed, the top of which was a little bald; his hair of a yellowish color, his
eyes rather small and deep-set, the nose long and slightly acquiline, his
mouth rather small, and not at all pretty. He was dressed in black, and a
large white cravat entirely hid his neck and chin; his having been afflicted
from childhood with salt-rheum was doubtless the cause of his chin being
so completely buried in the neckcloth. Upon the whole, he looked more
like one of our American Methodist parsons than any one I have seen in
this country. He entered freely into conversation with us. He said he
should be glad to attend my lecture that evening, but that he had long since
quit going out at night. He mentioned having heard William Lloyd Garrison some years before, and with whom he was well pleased. He said it

had long been a puzzle to him how Americans could hold slaves and still retain their membership in the churches. When we rose to leave, the old man took my hand between his two, and with tears in his eyes said, "Go on your Christian mission, and may the Lord protect and prosper you! Your enslaved countrymen have my sympathy, and shall have my prayers." Thus ended our visit to the bard of Sheffield. Long after I had quitted the presence of the poet, the following lines of his were ringing in my ears:

> "Wanderer, whither dost thou roam?
> Weary wanderer, old and gray,
> Wherefore hast thou left thine home,
> In the sunset of thy day?
> Welcome, wanderer, as thou art,
> All my blessings to partake;
> Yet thrice welcome to my heart,
> For thine injured people's sake.
> Wanderer, whither wouldst thou roam?
> To what region far away?
> Bend thy steps to find a home,
> In the twilight of thy day,
> Where a tyrant never trod,
> Where a slave was never known—
> But where Nature worships God
> In the wilderness alone."

Mr. Montgomery seems to have thrown his entire soul into his meditations on the wrongs of Switzerland. The poem which we have just quoted is unquestionably one of his best productions and contains more of the fire of enthusiasm than all his other works. We feel a reverence almost amounting to superstition for the poet who deals with nature. And who is more capable of understanding the human heart than the poet? Who has better known the human feelings than Shakspeare; better painted than Milton the grandeur of virtue; better sighed than Byron over the subtle weaknesses of Hope? Who ever had a sounder taste, a more exact intellect, than Dante? or who has ever tuned his harp more in favor of freedom than our own Whittier?

CHAPTER 9

"Now, this once gorgeous edifice, if reared
　　By piety, which sought with honest aim
The glory of the Lord, should be revered
　　Even for that cause, by those who seek the same.
Perchance the builders erred; but who shall blame
　　Error, nor feel that they partake it too?
Then judge with charity, whate'er thy name,
　　Be though a Pagan, Protestant, or Jew;
Nor with a scornful glance these Papal reliques view."

BARTON.

It was on a lovely morning that I found myself on board the little steamer *Wye*, passing out of Bristol harbor. In going down the river, we saw on our right the stupendous rocks of St. Vincent towering some four or five hundred feet above our heads. By the swiftness of our fairy steamer, we were soon abreast of Cook's Folly, a singular tower, built by a man from whom it takes its name, and of which the following romantic story is told: "Some years since a gentleman, of the name of Cook, erected this tower, which has since gone by the name of 'Cook's Folly.' A son having been born, he was desirous of ascertaining, by means of astrology, if he would live to enjoy his property. Being himself a firm believer, like the poet Dryden, that certain information might be obtained from the above science, he caused the child's horoscope to be drawn, and found, to his dismay, that in his third, sixteenth, or twenty-first year, he would be in danger of meeting with some fearful calamity or sudden death, to avert which he caused the turret to be constructed, and the child placed therein. Secure, as he vainly thought, there he lived, attended by a faithful servant, their food and fuel being conveyed to them by means of a pulley-basket, until he was old enough to wait upon himself. On the eve of his twenty-first year his parent's hopes rose high, and great were the rejoicings prepared to welcome the young heir to his home. But, alas! no human skill could avert the dark fate which clung to him. The last night he had to pass alone in the turret, a bundle of fagots was conveyed to him as usual, in which lay concealed a viper, which clung to his hand. The bite was fatal; and, instead of being borne in triumph, the dead body of his only son was the sad spectacle which met the sight of his father."

We crossed the channel, and soon entered the mouth of that most picturesque of rivers, the Wye. As we neared the town of Chepstow the old castle made its appearance, and a fine old ruin it is. Being previously provided with a letter of introduction to a gentleman in Chepstow, I lost no time in finding him out. This gentleman gave me a cordial reception, and did what Englishmen seldom ever do, lent me his saddle-horse to ride to the abbey. While lunch was in preparation I took a stroll through the castle which stood near by. We entered the castle through the great doorway, and were soon treading the walls that had once sustained the cannon and the sentinel, but were now covered with weeds and wild-flowers. The drum and fife had once been heard within these walls—the only music now is the cawing of the rook and daw. We paid a hasty visit to the various apartments, remaining longest in those of most interest. The room in which Martin the Regicide was imprisoned nearly twenty years was pointed out to us. The Castle of Chepstow is still a magnificent pile, towering upon the brink of a stupendous cliff, on reaching the top of which, we had a splendid view of the surrounding country. Time, however, compelled us to retrace our steps, and after partaking of a lunch, we mounted a horse for the first time in ten years, and started for Tintern Abbey. The distance from Chepstow to the abbey is about five miles, and the road lies along the banks of the river. The river is walled in on either side by hills of much beauty, clothed from base to summit with the richest verdure. I can conceive of nothing more striking than the first appearance of the abbey. As we rounded a hill, all at once we saw the old ruin standing before us in all its splendor. This celebrated ecclesiastical relic of the olden time is doubtless the finest ruin of its kind in Europe. Embosomed amongst hills, and situated on the banks of the most fairy-like river in the world, its beauty can scarcely be surpassed. We halted at the "Beaufort Arms," left our horse, and sallied forth to view the abbey. The sun was pouring a flood of light upon the old gray walls, lighting up its dark recesses, as if to give us a better opportunity of viewing it. I gazed with astonishment and admiration at its many beauties, and especially at the superb Gothic windows over the entrance-door. The beautiful Gothic pillars, with here and there a representation of a praying priest, and mailed knights, with saints and Christian martyrs, and the hundreds of Scriptural representations, all indicate that this was a place of considerable importance in its palmy days. The once stone floor had disappeared, and we found ourselves standing on a floor of unbroken green grass, swelling back to the old walls, and looking so verdant and silken that it seemed the very floor of fancy. There are more romantic and wilder places than this in the world, but none more beautiful. The preservation of these old abbeys should claim the attention of those under whose charge they are, and we felt like joining with the poet, and saying—

> "O ye who dwell
> Around yon ruins, guard the precious charge
> From hands profane! O save the sacred pile—
> O'er which the wing of centuries has flown
> Darkly and silently, deep-shadowing all
> Its pristine honors from the ruthless grasp
> Of future violation!"

In contemplating these ruins more closely, the mind insensibly reverts to the period of feudal and regal oppression, when structures like that of Tintern Abbey necessarily became the scenes of stirring and highly-important events. How altered is the scene! Where were formerly magnificence and splendor, the glittering array of priestly prowess, the crowded halls of haughty bigots, and the prison of religious offenders, there is now but a heap of mouldering ruins. The oppressed and the oppressor have long since lain down together in the peaceful grave. The ruin, generally speaking, is unusually perfect, and the sculpture still beautifully sharp. The outward walls are nearly entire, and are thickly clad with ivy. Many of the windows are also in a good state of preservation; but the roof has long since fallen in. The feathered songsters were fluttering about, and pouring forth their artless lays as a tribute of joy; while the lowing of the herds, the bleating of flocks, and the hum of bees upon the farm near by, all burst upon the ear, and gave the scene a picturesque sublimity that can be easier imagined than described. Most assuredly Shakspeare had such ruins in view when he exclaimed,

> "The cloud-capped towers, the gorgeous palaces,
> The solemn temples, the great globe itself,
> Yes, all which it inherit, shall dissolve,
> And, like the baseless fabric of a vision,
> Leave not a wreck behind."

In the afternoon we returned to Bristol, and I spent the greater part of the next day in examining the interior of Redcliffe Church. Few places in the west of England have greater claims upon the topographer and historian than the church of St. Mary's, Redcliffe. Its antiquity, the beauty of its architecture, and, above all, the interesting circumstances connected with its history, entitle it to peculiar notice. It is also associated with the enterprise of genius; for its name has been blended with the reputation of Rowley, of Ganynge, and of Chatterton, and no lover of poetry and admirer of art can visit it without a degree of enthusiasm. And, when the old building shall have mouldered into ruins, even these will be trodden with veneration, as sacred to the recollection of genius of the highest order. Ascending a winding stair, we were shown into the treasury room. The room forms an irregular octagon, admitting light through narrow, unglazed apertures, upon the broken and scattered fragments of the famous Rowleian chests, that, with the rubble and dust of centuries, cover the floor. It is here creative fancy pictures forth the sad image of the spirit of the spot—the ardent boy, flushed and fed by hope, musing on the brilliant deception he had conceived, whose daring attempt has left his name unto the intellectual world as a marvel and a mystery.

That a boy under twelve years of age should write a series of poems, imitating the style of the fifteenth century, and palm these poems off upon the world as the work of a monk, is indeed strange; and that these should become the object of interesting contemplation to the literary world, and should awaken inquiries, and exercise the talents of a Southey, a Bryant, a Miller, a Mathias, and others, savors more of romance than reality. I had visited the room in a garret in High Holborn where this poor boy died; I had stood over a grave in the burial-ground of Shoe-Lane Workhouse, which was pointed out to me as the last resting-place of Chatterton; and now I was in the room where, it was alleged, he obtained the manuscripts that gave him such notoriety. We descended and viewed other portions of the church. The effect of the chancel, as seen behind the pictures, is very singular, and suggestive of many swelling thoughts. We look at the great east window—it is unadorned with its wonted painted glass; we look at the altar-screen beneath, on which the light of day again falls, and behold the injuries it has received at the hands of time. There is a dreary mournfulness in the scene which fastens on the mind, and is in unison with the time-worn mouldering fragments that are seen all around us. And this dreariness is not removed by our tracing the destiny of man on the storied pavements or on the graven brass, that still bears upon its surface the names of those who obtained the world's regard years back. This old pile is not only an ornament to the city, but it stands a living monument to the genius of its founder. Bristol has long sustained a high position, as a place from which the American abolitionists have received substantial encouragement in their arduous labors for the emancipation of the slaves of that land; and the writer of this received the best evidence that in this respect the character of the people had not been exaggerated, especially as regards the "Clifton Ladies' Anti-Slavery Society." From Bristol I paid a hasty visit to the Scotch capital.

Edinburgh is the most picturesque of all the towns which I have visited since my arrival in the father-land. Its situation has been compared to that of Athens; but it is said that the modern Athens is superior to the ancient. I was deeply impressed with the idea that I had seen the most beautiful of cities after beholding those fashionable resorts, Paris and Versailles. I have seen nothing in the way of public grounds to compare with the gardens of Versailles, or the Champs Elysees, at Paris; and as for statuary, the latter place is said to take the lead of the rest of the world.

The general appearance of Edinburgh prepossesses one in its favor. The town, being built upon the brows of a large terrace, presents the most wonderful perspective. Its first appearance to a stranger, and the first impression, can scarcely be but favorable. In my first walk through the town I was struck with the difference in the appearance of the people from the English. But the difference between the Scotch and the Americans is very great. The cheerfulness depicted in the countenances of the people here, and their free-and-easy appearance, is very striking to a stranger. He who taught the sun to shine, the flowers to bloom, the birds to sing, and blesses us with rain, never intended that his creatures should look sad. There is a wide difference between the Americans and any other people which I have seen. The Scotch are healthy and robust, unlike the long-faced, sickly-looking Americans.

While on our journey from London to Paris, to attend the Peace Congress, I could not but observe the marked difference between the English and American delegates. The former looked as if their pockets had been filled with sandwiches, made of good bread and roast beef; while the latter appeared as if their pockets had been filled with Holloway's pills and Mrs. Kidder's cordial.

I breakfasted this morning in a room in which the poet Burns, as I was informed, had often sat. The conversation here turned upon Burns. The lady of the house pointed to a scrap of poetry which was in a frame hanging on the wall, written, as she said, by the poet, on hearing the people rejoicing in a church over the intelligence of a victory. I copied it, and will give it to you:

> "Ye hypocrites! are these your pranks,
> To murder men and give God thanks?

For shame! give o'er, proceed no further;
God won't accept your thanks for murder."

The fact that I was in the room where Scotland's great national poet had been a visitor caused me to feel that I was on classic, if not hallowed ground. On returning from our morning visit, we met a gentleman with a colored lady on each arm. C—— remarked, in a very dry manner, "If they were in Georgia, the slaveholders would make them walk in a more hurried gait than they do." I said to my friend that, if he meant the pro-slavery prejudice would not suffer them to walk peaceably through the streets, they need go no further than the pro-slavery cities of New York and Philadelphia. When walking through the streets, I amused myself by watching C——'s countenance; and, in doing so, imagined I saw the changes experienced by every fugitive slave in his first month's residence in this country. A sixteen months' residence has not yet familiarized me with the change.

*   *   *   *   *   *

I remained in Edinburgh a day or two which gave me an opportunity of seeing some of the lions in the way of public buildings, &c., in company with our friend C——. I paid a visit to the Royal Institute, and inspected the very fine collection of paintings, statues, and other productions of art. The collection in the Institute is not to be compared to the British Museum at London, or the Louvre at Paris, but is probably the best in Scotland. Paintings from the hands of many of the masters, such as Sir A. Vandyke, Tiziano, Vercellio and Van Dellen, were hanging on the wall, and even the names of Rubens and Titian were attached to some of the finer specimens. Many of these represent some of the nobles and distinguished families of Rome, Athens, Greece, &c. A beautiful one, representing a group of the Lomellini family of Genoa, seemed to attract the attention of most of the visitors.

In visiting this place, we passed close by the monument of Sir Walter Scott. This is the most exquisite thing of the kind that I have seen since coming to this country. It is said to be the finest monument in Europe. There sits the author of "Waverley," with a book and pencil in hand, taking notes. A beautiful dog is seated by his side. Whether this is meant to represent his favorite dog, Camp, at whose death the poet shed so many tears, we were not informed; but I was of the opinion that it might be the faithful Percy, whose monument stands in the grounds at Abbotsford. Scott was an admirer of the canine tribe. One may form a good idea of the appearance of this distinguished writer when living, by viewing this remarkable statue. The statue is very beautiful, but not equal to the one of Lord Byron, which was executed to be placed by the side of Johnson, Milton and Addison, in Poets' Corner, Westminster Abbey; but the vestry not allowing it a place there, it now stands in one of the colleges at Cambridge. While viewing the statue of Byron, I thought he, too, should have been represented with a dog by his side; for he, like Scott, was remarkably fond of dogs; so much so that he intended to have his favorite, Boatswain, interred by his side.

We paid a short visit to the monuments of Burns and Allan Ramsay, and the renowned old Edinburgh Castle. The castle is now used as a barrack for infantry. It is accessible only from the High Street, and must have been impregnable before the discovery of gunpowder. In the wars with the English, it was twice taken by stratagem: once in a very daring manner, by climbing up the most inaccessible part of the rock upon which it stands, and where a foe was least expected, and putting the guard to death; and at another time, by a party of soldiers disguising themselves as merchants, and obtaining admission inside the castle gates. They succeeded in preventing the gates from being closed until reinforced by a party of men under Sir Wm. Douglas, who soon overpowered the occupants of the castle.

We could not resist the temptation held out to see the palace of Holyrood. It was in this place that the beautiful but unfortunate Mary Queen of Scots resided for a number of years. On reaching the palace, we were met at the door by an elderly-looking woman, with a red face, garnished with a pair of second-hand curls, the whole covered with a cap having the widest border that I had seen for years. She was very kind in showing us about the premises, especially as we were foreigners, no doubt expecting an extra fee for politeness. The most interesting of the many rooms in this ancient castle is the one which was occupied by the queen, and where her Italian favorite, Rizzio, was murdered.

But by far the most interesting object which we visited while in Edinburgh was the house where the celebrated Reformer, John Knox, resided.[10] It is a queer-looking old building, with a pulpit on the outside, and above the door are the nearly obliterated remains of the following inscription: "Lufe. God. Above. Al. And. your. Nichbour. As you. Self." This was probably traced under the immediate direction of the great Reformer. Such an inscription put upon a house of worship at the present day would be laughed at. I have given it to you, punctuation and all, just as it stands.

The general architecture of Edinburgh is very imposing, whether we regard the picturesque disorder of the buildings in the Old Town, or the symmetrical proportions of the streets and squares in the New. But on viewing this city, which has the reputation of being the finest in Europe, I was surprised to find that it had none of those sumptuous structures which, like St. Paul's, or Westminster Abbey, York Minster, and some other of the English provincial cathedrals, astonish the beholder alike by their magnitude and their architectural splendor. But in no city which I have visited in the kingdom is the general standard of excellence better maintained than in Edinburgh.

CHAPTER 10

"I was a traveller then upon the moor;
I saw the hare that raced about with joy;
I heard the woods and distant waters roar,
Or heard them not, as happy as a boy."

WORDSWORTH.

I am glad once more to breathe an atmosphere uncontaminated by the fumes and smoke of a city with its population of three hundred thousand inhabitants. In company with my friend C——, I left Glasgow on the afternoon of the 23d inst., for Dundee, a beautiful town situated on the banks of the river Tay. One like myself, who has spent the best part of an eventful life in cities, and who prefers, as I do, a country to a town life, feels a greater degree of freedom when surrounded by forest trees, or country dwellings, and looking upon a clear sky, than when walking through the thronged thoroughfares of a city, with its dense population, meeting every moment a new or strange face, which one has never seen before, and never expects to see again.

Although I had met with one of the warmest public receptions with which I have been greeted since my arrival in the country, and had had an opportunity of shaking hands with many noble friends of the slave, whose names I had often seen in print, yet I felt glad to see the tall chimneys and smoke of Glasgow receding in the distance, as our "iron-horse" was taking us with almost lightning speed from the commercial capital of Scotland.

The distance from Glasgow to Dundee is some seventy or eighty miles, and we passed through the finest country which I have seen in this portion of the queen's dominions. We passed through the old town of Stirling, which lies about thirty miles distant from Glasgow, and is a place much frequented by those who travel for pleasure. It is built on the brow of a hill, and the castle from which it most probably derived its name may be seen from a distance. Had it not been for a "professional" engagement the same evening at Dundee, I would most assuredly have halted to take a look at the old building.

The castle is situated or built on an isolated rock, which seems as if nature had thrown it there for that purpose. It was once the retreat of the Scottish kings, and famous for its historical associations. Here the "Lady of the Lake," with the magic ring, sought the monarch to intercede for her father; here James II. murdered the Earl of Douglas; here the beautiful but unfortunate Mary was made queen; and here John Knox, the Reformer, preached the coronation sermon of James VI. The Castle Hill rises from the valley of the Forth, and makes an imposing and picturesque appearance. The windings of the noble river, till lost in the distance, present pleasing contrasts, scarcely to be surpassed.

The speed of our train, after passing Stirling, brought before us, in quick succession, a number of fine villas and farm-houses. Every spot seemed to have been arrayed by nature for the reception of the cottage of some happy family. During this ride we passed many sites where the lawns were made, the terraces defined and levelled, the groves tastefully clumped, the ancient trees, though small when compared to our great forest oaks, were beautifully sprinkled here and there, and in everything the labor of art seemed to have been anticipated by nature. Cincinnatus could not have selected a prettier situation for a farm than some which presented themselves during this delightful journey. At last we arrived at the place of our destination, where our friends were in waiting for us.

As I have already forwarded to you a paper containing an account of the Dundee meeting, I shall leave you to judge from these reports the character of the demonstration. Yet I must mention a fact or two connected with our first evening's visit to this town. A few hours after our arrival in the place, we were called upon by a gentleman whose name is known wherever the English language is spoken—one whose name is on the tongue of every student and school-boy in this country and America, and what lives upon their lips will live and be loved forever.

We were seated over a cup of strong tea, to revive our spirits for the evening, when our friend entered the room, accompanied by a gentleman, small in stature, and apparently seventy-five years of age, yet he appeared as active as one half that age. Feeling half drowsy from riding in the cold, and then the sudden change to a warm fire, I was rather inclined not to move on the entrance of the stranger. But the name of Thomas Dick, LL.D., roused me in a moment from my lethargy; I could scarcely believe that I was in the presence of the "Christian Philosopher." Dr. Dick is one of the men to whom the age is indebted. I never find myself in the presence of one to whom the world owes so much, without feeling a thrilling emotion, as if I were in the land of spirits. Dr. Dick had come to our lodgings to see and congratulate William and Ellen Craft upon their escape from the republican Christians of the United States;[11] and as he pressed the hand of the "white slave," and bid her "welcome to British soil," I saw the silent tear stealing down the cheek of this man of genius. How I wished that the many slaveholders and pro-slavery professed Christians of America, who have read and pondered the philosophy of this man, could have been present! Thomas Dick is an abolitionist—one who is willing that the world should know that he hates the "peculiar institution." At the meeting that evening, Dr. Dick was among the most prominent. But this was not the only distinguished man who took part on that occasion.

Another great mind was on the platform, and entered his solemn protest in a manner long to be remembered by those present. This was the Rev. George Gilfillan, well known as the author of the "Portraits of Literary Men." Mr. Gilfillan is an energetic speaker, and would have been the lion of the evening, even if many others who are more distinguished as platform orators had been present. I think it was Napoleon who said that the enthusiasm of others abated his own. At any rate, the spirit with which each speaker entered upon his duty for the evening abated my own enthusiasm for the time being. The last day of our stay in Dundee, I paid a visit, by invitation, to Dr. Dick, at his residence in the little village of Broughty Ferry. We found the great astronomer in his parlor waiting for us. From the parlor we went to the new study, and here I felt more at ease, for I went to see the philosopher in his study, and not in his drawing-room. But even this room had too much the look of nicety to be an author's *sanctum;* and I inquired and was soon informed by Mrs. Dick, that I should have a look at the *"old study."*

During a sojourn of eighteen months in Great Britain, I have had the good fortune to meet with several distinguished literary characters, and have always managed, while at their places of abode, to see the table and favorite chair. William and Ellen Craft were seeing what they could see through a microscope, when Mrs. Dick returned to the room, and intimated that we could now see the old literary workshop. I followed, and was soon in a room about fifteen feet square, with but one window, which occupied one side of the room. The walls of the other three sides were lined with books, and many of these looked the very personification of age. I took my seat in the *"old arm-chair;"* and here, thought I, is the place and the seat in which this distinguished man sat while weaving the radiant wreath of renown which now, in his old age, surrounds him, and whose labors will be more appreciated by future ages than the present.

I took a farewell of the author of the "Solar System," but not until I had taken a look through the great telescope in the observatory. This instrument, through which I tried to see the heavens, was not the one invented by Galileo, but an improvement upon the original. On leaving this learned man, he shook hands with us, and bade us "God speed" in our mission; and I left the philosopher, feeling I had not passed an hour more agreeably with a literary character since the hour which I spent with the poet Montgomery a few months since. And, by-the-by, there is a resemblance between the poet and the philosopher. In becoming acquainted with great men I have become a convert to the opinion that a big nose is an almost necessary appendage to the form of a man with a giant intellect. If those whom I have seen be a criterion, such is certainly the case. But I have spun out this too long, and must close.

CHAPTER 11

"Why weeps the Muse for England? What appears
In England's case to move the Muse to tears?
From side to side of her delightful isle
Is she not clothed with a perpetual smile?
Can nature add a charm, or art confer
A new-found luxury, not seen in her?"

COWPER.

My last left me under the hospitable roof of Harriet Martineau.[12] I had long had an invitation to visit this distinguished friend of our race, and as the invitation was renewed during my tour through the north, I did not feel disposed to decline it, and thereby lose so favorable an opportunity of meeting with one who had written so much in behalf of the oppressed of our land. About a mile from the head of Lake Windermere, and immediately under Wonsfell, and encircled by mountains on all sides except the south-west, lies the picturesque little town of Ambleside; and the brightest spot in the place is "The Knoll," the residence of Miss Martineau.

We reached "The Knoll" a little after night-fall, and a cordial shake of the hand by Miss M., who was waiting for us, trumpet in hand, soon assured us that we had met with a warm friend.

It is not my intention to lay open the scenes of domestic life at "The Knoll," nor to describe the social parties of which my friends and I were partakers during our sojourn within the hospitable walls of this distinguished writer; but the name of Miss M. is so intimately connected with the Anti-slavery movement by her early writings, and those have been so much admired by the friends of the slave in the United States, that I deem it not at all out of place for me to give my readers some idea of the authoress of "Political Economy," "Travels in the East," "The Hour and the Man," &c.

The dwelling is a cottage of moderate size, built after Miss M.'s own plan, upon a rise of land, from which it derives the name of "The Knoll." The library is the largest room in the building, and upon the walls of it were hung some beautiful engravings and a continental map. On a long table, which occupied the centre of the room, were the busts of Shakspeare, Newton, Milton, and a few other literary characters of the past. One side of the room was taken up with a large case, filled with a choice collection of books; and everything indicated that it was the home of genius and of taste.

The room usually occupied by Miss M., and where we found her on the evening of our arrival, is rather small, and lighted by two large windows. The walls of this room were also decorated with prints and pictures, and on the mantel-shelf were some models in terra cotta of Italian groups. On a circular table lay casts, medallions, and some very choice water-color drawings. Under the south window stood a small table covered with newly-opened letters, a portfolio, and several new books, with here and there a page turned down, and one with a paperknife between its leaves, as if it had only been half read. I took up the last-mentioned, and it proved to be the "Life and Poetry of Hartley Coleridge," son of S. T. Coleridge. It was just from the press, and had, a day or two before, been forwarded to her by the publisher. Miss M. is very deaf, and always carries in her left hand a trumpet; and I was not a little surprised on learning from her that she had never enjoyed the sense of smell, and only on one occasion the sense of taste, and that for a single moment. Miss M. is loved with a sort of idolatry by the people of Ambleside, and especially the poor, to whom she gives a course of lectures every winter gratuitously. She finished her last course the day before our arrival. She was much pleased with Ellen Craft, and appeared delighted with the story of herself and husband's escape from slavery, as related by the latter, during the recital of which I several times saw the silent tear stealing down her cheek, and which she tried in vain to hide from us.

When Craft had finished, she exclaimed, "I would that every woman in the British empire could hear that tale as I have, so that they might know how their own sex was treated in that boasted land of liberty." It seems strange to the people of this country, that one so white and so ladylike as Mrs. Craft should have been a slave, and forced to leave the land of her nativity and seek an asylum in a foreign country.

The morning after our arrival I took a stroll by a circuitous pathway to the top of Loughrigg Fell. At the foot of the mount I met a peasant, who very kindly offered to lend me his donkey, upon which to ascend the mountain. Never having been upon the back of one of these long-eared animals, I felt some hesitation about trusting myself upon so diminutive looking a creature. But, being assured that if I would only resign myself to his care, and let him have his own way, I would be perfectly safe, I mounted, and off we set. We had, however, scarcely gone fifty rods, when, in passing over a narrow part of the path and overlooking a deep chasm, one of the hind feet of the donkey slipped, and with an involuntary shudder I shut my eyes to meet my expected doom; but, fortunately, the little fellow gained his foothold, and in all probability saved us both from a premature death. After we had passed over this dangerous place I dismounted; and, as soon as my feet had once more gained terra firma, I resolved that I would never again yield my own judgment to that of any one, not even to a donkey.

It seems as if nature had amused herself in throwing these mountains together. From the top of Loughrigg Fell the eye loses its power in gazing upon the objects below. On our left lay Rydal Mount, the beautiful seat of the late poet Wordsworth; while to the right, and away in the dim distance, almost hidden by the native trees, was the cottage where once resided Mrs. Hemans. And below us lay Windermere, looking more like a river than a lake, and which, if placed by the side of our own Ontario, Erie or Huron, would be lost in the fog. But here it looks beautiful in the extreme, surrounded as it is by a range of mountains that have no parallel in the United States for beauty. Amid a sun of uncommon splendor, dazzling the eye with the reflection upon the water below, we descended into the valley, and I was soon again seated by the fireside of our hospitable hostess. In the afternoon of the same day we took a drive to the "Dove's Nest," the home of the late Mrs. Hemans.

We did not see the inside of the house, on account of its being occupied by a very eccentric man, who will not permit a woman to enter the house; and it is said that he has been known to run when a female had unconsciously intruded herself upon his premises. As our company was in part composed of ladies, we had to share their fate, and therefore were prevented from seeing the interior of the "Dove's Nest." The exhibitor of such a man would be almost sure of a prize at the Great Exhibition.

At the head of Grassmere Lake, and surrounded by a few cottages, stands an old, gray, antique-looking parish church, venerable with the lapse of centuries, and the walls partly covered with ivy, and in the rear of which is the parish burial-ground. After leaving the "Dove's Nest," and having a pleasant ride over the hills and between the mountains, and just as the sun was disappearing behind them, we arrived at the gate of

Grassmere Church; and, alighting and following Miss M., we soon found ourselves standing over a grave, marked by a single stone, and that, too, very plain, with a name deeply cut. This announced to us that we were standing over the grave of William Wordsworth. He chose his own grave, and often visited the spot before his death. He lies in the most sequestered spot in the whole grounds; and the simplicity and beauty of the place were enough to make one in love with it, to be laid so far from the bustle of the world, and in so sweet a place. The more one becomes acquainted with the literature of the Old World, the more he must love her poets. Among the teachers of men, none are more worthy of study than the poets; and, as teachers, they should receive far more credit than is yielded to them. No one can look back upon the lives of Dante, Shakspeare, Milton, Goethe, Cowper, and many others that we might name, without being reminded of the sacrifices which they made for mankind, and which were not appreciated until long after their deaths. We need look no further than our own country to find men and women wielding the pen practically and powerfully for the right. It is acknowledged on all hands, in this country, that England has the greatest dead poets, and America the greatest living ones. The poet and the true Christian have alike a hidden life. Worship is the vital element of each. Poetry has in it that kind of utility which good men find in their Bible, rather than such convenience as bad men often profess to draw from it. It ennobles the sentiments, enlarges the affections, kindles the imagination, and gives to us the enjoyment of a life in the past, and in the future, as well as in the present. Under its light and warmth, we wake from our torpidity and coldness, to a sense of our capabilities. This impulse once given, a great object is gained. Schiller has truly said, "Poetry can be to a man what love is to a hero. It can neither counsel him, nor smite him, nor perform any labor for him; but it can bring him up to be a hero, can summon him to deeds, and arm him with strength for all he ought to be." I have often read with pleasure the sweet poetry of our own Whitfield, of Buffalo, which has appeared from time to time in the columns of the newspapers. I have always felt ashamed of the fact the he should be compelled to wield the razor instead of the pen for a living. Meaner poets than James M. Whitfield are now living by their compositions; and were he a white man he would occupy a different position.

Near the grave of Wordsworth is that of Hartley Coleridge. This name must be lifted up as a beacon, with all its pleasant and interesting associations; it must be added to the list in which some names of brighter fame are written—Burns, Byron, Campbell, and others their compeers. They had all the rich endowment of genius, and might, in achieving fame for themselves, have gained glory for God, and great good for man. But they looked "upon the wine when it was red," and gave life and fame, and their precious gifts, and God's blessing, for its false and ruinous joys. We would not drag forth their names that we may gloat over their infirmities. We pity them for their sad fall. We acknowledge the strength of their temptations, and walking backwards, would throw a mantle over their frailties. But these men are needed, also, as warnings. The moral world must have its light-houses. Thousands of young men are running down upon the same rocks on which they were cast away. If the light of their genius has made them conspicuous, let us then use their conspicuity, and throw a ray from them, as from a beacon, far out upon the dim and perilous sea.

Hartley Coleridge was the eldest son of Samuel Taylor Coleridge, poet and metaphysician. He had some of his father's gifts, particularly his captivating conversational power, and his propensity for novel and profound speculation. He had also his father's infirmity of purpose. In the case of the son, the reason, as the world is now informed in a biography written by his brother, was that he early became the slave of intemperate habits, from which no aspirations of his own heart, no struggles with the enslaving appetite, and no efforts of sympathizing and sorrowful friends, could ever deliver him. He gained a fellowship in Oriel College, Oxford, and forfeited it in consequence of these habits. He then cast himself, as a literary adventurer, into the wild vortex of London life; failed sadly in all his projects; drank deep of the treacherous wine-cup, often to his own shame and the chagrin of his friends, from whom he would sometimes hide himself in places where restraint was unknown and shame forgotten, that he might be delivered from their reproachful pity. In the end, he betook himself to a cottage near Grassmere, and where, on the 6th of January, 1849, he died, not, we trust, without penitence and faith in the Redeemer of guilty and wretched men.

Hartley Coleridge tells us, in one of his confessions, that his first resort to wine was for the purpose of seeking relief from the sting of defeated ambition. This temptation was necessarily brief in its duration; for time would gradually extract this sting from his sensitive mind and heart. This, therefore, was not the doorway of the path which led him down to the gulf. The "wine parties" of Oxford were the scenes in which Hartley Coleridge was betrayed and lost. We have but a momentary glimpse of these things in the biography; but that glimpse is sufficient. It reveals to us what in popular language is called a gay scene, but which to us, and in reality, is sombre as death. In the midst of it there sits a bright-eyed, enthusiastic, impetuous young man, heated with repeated draughts of wine, urged by his fellow-revellers to drink deeper, yielding readily to their solicitations, and pouring forth all the while a stream of continuous and sparkling discourse, which fascinated his companions by its wit, its facility and its beauty. Alas! how many of those companions, it may be, are with him in graves where men can only weep and be silent!

It has often been said, and with much truth, that there is no more dangerous gift for a young man than to be able to sing a good song. It is equally dangerous, we think, to be known as a good talker. The gift of rapid, brilliant, mirth-moving speech, is a perilous possession. The dullards, for whose amusement this gift is so often invoked, know well that to ply its possessor with wine is the readiest way to bring out its power. But in the end the wine destroys the intellect, and the man of wit degenerates into a buffoon, and dies a drunkard. Such is the brief life and history of many a young man, who, behind the stained-glass windows of the fashionable *restaurant,* or in the mirrored and cushioned rooms of the club-house, was hailed as the "prince of good fellows," and the rarest of wits. The laughing applauders pass on, each in his own way, and he who made them sport is left to struggle in solitude with the enemy they have helped to fasten upon him. Let every young man who longs for these gifts, and envies their possessors, remember "poor Hartley Coleridge." Let them be warned by the fate of one who was caught in the toils they are weaving around themselves, and perished therein, leaving behind him the record of a life of unfulfilled purposes, and of great departures from the path of duty and peace.

After remaining a short time, and reading the epitaphs of the departed, we again returned to "The Knoll." Nothing can be more imposing than the beauty of English park scenery, and especially in the vicinity of the Lakes. Magnificent lawns that extend like sheets of vivid green, with here and there a sprinkling of fine trees, heaping up rich piles of foliage, and then the forest with the hare, the deer, and the rabbit, "bounding away to the covert, or the pheasant suddenly bursting upon the wing—the artificial stream, the brook taught to wind in natural meanderings, or expand into the glassy lake, with the yellow leaf sleeping upon its bright waters, and occasionally a rustic temple or sylvan statue grown green and dark with age," give an air of sanctity and picturesque beauty to English scenery that is unknown in the United States. The very laborer with his thatched cottage and narrow slip of ground-plot before the door, the little flower-bed, the woodbine trimmed against the wall, and hanging its blossoms about the windows, and the peasant seen trudging home at nightfall with the avails of the toil of the day upon his back—all this tells us of the happiness both of rich and poor in this country. And yet there are those who would have the world believe that the laborer of England is in a far worse condition than the slaves of America. Such persons know nothing of the real condition of the working classes of this country. At any rate, the poor here, as well as the rich, are upon a level, as far as the laws of the country are concerned. The more one becomes acquainted with the English people, the more one has to admire them. They are so different from the people of our own country. Hospitality, frankness and good humor, are always to be found in an Englishman. After a ramble of three days about the Lakes, we mounted the coach, bidding Miss Martineau farewell, and quitted the lake district.

CHAPTER 12

"And there are dresses splendid but fantastical,
  Masks of all times and nations, Turks and Jews,
And Harlequins and Clowns with feats gymnastical;
  Greeks, Romans, Yankee-doodles, and Hindoos."

Presuming that you will expect from me some account of the Great World's Fair, I take my pen to give you my own impressions, although I am afraid that anything which I may say about this "lion of the day" will fall far short of a description. On Monday last, I quitted my lodgings at an early hour, and started for the Crystal Palace. The day was fine, such as we seldom experience in London, with a clear sky, and invigorating air, whose vitality was as rousing to the spirits as a blast from the "horn of Astolpho." Although it was not yet ten o'clock when I entered Piccadilly, every omnibus was full, inside and out, and the street was lined with one living stream, as far as the eye could reach, all wending their way to the "Glass House." No metropolis in the world presents such facilities as London for the reception of the Great Exhibition now collected within its walls. Throughout its myriads of veins the stream of industry and toil pulses with sleepless energy. Every one seems to feel that this great capital of the world is the fittest place wherein they might offer homage to the dignity of toil. I had already begun to feel fatigued by my pedestrian excursions as I passed "Apsley House," the residence of the Duke of Wellington, and emerged into Hyde Park.

I had hoped that on getting into the Park I would be out of the crowd that seemed to press so heavily in the street. But in this I was mistaken. I here found myself surrounded by and moving with an overwhelming mass, such as I had never before witnessed. And, away in the distance, I beheld a

163

dense crowd, and above every other object was seen the lofty summit of the Crystal Palace. The drive in the Park was lined with princely-looking vehicles of every description. The drivers in their bright red and gold uniforms, the pages and footmen in their blue trousers and white silk stockings, and the horses dressed up in their neat, silver-mounted harness, made the scene altogether one of great splendor. I was soon at the door, paid my shilling, and entered the building at the south end of the transept. For the first ten or twenty minutes, I was so lost in astonishment, and absorbed in pleasing wonder, that I could do nothing but gaze up and down the vista of the noble building. The Crystal Palace resembles in some respects the interior of the cathedrals of this country. One long avenue from east to west is intercepted by a transept, which divides the building into two nearly equal parts. This is the greatest building the world ever saw, before which the Pyramids of Egypt, and the Colossus of Rhodes must hide their diminished heads. The palace was not full at any time during the day, there being only sixty-four thousand persons present. Those who love to study the human countenance in all its infinite varieties can find ample scope for the indulgence of their taste, by a visit to the World's Fair. All countries are there represented—Europeans, Asiatics, Americans and Africans, with their numerous subdivisions. Even the exclusive Chinese, with his hair braided, and hanging down his back, has left the land of his nativity, and is seen making long strides through the Crystal Palace, in his wooden-bottomed shoes. Of all places of curious costumes and different fashions, none has ever yet presented such a variety as this Exhibition. No dress is too absurd to be worn in this place.

There is a great deal of freedom in the Exhibition. The servant who walks behind his mistress through the Park feels that he can crowd against her in the Exhibition. The queen and the day laborer, the prince and the merchant, the peer and the pauper, the Celt and the Saxon, the Greek and the Frank, the Hebrew and the Russ, all meet here upon terms of perfect equality. This amalgamation of rank, this kindly blending of interests, and forgetfulness of the cold formalities of ranks and grades, cannot but be attended with the very best results. I was pleased to see such a goodly sprinkling of my own countrymen in the Exhibition—I mean colored men and women—well-dressed, and moving about with their fairer brethren. This, some of our pro-slavery Americans did not seem to relish very well. There was no help for it. As I walked through the American part of the Crystal Palace some of our Virginia neighbors eyed me closely and with jealous looks, especially as an English lady was leaning on my arm. But their sneering looks did not disturb me in the least. I remained the longer in their department, and criticized the bad appearance of their goods the more. Indeed, the Americans, as far as appearance goes, are behind every other country in the Exhibition. The "Greek Slave" is the only production of art which the United States has sent. And it would have been more to their credit had they kept that at home. In so vast a place as the Great Exhibition one scarcely knows what to visit first, or what to look upon last. After wandering about through the building for five hours, I sat down in one of the galleries and looked at the fine marble statue of Virginius, with the knife in his hand and about to take the life of his beloved and beautiful daughter, to save her from the hands of Appius Claudius. The admirer of genius will linger for hours among the great variety of statues in the long avenue. Large statues of Lords Eldon and Stowell, carved out of solid marble, each weighing above twenty tons, are among the most gigantic in the building.

I was sitting with my four hundred paged guide-book before me, and looking down upon the moving mass, when my attention was called to a small group of gentlemen standing near the statue of Shakspeare, one of whom wore a white coat and hat, and had flaxen hair, and trousers rather short in the legs. The lady by my side, and who had called my attention to the group, asked if I could tell what country this odd-looking gentleman was from. Not wishing to run the risk of a mistake, I was about declining to venture an opinion, when the reflection of the sun against a mirror, on the opposite side, threw a brilliant light upon the group and especially on the face of the gentleman in the white coat, and I immediately recognized under the brim of the white hat the features of Horace Greeley, Esq., of the New York *Tribune*. His general appearance was as much out of the English style as that of the Turk whom I had seen but a moment before, in his bag-like trousers, shuffling along in his slippers. But oddness in dress is one of the characteristics of the Great Exhibition.

Among the many things in the Crystal Palace, there are some which receive greater attention than others, around which may always be seen large groups of the visitors. The first of these is the Koh-i-noor, the "Mountain of Light." This is the largest and most valuable diamond in the world, said to be worth two million pounds sterling. It is indeed a great source of attraction to those who go to the Exhibition for the first time, but it is doubtful whether it obtains such admiration afterwards. We saw more than one spectator turn away with the idea that, after all, it was only a piece of glass. After some jamming, I got a look at the precious jewel; and although in a brass-grated cage, strong enough to hold a lion, I found it to be no larger than the third of a hen's egg. Two policemen remain by its side day and night.

The finest thing in the Exhibition is the "Veiled Vestal," a statue of a woman carved in marble, with a veil over her face, and so neatly done that it looks as if it had been thrown over after it was finished. The Exhibition presents many things which appeal to the eye and touch the heart, and altogether it is so decorated and furnished as to excite the dullest mind, and satisfy the most fastidious.

England has contributed the most useful and substantial articles; France, the most beautiful; while Russia, Turkey and the West Indies, seem to vie with each other in richness. China and Persia are not behind. Austria has also contributed a rich and beautiful stock. Sweden, Norway, Denmark, and the smaller states of Europe, have all tried to outdo themselves in sending goods to the World's Fair. In machinery, England has no competitor. In art, France is almost alone in the Exhibition, setting aside England.

In natural productions and provisions, America stands alone in her glory. There lies her pile of canvassed hams; whether they were wood or real, we could not tell. There are her barrels of salt beef and pork, her beautiful white lard, her Indian-corn and corn-meal, her rice and tobacco, her beef-tongues, dried peas, and a few bags of cotton. The contributors from the United States seemed to have forgotten that this was an exhibition of art, or they most certainly would not have sent provisions. But the United States takes the lead in the contributions, as no other country has sent in provisions. The finest thing contributed by our countrymen is a large piece of silk with an eagle painted upon it, surrounded by stars and stripes.

After remaining more than five hours in the great temple, I turned my back upon the richly-laden stalls, and left the Crystal Palace. On my return home I was more fortunate than in the morning, inasmuch as I found a seat for my friend and myself in an omnibus. And even my ride in the close omnibus was not without interest. For I had scarcely taken my seat, when my friend, who was seated opposite me, with looks and gesture informed me that we were in the presence of some distinguished person. I eyed the countenances of the different persons, but in vain, to see if I could find any one who by his appearance showed signs of superiority over his fellow-passengers. I had given up the hope of selecting the person of note, when another look from my friend directed my attention to a gentleman seated in the corner of the omnibus. He was a tall man, with strongly-marked features, hair dark and coarse. There was a slight stoop of the shoulder—that bend which is almost always a characteristic of studious men. But he wore upon his countenance a forbidding and disdainful frown, that seemed to tell one that he thought himself better than those about him. His dress did not indicate a man of high rank; and had we been in America, I would have taken him for an Ohio farmer.

While I was scanning the features and general appearance of the gentleman, the omnibus stopped and put down three or four of the passengers, which gave me an opportunity of getting a seat by the side of my friend, who, in a low whisper, informed me that the gentleman whom I had been eying so closely was no less a person than Thomas Carlyle. I had read his "Hero-worship," and "Past and Present," and had formed a high opinion of his literary abilities. But his recent attack upon the emancipated people of the West Indies, and his laborious article in favor of the reëstablishment of the lash and slavery, had created in my mind a dislike for the man, and I almost regretted that we were in the same omnibus. In some things Mr. Carlyle is right; but in many he is entirely wrong. As a writer, Mr. Carlyle is often monotonous and extravagant. He does not exhibit a new view of nature, or raise insignificant objects into importance; but generally takes commonplace thoughts and events, and tries to express them in stronger and statelier language than others. He holds no communion with his kind, but stands alone, without mate or fellow. He is like a solitary peak, all access to which is cut off. He exists not by sympathy, but by antipathy. Mr. Carlyle seems chiefly to try how he shall display his own powers, and astonish mankind, by starting new trains of speculation, or by expressing old ones so as not to be understood. He cares little what he says, so as he can say it differently from others. To read his works, is one thing; to understand them, is another. If any one thinks I exaggerate, let him sit for an hour over "Sartor Resartus," and if he does not rise from its pages, place his three or four dictionaries on the shelf, and say I am right, I promise never again to say a word against Thomas Carlyle. He writes one page in favor of reform, and ten against it. He would hang all prisoners to get rid of them; yet the inmates of the prisons and "workhouses are better off than the poor." His heart is with the poor; yet the blacks of the West Indies should be taught that if they will not raise sugar and cotton by their own free will, "Quashy should have the whip applied to him." He frowns upon the reformatory speakers upon the boards of Exeter Hall; yet he is the prince of reformers. He hates heroes and assassins; yet Cromwell was an angel, and Charlotte Corday a saint. He scorns everything, and seems to be tired of what he is by nature, and tries to be what he is not.

CHAPTER 13

"The time shall come, when free as seas or wind,
Unbounded Thames shall flow for all mankind
Whole nations enter with each swelling tide,
And seas but join the regions they divide;
Earth's distant ends our glories shall behold,
And the New World launch forth to meet the Old."

POPE.

The past six weeks have been of a stirring nature in this great metropolis. It commenced with the Peace Congress, the proceedings of which have long since reached you. And although that event has passed off, it may not be out of place here to venture a remark or two upon its deliberations.

A meeting upon the subject of peace, with the support of the monied and influential men who rally around the peace standard, could scarcely have been held in Exeter Hall without creating some sensation. From all parts of the world flocked delegates to this practical protest against war. And among those who took part in the proceedings were many men whose names alone would even on ordinary occasions, have filled the great hall. The speakers were chosen from among the representatives of the various countries, without regard to dialect or complexion; and the only fault which seemed to be found with the committee's arrangement was, that in their desire to get foreigners and Londoners, they forgot the country delegates, so that none of the large provincial towns were at all represented in the Congress, so far as speaking was concerned. Manchester, Leeds, Newcastle, and all the important towns in Scotland and Ireland, were silenced in the great meeting. I need not say that this was an oversight of the committee, and one, too, that has done some injury. Such men as the able chairman of the late Anti-Corn-Law League cannot be forgotten in such a meeting, without giving offence to those who sent him, especially when the committee brought forward, day after day, the same speakers, chosen from amongst the metropolitan delegation. However, the meeting was a glorious one, and will long be remembered with delight as a step onward in the cause of peace. Burritt's Brotherhood Bazaar followed close upon the heels of the Peace Congress; and this had scarcely closed, when that ever-memorable meeting of the American fugitive slaves took place in the Hall of Commerce.

The temperance people made the next reformatory move. This meeting took place in Exeter Hall, and was made up of delegates from the various towns in the kingdom. They had come from the North, East, West and South. There was the quick-spoken son of the Emerald Isle, with his pledge suspended from his neck; there, too, the Scot, speaking his broad dialect; also the representatives from the provincial towns of England and Wales, who seemed to speak anything but good English.

The day after the meeting had closed in Exeter Hall, the country societies, together with those of the metropolis, assembled in Hyde Park, and then walked to the Crystal Palace. Their number while going to the Exhibition was variously estimated at from fifteen thousand to twenty thousand, and was said to have been the largest gathering of teetotallers ever assembled in London. They consisted chiefly of the working classes, their wives and children—clean, well-dressed and apparently happy: their looks indicating in every way those orderly habits which, beyond question, distinguish the devotees of that cause above the common laborers of this country. On arriving at the Exhibition, they soon distributed themselves among the departments, to revel in its various wonders, eating their own lunch, and drinking from the Crystal Fountain.

And, now I am at the world's wonder, I will remain here until I finish this sheet. I have spent fifteen days in the Exhibition, and have conversed with those who have spent double that number amongst its beauties, and the general opinion appears to be that six months would not be too long to remain within its walls to enable one to examine its laden stalls. Many persons make the Crystal Palace their home, with the exception of night. I have seen them come in the morning, visit the dressing-room, then go to the refreshment-room, and sit down to breakfast as if they had been at their hotel. Dinner and tea would be taken in turn.

The Crystal Fountain is the great place of meeting in the Exhibition. There you may see husbands looking for lost wives, wives for stolen husbands, mothers for their lost children, and towns-people for their country friends; and, unless you have an appointment at a certain place at an hour, you might as well prowl through the streets of London to find a friend as in the Great Exhibition. There is great beauty in the "Glass House." Here, in the transept, with the glorious sunlight coming through that wonderful glass roof, may the taste be cultivated and improved, the mind edified, and the feelings chastened. Here, surrounded by noble creations in marble and bronze, and in the midst of an admiring throng, one may gaze at statuary which might fitly decorate the house of the proudest prince in Christendom.

He who takes his station in the gallery, at either end, and looks upon that wondrous nave, or who surveys the matchless panorama around him from the intersection of the nave and transept, may be said, without presumption or exaggeration, to see all the kingdoms of this world and the glory of them. He sees not only a greater collection of fine articles, but also a greater as well as more various assemblage of the human race, than ever before was gathered under one roof.

One of the beauties of this great international gathering is, that it is not confined to rank or grade. The million toilers from mine, and factory, and workshop, and loom, and office, and field, share with their more wealthy neighbors the feast of reason and imagination spread out in the Crystal Palace.

It is strange, indeed, to see so many nations assembled and represented on one spot of British ground. In short, it is one great theatre, with thousands of performers, each playing his own part. England is there, with her mighty engines toiling and whirring, indefatigable in her enterprises to shorten labor. India spreads her glitter and paint. France, refined and fastidious, is there every day, giving the last touch to her picturesque group; and the other countries, each in its turn doing what it can to show off. The distant hum of thousands of good-humored people, with occasionally a national anthem from some gigantic organ, together with the noise of the machinery, seems to send life into every part of the Crystal Palace.

When you get tired of walking you can sit down and write your impressions, and there is the "post" to receive your letter; or, if it be Friday or Saturday, you may, if you choose, rest yourself by hearing a lecture from Professor Anstead; and then, before leaving, take your last look, and see something that you have not before seen. Everything which is old in cities, new in colonial life, splendid in courts, useful in industry, beautiful in nature, or ingenious in invention, is there represented. In one place we have the Bible translated into one hundred and fifty languages; in another, we have saints and archbishops painted on glass; in another, old palaces, and the altars of a John Knox, a Baxter, or some other divines of olden time. In the old Temple of Delphi we read that every state of the civilized world had its separate treasury, where Herodotus, born two thousand years before his time, saw and observed all kinds of prodigies in gold and silver, brass and iron, and even in linen. The nations all met there on one common ground, and the peace of the earth was not a little promoted by their common interest in the sanctity and splendor of that shrine. As long as the Exhibition lasts, and its memory endures, we hope and trust that it may shed the same influence. With this hasty scrap I take leave of the Great Exhibition.

CHAPTER 14

"And gray walls moulder round, on which dull time
  Feeds, like slow fire upon a hoary brand;
And one keen pyramid, with wedge sublime,
  Stands o'er the dust of him who planned."

SHELLEY.

I have just finished a short visit to the far-famed city of Oxford, which has
not unaptly been styled the City of Palaces. Aside from this being one of
the principal seats of learning in the world, it is distinguished alike for its
religious and political changes in times past. At one time it was the seat of
Popery; at another, the uncompromising enemy of Rome. Here the tyrant
Richard the Third held his court; and when James the First and his son
Charles the First found their capital too hot to hold them, they removed to
their loyal city of Oxford. The writings of the great republicans were here
committed to the flames. At one time Popery sent Protestants to the stake
and fagot; at another, a Papist king found no favor with the people. A noble
monument now stands where Cranmer, Ridley and Latimer, proclaimed
their sentiments and faith, and sealed them with their blood. And now we
read upon the town treasurer's book—"For three loads of wood, one load
of fagots, one post, two chains and staples, to burn Ridley and Latimer,
£1.5s. 1d." Such is the information one gets by looking over the records of
books written three centuries ago.

It was a beautiful day on which I arrived at Oxford, and, instead of
remaining in my hotel, I sallied forth to take a survey of the beauties of the
city. I strolled into Christ Church Meadows, and there spent the evening in
viewing the numerous halls of learning which surround that splendid
promenade. And fine old buildings they are: centuries have rolled over

many of them, hallowing the old walls, and making them gray with age. They have been for ages the chosen homes of piety and philosophy. Heroes and scholars have gone forth from their studies here into the great field of the world, to seek their fortunes, and to conquer and be conquered. As I surveyed the exterior of the different colleges, I could here and there see the reflection of the light from the window of some student, who was busy at his studies, or throwing away his time over some trashy novel, too many of which find their way into the trunks or carpet-bags of the young men on setting out for college. As I looked upon the walls of these buildings I thought, as the rough stone is taken from the quarry to the finisher, there to be made into an ornament, so was the young mind brought here to be cultivated and developed. Many a poor, unobtrusive young man, with the appearance of little or no ability, is here moulded into a hero, a scholar, a tyrant, or a friend of humanity. I never look upon these monuments of education without a feeling of regret that so few of our own race can find a place within their walls. And, this being the fact, I see more and more the need of our people being encouraged to turn their attention more seriously to self-education, and thus to take a respectable position before the world by virtue of their own cultivated minds and moral standing.

Education, though obtained by a little at a time, and that, too, over the midnight lamp, will place its owner in a position to be respected by all, even though he be black. I know that the obstacles which the laws of the land and of society place between the colored man and education in the United States are very great, yet if *one* can break through these barriers more can; and if our people would only place the right appreciation upon education, they would find these obstacles are easier to be overcome than at first sight appears. A young man once asked Carlyle what was the secret of success. His reply was, "Energy; whatever you undertake, do it with all your might." Had it not been for the possession of energy, I might now have been working as a servant for some brainless fellow who might be able to command my labor with his money, or I might have been yet toiling in chains and slavery. But thanks to energy, not only for my being to-day in a land of freedom, but also for my dear girls being in one of the best seminaries in France, instead of being in an American school, where the finger of scorn would be pointed at them by those whose superiority rests entirely upon their having a whiter skin.

Oxford is, indeed, one of the finest located places in the kingdom, and every inch of ground about it seems hallowed by interesting associations. The university, founded by the good King Alfred, still throws its shadow upon the side-walk; and the lapse of ten centuries seems to have made but little impression upon it. Other seats of learning may be entitled to our admiration, but Oxford claims our veneration. Although the lateness of the night compelled me, yet I felt an unwillingness to tear myself from the scene of such surpassing interest. Few places in any country as noted as Oxford is are without some distinguished person residing within their precincts; and, knowing that the city of palaces was not an exception to this rule, I resolved to see some of its lions. Here, of course, is the head-quarters of the Bishop of Oxford, a son of the late William Wilberforce, Africa's noble champion. I should have been glad to have seen this distinguished pillar of the church; but I soon learned that the bishop's residence was out of town, and that he seldom visited the city, except on business. I then determined to see one who, although a lesser dignitary in the church, is, nevertheless, scarcely less known than the Bishop of Oxford. This was the Rev. Dr. Pusey, a divine whose name is known wherever the religion of Jesus is known and taught, and the acknowledged head of the Puseyites. On the second morning of my visit I proceeded to Christ Church Chapel, where the reverend gentleman officiates. Fortunately I had an opportunity of seeing the doctor, and following close in his footsteps to the church. His personal appearance is anything but that of one who is the leader of a growing and powerful party in the church. He is rather under the middle size, and is round-shouldered, or rather stoops. His profile is more striking than his front face, the nose being very large and prominent. As a matter of course, I expected to see a large nose, for all great men have them. He has a thoughtful and somewhat sullen brow, a firm and somewhat pensive mouth, a cheek pale, thin, and deeply furrowed. A monk fresh from the cloisters of Tinterran Abbey, in its proudest days, could scarcely have made a more ascetic and solemn appearance than did Dr. Pusey on this occasion. He is not apparently above forty-five, or, at most, fifty years of age, and his whole aspect renders him an admirable study for an artist. Dr. Pusey's style of preaching is cold and tame, and one looking at him would scarcely believe that such an apparently uninteresting man could cause such an eruption in the church as he has. I was glad to find that a colored young man was among the students at Oxford.

A few months since, I paid a visit to our countryman, Alexander Crummel who is still pursuing his studies at Cambridge,[13]—a place which, though inferior to Oxford as far as appearance is concerned, is yet said to be greatly its superior as a place of learning. In an hour's walk through the Strand, Regent-street or Piccadilly, in London, one may meet half a dozen colored men, who are inmates of the various colleges in the metropolis. These are all signs of progress in the cause of the sons of

Africa. Then let our people take courage, and with that courage let them apply themselves to learning. A determination to excel is the sure road to greatness, and that is as open to the black man as the white. It is that which has accomplished the mightiest and noblest triumphs in the intellectual and physical world. It is that which has made such rapid strides towards civilization, and broken the chains of ignorance and superstition which have so long fettered the human intellect. It was determination which raised so many worthy individuals from the humble walks of society, and from poverty, and placed them in positions of trust and renown. It is no slight barrier that can effectually oppose the determination of the will; —success must ultimately crown its efforts. "The world shall hear of me," was the exclamation of one whose name has become as familiar as household words. A Toussaint once labored in the sugar-field with his spelling-book in his pocket, amid the combined efforts of a nation to keep him in ignorance.[14] His name is now recorded among the list of statesmen of the past. A Soulouque was once a slave and knew not how to read. He now sits upon the throne of an empire.

In our own country there are men who once held the plough, and that too without any compensation, who are now presiding at the editor's table. It was determination that brought out the genius of a Franklin, and a Fulton, and that has distinguished many of the American statesmen, who, but for their energy and determination, would never have had a name beyond the precincts of their own homes.

It is not always those who have the best advantages, or the greatest talents, that eventually succeed in their undertakings: but it is those who strive with untiring diligence to remove all obstacles to success, and who, with unconquerable resolution, labor on until the rich reward of perseverance is within their grasp. Then again let me say to our young men, Take courage. "There is a good time coming." The darkness of the night appears greatest just before the dawn of day.

CHAPTER 15

"Blush ye not
To boast your equal laws, your just restraints,
Your rights defined, your liberties secured;
Whilst, with an iron hand, ye crush to earth
The helpless African, and bid him drink
That cup of sorrow which yourselves have dashed,
Indignant, from Oppression's fainting grasp?"

WILLIAM ROSCOE.

The love of freedom is one of those natural impulses of the human breast which cannot be extinguished. Even the brute animals of the creation feel and show sorrow and affection when deprived of their liberty. Therefore is a distinguished writer justified in saying, "Man is free, even were he born in chains." The Americans boast, and justly too, that Washington was the hero and model patriot of the American Revolution,—the man whose fame, unequalled in his own day and country, will descend to the end of time, the pride and honor of humanity. The American speaks with pride of the battles of Lexington and Bunker Hill; and, when standing in Faneuil Hall, he points to the portraits of Otis, Adams, Hancock, Quincy, Warren and Franklin, and tells you that their names will go down to posterity among the world's most devoted and patriotic friends of human liberty.

It was on the first of August, 1851, that a number of men, fugitives from that boasted land of freedom, assembled at the Hall of Commerce in the city of London, for the purpose of laying their wrongs before the British nation, and, at the same time, to give thanks to the God of freedom for the liberation of their West India brethren on the first of August, 1834. Little notice had been given of the intended meeting, yet it seemed to be known

177

in all parts of the city. At the hour of half-past seven, for which the meeting had been called, the spacious hall was well filled, and the fugitives, followed by some of the most noted English Abolitionists, entered the hall, amid the most deafening applause, and took their seats on the platform. The appearance of the great hall at this juncture was most splendid. Besides the committee of fugitives, on the platform there were a number of the oldest and most devoted of the slaves' friends. On the left of the chair sat Geo. Thompson, Esq., M.P.; near him was the Rev. Jabez Burns, D.D., and by his side the Rev. John Stevenson, M.A., Wm. Farmer, Esq., R. Smith, Esq.; while on the other side were Joseph Hume, Esq., M.P., John Lee, LL.D., Sir J. Walmsley, M.P., the Rev. Edward Matthews, John Cunliff, Esq., Andrew Paton, Esq., J. P. Edwards, Esq., and a number of colored gentlemen from the West Indies. The body of the hall was not without its distinguished guests. The Chapmans and Westons of Boston, U. S., were there. The Estlins and Tribes had come all the way from Bristol to attend the great meeting. The Patons, of Glasgow, had delayed their departure, so as to be present. The Massies had come in from Upper Clapton. Not far from the platform sat Sir Francis Knowles, Bart.; still further back was Samuel Bowly, Esq., while near the door were to be seen the greatest critic of the age, and England's best living poet. Macaulay had laid aside the pen, entered the hall, and was standing near the central door, while not far from the historian[15] stood the newly-appointed Poet Laureate.[16] The author of "In Memoriam" had been swept in by the crowd, and was standing with his arms folded, and beholding for the first time (and probably the last) so large a number of colored men in one room. In different parts of the hall were men and women from nearly all parts of the kingdom, besides a large number who, drawn to London by the Exhibition, had come in to see and hear these oppressed people plead their own cause.

The writer of this sketch was chosen chairman of the meeting, and commenced its proceedings by delivering the following address, which we cut from the columns of the *Morning Advertiser:*

"The chairman, in opening the proceedings, remarked that, although the metropolis had of late been inundated with meetings of various characters, having reference to almost every variety of subjects, yet that the subject they were called upon that evening to discuss differed from them all. Many of those by whom he was surrounded, like himself, had been victims to the inhuman institution of slavery, and were in consequence exiled from the land of their birth. They were fugitives from their native land, but not fugitives from justice; and they had not fled from a monarchical, but from a so-called republican government. They came from amongst a people who declared, as part of their creed, that all men were born free; but who, while they did so, made slaves of every sixth man, woman and child, in the country. (Hear, hear.) He must not, however, forget that one of the purposes for which they were met that night was to commemorate the emancipation of their brothers and sisters in the isles of the sea. That act of the British Parliament, and he might add in this case, with peculiar emphasis, of the British nation, passed on the twelfth day of August, 1833, to take effect on the first day of August, 1834, and which enfranchised eight hundred thousand West Indian slaves, was an event sublime in its nature, comprehensive and mighty in its immediate influences and remote consequences, precious beyond expression to the cause of freedom, and encouraging beyond the measure of any government on earth to the hearts of all enlightened and just men. This act was the result of a long course of philanthropic and Christian efforts on the part of some of the best men that the world ever produced. It was not his intention to go into a discussion or a calculation of the rise and fall of property, or whether sugar was worth more or less by the act of emancipation. But the abolition of slavery in the West Indies was a blow struck in the right direction, at that most inhuman of all traffics, the slave-trade—a trade which would never cease so long as slavery existed; for where there was a market there would be merchandise; where there was demand there would be a supply; where there were carcasses there would be vultures; and they might as well attempt to turn the water, and make it run up the Niagara river, as to change this law.

"It was often said by the Americans that England was responsible for the existence of slavery there, because it was introduced into that country while the colonies were under the British crown. If that were the case, they must come to the conclusion that, as England abolished slavery in the West Indies, she would have done the same for the American States if she had had the power to do it; and if that was so, they might safely say that the separation of the United States from the mother country was (to say the least) a great misfortune to one sixth of the population of that land. England had set a noble example to America, and he would to heaven his countrymen would follow the example. The Americans boasted of their superior knowledge; but they needed not to boast of their superior guilt, for that was set upon a hill-top, and that, too, so high, that it required not the lantern of Diogenes to find it out. Every breeze from the western world brought upon its wings the groans and cries of the victims of this guilt. Nearly all countries had fixed the seal of disapprobation on slavery; and when, at some future age, this stain on the page of history shall be pointed at, posterity will blush as the discrepancy between American profession and American practice. What was to be thought of a people boasting of their liberty, their humanity, their Christianity, their love of justice, and at the same time keeping in slavery nearly four millions of God's children, and shutting out from them the light of the Gospel, by denying the Bible to the slave! (Hear, hear.) No education, no marriage, everything done to keep the mind of the slave in darkness. There was a wish on the part of the people of the Northern States to shield themselves from the charge of slaveholding; but, as they shared in the guilt, he was not satisfied with letting them off without their share in the odium.

"And now a word about the Fugitive Slave Bill. That measure was in every respect an unconstitutional measure. It set aside the right formerly enjoyed by the fugitive of trial by jury; it afforded to him no protection, no opportunity of proving his right to be free; and it placed every free colored person at the mercy of any unprincipled individual who might wish to lay claim to him. (Hear.) That law is opposed to the principles of Christianity—foreign alike to the laws of God and man. It had converted the whole population of the Free States into a band of slave-catchers, and every rood of territory is but so much hunting-ground, over which they might chase the fugitive. But while they were speaking of slavery in the United States, they must not omit to mention that there was a strong feeling in that land, not only against the Fugitive Slave Law, but also against the existence of slavery in any form. There was a band of fearless men and women in the United States, whose labors for the slave had resulted in good beyond calculation. This noble and heroic class had created an agitation in the whole country, until their principles have taken root in almost every association in the land, and which, with God's blessing, will, in due time, cause the Americans to put into practice what they have so long professed. (Hear, hear.) He wished it to be continually held up before the country, that the Northern States are as deeply implicated in the guilt of slavery as the South. The North had a population of 13,553,328 freemen; the South had a population of only 6,393,756 freemen; the North has 152 representatives in the House, the South only 81; and it would be seen by this that the balance of power was with the Free States. Looking, therefore, at the question in all its aspects, he was sure that there was no one in this country but who would find out that the slavery of the United States of America was a system the most abandoned and the most tyrannical. (Hear, hear.)"

At the close of this address, the Rev. Edward Matthews, from Bristol, but who had recently returned from the United States, where he had been

maltreated on account of his fidelity to the cause of freedom, was introduced, and made a most interesting speech. The next speaker was George
Thompson, Esq., M.P.; and we need only say that his eloquence, which
has seldom if ever been equalled, and never surpassed, exceeded, on this
occasion, the most sanguine expectations of his friends. All who sat under
the thundering anathemas which he hurled against slavery seemed in-
structed, delighted, and animated. Scarcely any one could have remained
unmoved by the pensive sympathies that pervaded the entire assembly.
There were many in the meeting who had never seen a fugitive slave
before, and when any of the speakers would refer to those on the platform
the whole audience seemed moved to tears. No meeting of the kind held in
London for years created a greater sensation than this gathering of ref-
ugees from the "Land of the free, and the home of the brave."

The Rev. J. Burns, D.D., next made an eloquent speech, and was
followed by J. P. Edwards, Esq.

CHAPTER 16

"For 'tis the mind that makes the body rich;
And as the sun breaks through the darkest clouds,
So Honor peereth in the meanest habit."

SHAKSPEARE.

After strolling, for more than two hours, through the beautiful town of Lemington, in which I had that morning arrived, a gentleman, to whom I had a letter of introduction, asked me if I was not going to visit Shakspeare's House. It was only then that I called to mind the fact that I was within a few miles of the birthplace of the world's greatest literary genius. A horse and chaise was soon procured, and I on my way to Stratford. A quick and pleasant ride brought me to the banks of the Avon, and a short time after, to the little but picturesque town of Stratford. I gave the horse in charge of the man-of-all-work at the inn, and then started for the much-talked-of and celebrated cottage. I found it to be a small mean-looking house of wood and plaster, the walls of which are covered with names, inscriptions and hieroglyphics, in every language, by people of all nations, ranks and conditions, from the highest to the lowest, who have made their pilgrimage there. The old shattered and worn-out stock of the gun with which Shakspeare shot Sir Thomas Lucy's deer was shown to us. The old-fashioned tobacco-box was also there. The identical sword with which he played Hamlet, the lantern with which Romeo and Juliet were discovered, lay on the table. A plentiful supply of Shakspeare's mulberry-tree was there, and we were asked if we did not want to purchase; but, fearing that it was not the genuine article, we declined. In one of the most gloomy and dilapidated rooms is the old chair in which the poet used to sit. After viewing everything of interest, and paying the elderly young woman (old maid) her accustomed fee, we left the poet's birthplace to visit his grave. We were soon standing in the chancel of the parish church, a large and venerable edifice, mouldering with age, but finely ornamented within, and the ivy clinging around without. It stands in a beautiful situation on the banks of the Avon. Garrick has most truthfully said:

"Thou soft-flowing Avon, by thy silver stream
Of things more than mortal sweet Shakspeare would dream;
The fairies by moonlight dance round his green bed,
For hallowed the turf is which pillowed his head."

The picturesque little stream runs murmuring at the foot of the church-yard, disturbed only by the branches of the large elms that stand on the banks, and whose limbs droop down. A flat stone is the only thing that marks the place where the poet lies buried. I copied the following verse from the stone, and which is said to have been written by the bard himself:

"Good friend, for Jesus' sake, forbeare
To dig the dust enclosed here:
Blessed be he that spares these stones,
And cursed be he that moves my bones."

Above the grave, in a niche in the wall, is a bust of the poet, placed there not long after his death, and which is supposed to bear some resemblance. Shakspeare's wife and daughter lie near him. After beholding everything of any possible interest, we stepped into our chaise and were soon again in Lemington; which, by the by, is the most beautiful town in all Great Britain, not excepting Cheltenham. In the evening I returned to Coventry, and was partaking of the hospitality of my excellent friend, Joseph Cash, Esq., of Sherburne House, and had stretched myself out on a sofa, with Carlyle's Life of Stirling in my hands, when I was informed that the younger members of the family were preparing to attend a lecture at the Mechanics' Institution. I did not feel inclined to stir from my easy position, after the fatigues of the day; but learning that the lecturer was George Dawson, Esq., I resolved to join the company.

The hall was nearly filled when we reached it, which was only a few minutes before the commencement of the lecture. The stamping of feet and clapping of hands—which is the best evidence of an Englishman's impatience—brought before us a thin-faced, spare-made, wiry-looking man, with rather a dark complexion for an Englishman, but with pre-possessing features. I must confess that I entered the room with some little prejudice against the speaker, caused by an unfavorable criticism from the pen of George Gilfillan, the essayist. However, I was happily disappointed.

His style is witty, keen and gentle, with the language of the drawing-room. His smiling countenance, piercing glance and musical voice, captivated his audience. Mr. Dawson's subject was "The Rise and Spread of the Anglo-Saxon Race," and he showed that he understood his task. During his discourse he said:

"The Greeks and Romans sent out colonies; but no nation but England ever before gave a nation birth. The Americans are a nation, with no language, no creed, no grave-yards. Their names are a derivation; and it is laughable to see the pains an American takes to appear national. He will soon explain to you that he is not an Englishman, but a free-born citizen of the U-nited States, with a pretty considerable contempt for them British-ers. These notions make an Englishman smile; the Americans are a nation without being a nation; they are impressed with an idea that they have characteristics,—they are odd, not national, and remind one of a long, slender youth, somewhat sallow, who has just had a new watch, conse-quently blasphemes the old one; and as for the watch his father used, what is it?—a turnip; by this means he assumes the independent. The American *is* independent; he flaunts it in your face, and surprises you with his galvanic attempts at showing off his nationality. They have, in fact, no literature; we don't want them to have any, as long as they can draw from the old country; the feeling is kindly, and should be cherished; it is like the boy at Christmas coming home to spend the holidays. Long may they draw inspiration from Shakspeare and Milton, and come again and again to the old well. Walking down Broadway is like looking at a page of the Polyglot Bible. America was founded in a great thought, peopled through liberty; and long may that country be the noblest thing that England has to boast of.

"Some people think that we, as a nation, are going down; that we have passed the millennium; but there is no reason yet. We have work to do,—gold mines to dig, railways to construct, &c. &c. When all the work is done, then, and not till then, will the Saxon folk have finished their destiny. We have continents to fill yet; our work is not done till Europe is free. When Emerson visited us, he said that England was not an old country, but had the two-fold character of youth and age; he saw new cities, new docks; a good day's work yet to be done, and many vast undertakings only just begun. The coal, the iron and the gold, are ours; we have noble days in store, but we must labor more than we have yet done. Talk of going down!—we have hardly arrived at our meridian. We have our faults; any Frenchman or German may point them out. We have our duties, and often waste our precious moments by indulging in one eternal grumble at what we do, compared to what we ought to do. A little praise is good sometimes,—we walk the taller for it, and work the better. Only as we know our work here, and do it as our fathers did, shall we promote good; working heartily, and not faltering until the object is gained. The more we add to the happiness of a people, the more we shall be worthy of the good gifts of God."

As an orator, Mr. Dawson stands deservedly high; and was on several occasions applauded to the echo. He was educated for the ministry in the Orthodox persuasion, but left it and became a Unitarian, and has since gone a step further. Mr. Dawson resides in Birmingham, where he has a fine chapel, and a most intellectual congregation, and is considered the Theodore Parker of England.[17]

It is indeed strange, the impression which a mind well cultivated can make upon those about it; and in this we see more clearly the need of education. In whatever light we view education, it cannot fail to appear the most important subject that can engage the attention of mankind. When we contrast the ignorance, the rudeness and the helplessness of the savage, with the knowledge, the refinement and the resources of civilized man, the difference between them appears so wide, that they can scarcely be regarded as of the same species; yet compare the infant of the savage with that of the educated and enlightened philosopher, and you will find them in all respects the same. The same *high, capacious powers* of the mind lie folded up in both, and in both the organs of sensation adapted to these mental powers are exactly similar. All the difference which is afterwards to distinguish them depends entirely upon their education, energy and self-culture.

CHAPTER 17

"Proud pile! that rearest thy hoary head,
In ruin vast, in silence dread,
    O'er Teme's luxuriant vale,
Thy moss-grown halls, thy precincts drear,
To musing Fancy's pensive ear
    Unfold a varied tale."

It was in the latter part of December, and on one of the coldest nights that I have experienced, that I found myself seated before the fire, and alone, in the principal hotel in the town of Ludlow, and within a few minutes' walk of the famous old castle from which the town derives its name. A ride of one hundred and fifty miles by rail, in such uncomfortable carriages as no country except Great Britain furnishes for the weary traveller, and twenty miles on the top of a coach, in a drenching rain, caused me to remain by the fire's side to a later hour than I otherwise would have done. "Did you ring, sir?" asked the waiter, as the clock struck twelve. "No," I replied; but I felt that this was the servant's mode of informing me that it was time for me to retire to bed and consequently I asked for a candle, and was shown to my chamber, and was soon in bed. From the weight of the covering on the bed, I felt sure that the extra blanket which I had requested to be put on was there; yet I was shivering with cold. As the sheets began to warm, I discovered, to my astonishment, that they were damp; indeed, wet. My first thought was to ring the bell for the chambermaid, and have them changed; but, after a moment's consideration, I resolved to adopt a different course. I got out of bed, pulled the sheets off, rolled them up, raised the window, and threw them into the street. After disposing of the wet sheets, I returned to bed and got in between the blankets, and lay there trembling with cold till Morpheus came to my relief. The next morning I said nothing about the uncomfortable night I had experienced, and determined to leave it until they discovered the loss of the sheets. As soon as I had breakfasted, I went out to view the castle. For many years this was one of the strongest baronial fortifications in England. It was from Ludlow Castle that Edward, Prince of Wales, and his brother, were taken to London and put to death in the Tower, by order of their uncle, Richard III., before that villain seized upon the crown. The family of Mortimer for centuries held the castle, and, consequently, ruled Herefordshire. The castle rises from the point of a headland, and its foundations are ingrafted into a bare gray rock. The front consists of square towers, with high connecting walls. The castle is a complete ruin, and has been for centuries; large trees are still growing in the midst of the old pile, which give it a picturesque appearance. It was here that the exquisite effusion of the youthful genius of Milton—The Masque of Comus—was composed, and performed before His Majesty Charles I., in 1631. Little did the king think that the poet would one day be secretary to the man who should put him to death and rule his kingdom. Although a ruin, this fact is enough to excite interest, and to cause one to venerate the old building, and to do homage to the memory of the divine poet who hallowed it with his immortal strains. From a visitor's book that is kept at the gatehouse, I copied the following verses:

> "Here Milton sung; what needs a greater spell
>   To lure thee, stranger, to these far-famed walls?
> Though chroniclers of other ages tell
>   That princes oft have graced fair Ludlow's halls,
> Their honors glide along oblivion's stream,
>   And o'er the wreck a tide of ruin drives;
> Faint and more faint the rays of glory beam
>   That gild their course—the bard alone survives.
> And, when the rude, unceasing shocks of Time
>   In one vast heap shall whelm this lofty pile,
> Still shall his genius, towering and sublime,
>   Triumphant o'er the spoils of grandeur smile;
> Still in these haunts, true to a nation's tongue,
> Echo shall love to dwell, and say, Here Milton sung."

I lingered long in the room pointed out to me as the one in which Milton wrote his "Comus." The castle was not only visited by the author of "Paradise Lost," but here, amidst the noise and bustle of civil dissensions, Samuel Butler, the satirical author of "Hudibras," found an asylum. The part of the tower in which it is said he composed his "Hudibras" was shown to us. In looking over the different apartments, we passed through a cell with only one small window through which the light found its way. On a stone, chiselled with great beauty, was a figure in a weeping position, and underneath it some one had written with pencil, in a legible hand:

"The Muse, too, weeps; in hallowed hour
Here sacred Milton owned her power,
    And woke to nobler song."

The weather was exceedingly cold, and made more so by the stone walls partly covered with snow and frost around us; and I returned to the inn. It being near the time for me to leave by the coach for Hereford, I called for my bill. The servant went out of the room; but soon returned, and began stirring up the fire with the poker. I again told him that the coach would shortly be up, and that I wanted my bill. "Yes, sir, in a moment," he replied, and left in haste. Ten or fifteen minutes passed away, and the servant once more came in, walked to the window, pulled up the blinds, and then went out. I saw that something was in the wind; and it occurred to me that they had discovered the loss of the sheets. The waiter soon returned again, and, in rather an agitated manner, said, "I beg your pardon, sir, but the landlady is in the hall, and would like to speak to you." Out I went, and found the finest specimen of an English lady that I had seen for many a day. There she stood, nearly as thick as she was high, with a red face, garnished around with curls, that seemed to say, "I have just been brushed and oiled." A neat apron covered a black alpacca dress that swept the ground with modesty, and a bunch of keys hung at her side. O, that smile! such a smile as none but a woman who had often been before a mirror could put on. However, I had studied human nature too successfully not to know that thunder and lightning were concealed under that smile; and I nerved myself up for the occasion. "I am sorry to have to name it, sir," said she, "but the sheets are missing off your bed." "O, yes," I replied; "I took them off last night." "Indeed!" exclaimed she; "and pray what have you done with them?" "I threw them out of the window," said I. "What! into the street?" "Yes, into the street," I said. "What did you do that for?" "They were wet; and I was afraid that if I left them in the room they would be put on at night, and give somebody else a cold." And here I coughed with all my might, to remind her that I had suffered from the negligence of her chambermaid. The heaving of the chest and panting for breath which the lady was experiencing at this juncture told me plainly that an explosion was at hand; and the piercing glance of those wicked-looking black eyes, and the rapid changes that came over that never-to-be-forgotten face, were enough to cause the most love-sick man in the world to give up all ideas of matrimony, and to be contented with being his own master. "Then, sir," said the landlady, "you will have to pay for the sheets." "O, yes," replied I; "I will pay for them; put them in the bill, and I will send the bill to *The Times,* and have it published, and let the travelling public know how much you charge for wet sheets!" and I turned upon my heel and walked into the room.

A few minutes after, the servant came in and laid before me the bill. I looked, but in vain, to see how much I had been charged for my hasty indiscretion the previous night. No mention was made of the sheets; and I paid the bill as it stood. The blowing of the coachman's horn warned me that I must get ready; and I put on my top coat. As I was passing through the hall, there stood the landlady just where I had left her, looking as if she had not stirred a single peg. And that smile, that had often cheered or carried consternation to many a poor heart, was still to be seen. I would rather have gone without my dinner than to have looked her in the face, such is my timidity. But common courtesy demanded that I should at least nod as I passed by; and therefore I was thrown back upon my manners, and unconsciously found myself giving her one of my best bows. Whether this bow was the result of my early training while in slavery, the domestic discipline that I afterwards experienced in freedom, or the terror with which every nerve was shaken on first meeting the landlady, I am still unaware. However, the bow was made and the ice broken, and the landlady smilingly said, "You do not know, sir, how much I am grieved at your being put to so much trouble last night, with those wet sheets; it was all the fault of the chambermaid, and I have given her warning, and shall dismiss her a month from to-day. And I do hope, sir, that if you should ever mention this circumstance you will not name the house in which it occurred." How could I do otherwise than to acquiesce in her wishes? Yes, I promised that I would never name the inn at which I had caught the rheumatism; and, therefore, reader, you may ask me, but in vain,—I will not tell you. One more bow, and out I went, and mounted the coach. As the driver was pulling up his reins, and raising his whip in the air, I turned to take a farewell glance of the inn, when, to my surprise, I beheld the landlady at the door with a white handkerchief in her hand, and a countenance beaming with smiles that I still see in my mind's eye. I raised my hat, she nodded, and away went the coach. Although the ride was a cold and dreary one, I often caught myself smiling over the fright in which I had put the landlady by threatening to publish her house.

After a fatiguing stage twenty miles or more, over a bad road, we reached Hereford, a small city, situated in a fertile plain, bounded on all sides with orchards, and watered by the translucent Wye. I spent the greater part of the next day in seeing the lions of the little city. I first visited, what most strangers do, the cathedral; a building partly Gothic and partly Saxon in its architecture, the interior of which is handsome, and contains an excellent organ, a piece of furniture that often calls more hearers to a place of worship than the preacher. In passing through the cathedral I stood a moment or two over the grave of the poet Phillips, the author of the "Splendid Shilling," "Cider," etc. While in the library the verger showed me a manuscript Bible of Wickliffe's, the first in use, written on vellum in the old black letter, full of abbreviations. He also pointed out some Latin manuscripts, in various parts beautifully illuminated with most ingenious penmanship, the coloring of the figures very bright. After all, there is a degree of pleasure in handling these old and laid-aside books. Hereford is noted for having been the birthplace of several distinguished persons. I was shown the house in which David Garrick was born. From Hereford he was removed to Litchfield and became the pupil of Dr. Johnson, and eventually both master and pupil went to London in search of bread, one became famous as an actor, the other noted as *surly Sam Johnson*. An obscure cottage in Pipe-lane was pointed out as the birthplace of the celebrated Nell Gwynne, who first appeared in London in the pit of Drury-lane Theatre as an apple-girl, and afterwards became an actress, in which position she was seen by King Charles II., who took her to his bed and board, and created her Duchess of St. Albans. However, she had many crooked paths to tread, after becoming an actress, before she captivated the heart of the *Merry Monarch*. The following story of her life, told by herself, is too good to be lost; so I insert it here.

"When I was a poor girl," said the Duchess of St. Albans, "working very hard for my thirty shillings a week, I went down to Liverpool during the holidays, where I was always well received. I was to perform in a new piece, something like those pretty little affecting dramas they get up now at our minor theatres; and in my character I represented a poor, friendless orphan-girl, reduced to the most wretched poverty. A heartless tradesman prosecutes the sad heroine for a heavy debt, and insists on putting her in prison, unless some one will be bail for her. The girl replies, 'Then I have no hope; I have not a friend in the world.' 'What! will no one be bail for you, to save you from going to prison?' asks the stern creditor. 'I have told you I have not a friend on earth,' was the reply. But just as I was uttering the words, I saw a sailor in the upper gallery springing over the railing, letting himself down from one tier to another, until he bounded clear over the orchestra and footlights, and placed himself beside me in a moment. 'Yes, you shall have *one* friend at least, my poor young woman,' said he, with the greatest expression in his honest, sunburnt countenance; I will go bail for you to any amount. And as for *you,*' turning to the frightened actor, 'if you don't bear a hand and shift your moorings, you lubber, it will be worse for you when I come athwart your bows!' Every creature in the house rose; the uproar was indescribable—peals of laughter, screams of terror, cheers from his tawny messmates in the gallery, preparatory scrapings of violins from the orchestra; and, amidst the universal din, there stood the unconscious cause of it, sheltering me, 'the poor, distressed young woman,' and breathing defiance and destruction against my mimic persecutor. He was only persuaded to relinquish his care of me, by the manager pretending to arrive and rescue me, with a profusion of theatrical bank-notes."

Hereford was also the birthplace of Mrs. Siddons, the unequalled tragic actress. The views around Hereford are very sylvan, and from some points, where the Welsh mountains are discernible, present something of the magnificent. All this part of the country still shows unmistakable evidence that war has had its day here. In those times the arts and education received no encouragement. The destructive exploits of conquerors may dazzle for a while, but the silent labors of the student and the artist, of the architect and the husbandman, which embellish the earth, and convert it into a terrestrial paradise, although they do not shine with so conspicuous a glare, diversify the picture with milder colors and more beautiful shades.

CHAPTER 18

"To him no author was unknown
Yet what he writ was all his own;
Horace's wit, and Virgil's state,
He did not steal, but emulate;
And when he would like them appear,
Their form, but not their clothes, did wear."

DENHAM.

If there be an individual living who has read the "Essay on Man," or "The Rape of the Lock," without a wish to become more acquainted with the writings of the gifted poet that penned those exquisite poems, I confess that such an one is made of different materials from myself.

It is possible that I am too great a devotee to authors, and especially poets; yet such is my reverence for departed writers, that I would rather walk five miles to see a poet's grave than to spend an evening at the finest entertainment that could be got up.

It was on a pleasant afternoon in September, that I had gone into Surrey to dine with Lord C—, that I found myself one of a party of nine, and seated at a table loaded with everything that the heart could wish. Four men-servants, in livery, with white gloves, waited upon the company.

After the different courses had been changed, the wine occupied the most conspicuous place on the table, and all seemed to drink with a relish unappreciated except by those who move in the higher walks of life. My glass was the only one on the table in which the juice of the grape had not been poured. It takes more nerve than most men possess to cause one to decline taking a glass of wine with a lady; and in English society they don't appear to understand how human beings can live and enjoy health without taking at least a little wine. By my continued refusal to drink with first one and then another of the company, I had become rather an object of pity than otherwise.

A lady of the party, and in company with whom I had dined on a previous occasion, and who knew me to be an abstainer, resolved to relieve me from the awkward position in which my principles had placed me, and therefore caused a decanter of raspberry vinegar to be adulterated and brought on the table. A note in pencil from the lady informed me of the contents of the new bottle. I am partial to this kind of beverage, and felt glad when it made its appearance. No one of the party, except the lady, knew of the fraud; and I was able, during the remainder of the time, to drink with any of the company. The waiters, as a matter of course, were in the secret; for they had to make the change while passing the wine from me to the person with whom I drank.

After a while, as is usual, the ladies all rose and left the room. The retiring of the fair sex left the gentlemen in a more free-and-easy position, and consequently the topics of conversation were materially changed, but not for the better. The presence of women is always a restraint in the right direction. An hour after the ladies had gone, the gentlemen were requested to retire to the drawing-room, where we found tea ready to be served up. I was glad when the time came to leave the dining-room, for I felt it a great bore to be compelled to remain at the table *three hours*. Tea over, the wine again brought on, and the company took a stroll through the grounds at the back of the villa. It was a bright moonlight night, and the stars were out, and the air came laden with the perfume of sweet flowers, and there were no sounds to be heard, except the musical splashing of the little cascade at the end of the garden, and the song of the nightingale, that seemed to be in one of the trees near by. How pleasant everything looked with the flowers creeping about the summer-house, and the windows opening to the velvet lawn, with its modest front, neat trellis-work, and meandering vine! The small smooth fish-pond, and the life-like statues standing or kneeling in different parts of the grounds, gave it the appearance of a very paradise.

"There," said his lordship, "is where Cowley used to sit under that tree, and read."

This reminded me that I was near Chertsey, where the poet spent his last days; and, as I was invited to spend the night within a short ride of that place, I resolved to visit it the next day. We returned to the drawing-room, and a few moments after the party separated, at ten o'clock.

After breakfast the following morning, I drove over to Chertsey, a pretty little town, with but two streets of any note. In the principal street, and not far from the railway station, stands a low building of wood and plaster, known as the *Porch House*. It was in this cottage that Abraham Cowley, the poet, resided, and died in 1667, in the forty-ninth year of his age. It being the residence of a gentleman who was from home, I did not have an opportunity of seeing the interior of the building, which I much regretted. Having visited Cowley's house, I at once determined to do what I had long promised myself; that was, to see Pope's villa, at Twickenham; and I returned to London, took the Richmond boat, and was soon gliding up the Thames.

I have seldom had a pleasanter ride by water than from London Bridge to Richmond; the beautiful panoramic view which unfolds itself on either side of the river can scarcely be surpassed by the scenery in any country. In the centre of Twickenham stands the house made celebrated from its having been the residence of Alexander Pope. The house is not large, but occupies a beautiful site, and is to be seen to best advantage from the river. The garden and grounds have undergone some change since the death of the poet. The grotto leading from the villa to the Thames is in a sad condition.

The following lines, written by Pope soon after finishing this idol of his fancy, show in what estimate he held it, and should at least have preserved it from decay:

> "Thou who shalt stop where *Thames'* translucent wave
> Shines a broad mirror through the shadowy cave;
> Where lingering drops from mineral roofs distill,
> And pointed crystals break the sparkling rill;
> Unpolished gems no ray on pride bestow,
> And latent metals innocently glow—
> Approach! Great nature studiously behold!
> And eye the mine without a wish for gold.
> Approach—but awful! Lo! The Ægerian grot,
> Where, nobly pensive, St. John sate and thought;
> Where *British* sighs from dying Wyndham stole,
> And the bright flame was shot through Marchmont's soul.
> Let such—such only—tread this sacred floor,
> Who dare to love their country and be poor."

It is strange that there are some at the present day who deny that Pope was a poet; but it seems to me that such either show a want of appreciation of poetry, or themselves no judge of what constitutes poetry. Where can be found a finer effusion than the "Essay on Man"? Johnson, in his admirable Life of Pope, in drawing a comparison between him and Dryden, says, "If the flights of Dryden are higher, Pope continues longer on the wing; if of Dryden's fire the blaze is brighter, of Pope is the heat more regular and constant. Dryden often surpasses expectation, and Pope never falls below it; Dryden is read with frequent astonishment, and Pope with perpetual delight." In speaking of the "Rape of the Lock," the same great critic remarks that it "stands forward in the classes of literature, as the most exquisite example of ludicrous poetry." Another poet and critic of no mean authority calls him "The sweetest and most elegant of English poets, the severest chastiser of vice, and the most persuasive teacher of wisdom." Lord Byron terms him "the most perfect and harmonious of poets." How many have quoted the following lines without knowing that they were Pope's!

> "To look through Nature up to Nature's God."
> "An honest man's the noblest work of God."
> "Just as the twig is bent, the tree's inclined."
> "If to her share some female errors fall,
> Look on her face, and you'll forget them all."
> "For modes of faith let graceless zealots fight,
> His can't be wrong whose life is in the right."

Pope was certainly the most independent writer of his time; a poet who never sold himself, and never lent his pen to the upholding of wrong. And although a severe critic, the following verse will show that he did not wish to bestow his chastisement in a wrong direction:

> "Curst be the verse, how well soe'er it flow,
> That tends to make one honest man my foe,
> Give Virtue scandal, Innocence a fear,
> Or from the soft-eyed virgin steal a tear!"

No poet's pen was ever more thoroughly used to suppress vice than Pope's; and what he did was done conscientiously, as the following lines will show:

> "Ask you what provocation I have had?
> The strong antipathy of good to bad.
> When Truth or Virtue an affront endures,
> The affront is mine, my friend, and should be yours."

Pope is not a poet of a high order, but as yet he is the unsurpassed translator of Homer.

My visit to Pope's villa was a short one, but it was attended with many pleasing incidents. I have derived much pleasure from reading his Iliad and other translations. The verse from the pen of Lord Denham, that heads this chapter, conveys but a faint idea of my estimate of Pope's genius and talents.

CHAPTER 19

"The treasures of the deep are not so precious
As are the concealed comforts of a man
Locked up in woman's love. I scent the air
Of blessings, when I come but near the house.
What a delicious breath marriage sends forth! . . .
The violet bed's not sweeter."

MIDDLETON.

During a sojourn of five years in Europe, I have spent many pleasant hours in strolling through old church-yards, and reading the epitaphs upon the tombstones of the dead. Part of the pleasure was derived from a wish for solitude; and no place offers as quiet walks as a village burial-ground. And the curious epitaphs that are to be seen in a church-yard six or eight hundred years old are enough to cause a smile, even in so solemn a place as a grave-yard. While walking through Horsleydown church, in Cumberland, a short time since, I read an inscription over a tomb which I copied, and shall give in this chapter, although at the risk of bringing down upon my devoted head the indignation of the fair sex. Domestic enjoyment is often blasted by an intermixture of foibles with virtues of a superior kind; and if the following shall prove a warning to wives, I shall be fully compensated for my trouble.

Here lie the bodies of
THOMAS BOND, and MARY his wife.
She was temperate, chaste and charitable;
But
She was proud, peevish and passionate.
She was an affectionate wife and a tender mother;

But

Her husband and child, whom she loved, seldom saw her
countenance without a disgusting frown,
Whilst she received visitors, whom she despised, with an
endearing smile.
Her behavior was discreet toward strangers;

But

imprudent in her family.
Abroad, her conduct was influenced by good-breeding;

But

at home, by ill-temper.
She was a professed enemy to flattery, and was
Seldom known to praise or commend;

But

the talents in which she principally excelled were
difference of opinion, and discovering
flaws and imperfections.
She was an admirable economist,
and, without prodigality,
dispensed plenty to every person in her family;

But

would sacrifice their eyes to a farthing candle.
She sometimes made her husband happy with her good qualities;

But

Much more frequenlty miserable with her many failings;
Insomuch, that, in thirty years' cohabitation, he often
lamented that, maugre her virtues,
He had not, in the whole, enjoyed two years
of matrimonial comfort.
At length,
finding that she had lost the affections of her
husband, as well as the regard of her neighbors, family
disputes having been divulged by servants,
She died of vexation, July 20, 1768,
Aged 48 years.
Her worn-out husband survived her four months
and two days, and departed this life November 28, 1768,
in the 54th year of his age.
William Bond, brother to the deceased, erected
this stone,
a *weekly monitor* to the surviving wives of this
parish, that they may avoid the infamy
of having their memories handed down to posterity
with a *patch-work* character.

CHAPTER 20

"To where the broken landscape, by degrees
Ascending, roughens into rigid hills,
O'er which the Cambrian mountains, like far clouds
That skirt the blue horizon, dusky rise."

THOMSON.

I have visited few places where I found warmer friends, or felt myself more at home, than in Aberdeen. The dwellings, being built mostly of granite, remind one of Boston, especially in a walk down Union-street, which is thought to be one of the finest promenades in Europe. The town is situated on a neck of land between the rivers Dee and Don, and is the most important commercial place in the north of Scotland.

During our stay in the city we visited, among other places, the old bridge of Don, which is not only resorted to owing to its antique celebrity and peculiar appearance, but also for the notoriety that it has gained by Lord Byron's poem for the "Bridge of Don." His lordship spent several years here during his minority, and this old bridge was a favorite resort of his. In one of his notes he alludes to how he used to hang over its one arch, and the deep black salmon stream below, with a mixture of childish terror and delight. While we stood upon the melancholy bridge, and although the scene around was severely grand and terrific,—the river swollen, the wind howling amongst the leafless trees, the sea in the distance,—and although the walk where Hall and Mackintosh were wont to melt down hours to moments in high converse was in sight, it was, somehow or other, the figure of the mild lame boy leaning over the parapet that filled our fancy; and the chief fascination of the spot seemed to breathe from the genius of the author of "Childe Harold."

To Anthony Cruikshank, Esq., whose hospitality we shared in Aberdeen, we are indebted for showing us the different places of interest in the town and vicinity. An engagement, however, to be in Edinburgh, cut short our stay in the north. The very mild state of the weather, and a wish to see something of the coast between Aberdeen and Edinburgh, induced us to make the journey by water. Consequently, after delivering a lecture before the Mechanics' Institute, with His Honor the Provost in the chair, on the evening of February 15th, we went on board the steamer bound for Edinburgh. On reaching the vessel we found the drawing-saloon almost entirely at our service, and, prejudice against color being unknown, we had no difficulty in obtaining the best accommodation that the steamer afforded. This was so unlike the pro-slavery, negro-hating spirit of America, that my colored friends who were with me were almost bewildered by the transition. The night was a glorious one. The sky was cloudless, and the clear, bracing air had a buoyancy I have seldom seen. The moon was in its zenith; the steamer and surrounding objects were beautiful in the extreme. The boat left her moorings at half-past twelve, and we were soon out at sea. The "Queen" is a splendid craft, and, without the aid of sails, was able to make fifteen miles within the hour. I was up the next morning extremely early,—indeed, before any of my fellow-passengers,—and found the sea, as on the previous night, as calm and as smooth as a mirror.

> "There was no sound upon the deep,
>   The breeze lay cradled there;
> The motionless waters sank to sleep
>   Beneath the sultry air;
> Out of the cooling brine to leap
>   The dolphin scarce would dare."

It was a delightful morning, more like April than February; and the sun, as it rose, seemed to fire every peak of the surrounding hills. On our left lay the Island of May, while to the right was to be seen the small fishing-town of Anstruther, twenty miles distant from Edinburgh. Beyond these, on either side, was a range of undulating blue mountains, swelling, as they retired, into a bolder outline and a loftier altitude, until they terminated some twenty-five or thirty miles in the dim distance. A friend at my side pointed out a place on the right, where the remains of an old castle or look-out house, used in the time of the border wars, once stood, and which reminded us of the barbarism of the past.

But these signs are fast disappearing. The plough and roller have passed over many of these foundations, and the time will soon come when the antiquarian will look in vain for those places that history has pointed out to him as connected with the political and religious struggles of the past.

The steward of the vessel came round to see who of the passengers wished for breakfast; and as the keen air of the morning had given me an appetite, and there being no prejudice on the score of color, I took my seat at the table, and gave ample evidence that I was not an invalid. On our return to the deck again, I found that we had entered the Frith of Forth, and that "Modern Athens" was in sight; and far above every other object, with its turrets almost lost in the clouds, could be seen Edinburgh Castle.

After landing, and a pleasant ride over one of the finest roads in Scotland, with a sprinkling of beautiful villas on either side, we were once more at Cannon's Hotel. While in the city, on this occasion, we went on the Calton Hill, from which we had a delightful view of the place and surrounding country.

I had an opportunity, during my stay in Edinburgh, of visiting the Infirmary; and was pleased to see among the two or three hundred students three colored young men, seated upon the same benches with those of a fairer complexion, and yet there appeared no feeling on the part of the whites towards their colored associates, except of companionship and respect. One of the cardinal truths, both of religion and freedom, is the equality and brotherhood of man. In the sight of God and all just institutions, the whites can claim no precedence or privilege on account of their being white; and if colored men are not treated as they should be in the educational institutions in America, it is a pleasure to know that all distinction ceases by crossing the broad Atlantic. I had scarcely left the lecture-room of the Institute and reached the street, when I met a large number of the students on their way to the college, and here again were seen colored men arm in arm with whites. The proud American who finds himself in the splendid streets of Edinburgh, and witnesses such scenes as these, can but behold in them the degradation of his own country, whose laws would make slaves of these same young men, should they appear in the streets of Charleston or New Orleans.

During my stay in Edinburgh I accepted an invitation to breakfast with George Combe, Esq., the distinguished philosophical phrenologist, and author of "The Constitution of Man." Although not far from seventy years of age, I found him apparently as active and as energetic as many men of half that number of years. Mr. Combe feels a deep interest in the cause of the American slave. I have since become more intimately acquainted with him, and am proud to reckon him amongst the warmest of my friends. In all of Mr. Combe's philanthropic exertions he is ably seconded by his wife, a lady of rare endowments, of an attractive person and engaging manners, and whose greatest delight is in doing good. She took much interest in Ellen Craft, who formed one of the breakfast party; and was often moved to tears on the recital of the thrilling narrative of her escape from slavery.

CHAPTER 21

"Look here, upon this picture, and on this."

HAMLET.

No one accustomed to pass through Cheapside could fail to have noticed a good-looking man, neither black nor white, engaged in distributing bills to the thousands who throng that part of the city of London. While strolling through Cheapside, one morning, I saw, for the fiftieth time, Joseph Jenkins, the subject of this chapter, handing out his bills to all who would take them as he thrust them into their hands. I confess that I was not a little amused, and stood for some moments watching and admiring his energy in distributing his papers. A few days after, I saw the same individual in Chelsea, sweeping a crossing; here, too, he was equally as energetic as when I met him in the city. Some days later, while going through Kensington, I heard rather a sweet, musical voice singing a familiar psalm, and on looking round was not a little surprised to find that it was the Cheapside bill-distributor and Chelsea crossing-sweeper. He was now singing hymns, and selling religious tracts. I am fond of patronizing genius, and therefore took one of his tracts and paid him for a dozen.

During the following week, I saw, while going up the city road, that Shakespeare's tragedy of Othello was to be performed at the Eagle Saloon that night, and that the character of the Moor was to be taken by "*Selim, an African prince.*" Having no engagement that evening, I resolved at once to attend, to witness the performance of the "African Roscius," as he was termed on the bills. It was the same interest that had induced me to go to the Italian opera to see Madames Sontag and Grisi in Norma, and to visit Drury Lane to see Macready take leave of the stage. My expectations were screwed up to the highest point. The excitement caused by the publication of "Uncle Tom's Cabin" had prepared the public for anything in the African line, and I felt that the *prince* would be sure of a good audience; and in this I was not disappointed, for, as I took my seat in one of the boxes near the stage, I saw that the house was crammed with an orderly company. The curtain was already up when I entered, and Iago and Roderigo were on the stage. After a while Othello came in, and was greeted with thunders of applause, which he very gracefully acknowledged. Just black enough to take his part without coloring his face, and being tall, with a good figure and an easy carriage, a fine, full and musical voice, he was well adapted to the character of Othello. I immediately recognized in the countenance of the Moor a face that I had seen before, but could not at the moment tell where. Who could this "prince" be, thought I. He was too black for Douglass, not black enough for Ward, not tall enough for Garnet, too calm for Delany, figure, though fine, not genteel enough for Remond. However, I was soon satisfied as to who the *star* was. Reader, would you think it? it was no less a person than Mr. Jenkins, the bill-distributor from Cheapside, and crossing-sweeper from Chelsea! For my own part, I was overwhelmed with amazement, and it was some time before I could realize the fact. He soon showed that he possessed great dramatic power and skill; and his description to the senate of how he won the affections of the gentle Desdemona stamped him at once as an actor of merit. "What a pity," said a lady near me to a gentleman that was by her side, "that a prince of the royal blood of Africa should have to go upon the stage for a living! It it is indeed a shame!" When he came to the scene,

> "O, cursed, cursed slave!—whip me, ye devils,
> From the possession of this heavenly sight!
> Blow me about in winds, roast me in sulphur!
> Wash me in steep-down gulfs of liquid fire!
> O, Desdemona! Desdemona! dead?
> Dead? O! O! O!"

the effect was indeed grand. When the curtain fell, the prince was called upon the stage, where he was received with deafening shouts of approbation, and a number of *bouquets* thrown at his feet, which he picked up, bowed, and retired. I went into Cheapside the next morning, at an early hour, to see if the prince had given up his old trade for what I supposed to be a more lucrative one; but I found the hero of the previous night at his post, and giving out his bills as energetically as when I had last seen him. Having to go to the provinces for some months, I lost sight of Mr. Jenkins, and on my return to town did not trouble myself to look him up. More than a year after I had witnessed the representation of Othello at the Eagle, I was walking, one pleasant Sabbath evening, through one of the small streets in the borough, when I found myself in front of a little chapel, where a number of persons were going in. As I was passing on slowly, an elderly man said to me, "I suppose you have come to hear your colored brother preach." "No," I answered; "I was not aware that one was to be here." "Yes," said he; "and a clever man he is, too." As the old man offered to find me a seat, I concluded to go in and hear this son of Africa. The room, which was not large, was already full. I had to wait but a short time before the reverend gentleman made his appearance. He was nearly black, and dressed in a black suit, with high shirt-collar, and an intellectual-looking cravat, that nearly hid his chin. A pair of spectacles covered his eyes. The preacher commenced by reading a portion of Scripture; and then announced that they would sing the twenty-eighth hymn in "the arrangement." O, that voice! I felt sure that I had heard that musical voice before; but where, I could not tell. I was not aware that any of my countrymen were in London; but felt that, whoever he was, he was no discredit to the race; for he was a most eloquent and accomplished orator. His sermon was against the sale and use of intoxicating drinks, and the bad habits of the working classes, of whom his audience was composed.

Although the subject was intensely interesting, I was impatient for it to come to a close, for I wanted to speak to the preacher. But, the evening being warm, and the room heated, the reverend gentleman, on wiping the perspiration from his face (which, by the way, ran very freely), took off his spectacles on one occasion, so that I immediately recognized him, and saved me from going up to the pulpit at the end of the service. Yes; it was the bill-distributor of Cheapside, the crossing-sweeper of Chelsea, the tract-seller and psalm-singer of Kensington, and the Othello of the Eagle Saloon. I could scarcely keep from laughing right out when I discovered this to be the man that I had seen in so many characters. As I was about leaving my seat at the close of the services, the old man who showed me into the chapel asked me if I would not like to be introduced to the minister, and I immediately replied that I would. We proceeded up the aisle, and met the clergyman as he was descending. On seeing me, he did not wait for a formal introduction, but put out his hand and said, "I have seen you so often, sir, that I seem to know you." "Yes," I replied; "we have met several times, and under different circumstances." Without saying more, he invited me to walk with him towards his home, which was in the direction of my own residence. We proceeded; and, during the walk,

Mr. Jenkins gave me some little account of his early history. "You think me rather an odd fish, I presume," said he. "Yes," I replied. "You are not the only one who thinks so," continued he. "Although I am not as black as some of my countrymen, I am a native of Africa. Surrounded by some beautiful mountain scenery, and situated between Darfour and Abyssinia, two thousand miles in the interior of Africa, is a small valley going by the name of Tegla. To that valley I stretch forth my affections, giving it the endearing appellation of my native home and fatherland. It was there that I was born, it was there that I received the fond looks of a loving mother, and it was there that I set my feet, for the first time, upon a world full of cares, trials, difficulties and dangers. My father being a farmer, I used to be sent out to take care of his goats. This service I did when I was between seven and eight years of age. As I was the eldest of the boys, my pride was raised in no small degree when I beheld my father preparing a farm for me. This event filled my mind with the grand anticipation of leaving the care of the goats to my brother, who was then beginning to work a little. While my father was making these preparations, I had the constant charge of the goats; and, being accompanied by two other boys, who resided near my father's house, we wandered many miles from home, by which means we acquired a knowledge of the different districts of our country.

"It was while in these rambles with my companions that I became the victim of the slave-trader. We were tied with cords, and taken to Tegla, and thence to Kordofan, which is under the jurisdiction of the Pacha of Egypt. From Kordofan I was brought down to Dongola and Korti, in Nubia, and from thence down the Nile to Cairo; and, after being sold nine times, I became the property of an English gentleman, who brought me to this country and put me into school. But he died before I finished my education, and his family feeling no interest in me, I had to seek a living as best I could. I have been employed for some years in distributing hand-bills for a barber in Cheapside in the morning, go to Chelsea and sweep a crossing in the afternoon, and sing psalms and sell religious tracts in the evening. Sometimes I have an engagement to perform at some of the small theatres, as I had when you saw me at the Eagle. I preach for this little congregation over here, and charge them nothing; for I want that the poor should have the Gospel without money and without price. I have now given up distributing bills; I have settled my son in that office. My eldest daughter was married about three months ago; and I have presented her husband with the Chelsea crossing, as my daughter's wedding portion." "Can he make a living at it?" I eagerly inquired. "O, yes! that crossing at Chelsea is worth thirty shillings a week, if it is well swept," said he. "But what do you do for a living for yourself?" I asked. "I am the leader of a band," he continued; "and we play for balls and parties, and three times a week at the Holborn Casino."

By this time we had reached a point where we had to part; and I left Joseph Jenkins, impressed with the idea that he was the greatest genius that I had met in Europe.

CHAPTER 22

"Dull rogues affect the politician's part,
And learn to nod, and smile, and shrug, with art;
Who nothing has to lose, the war bewails;
And he who nothing pays, at taxes rails."

CONGREVE.

The Abbey clock was striking nine, as we entered the House of Commons, and, giving up our ticket, were conducted to the strangers' gallery. We immediately recognized many of the members, whom we had met in private circles or public meetings. Just imagine, reader, that we are now seated in the strangers' gallery, looking down upon the representatives of the people of the British empire.

There, in the centre of the room, shines the fine, open, glossy brow and speaking face of Alexander Hastie, a Glasgow merchant, a mild and amiable man, of modest deportment, liberal principles, and religious profession. He has been twice elected for the city of Glasgow, in which he resides. He once presided at a meeting for us in his own city.

On the right of the hall, from where we sit, you see that small man, with fair complexion, brown hair, gray eyes, and a most intellectual countenance. It is Layard, with whom we spent a pleasant day at Hartwell Park, the princely residence of John Lee, Esq., LL.D. He was employed as consul at Bagdad, in Turkey. While there he explored the ruins of ancient Nineveh, and sent to England the Assyrian relics now in the British Museum. He is member for Aylesbury. He takes a deep interest in the Eastern question, and censures the government for their want of energy in the present war.

Not far from Layard you see the large frame and dusky visage of Joseph

Hume. He was the son of a poor woman who sold apples in the streets of London. Mr. Hume spent his younger days in India, where he made a fortune; and then returned to England, and was elected a member of the House of Commons, where he has been ever since, with the exception of five or six years. He began political life as a tory, but soon went over to radicalism. He is a great financial reformer, and has originated many of the best measures of a practical character that have been passed in Parliament during the last thirty years. He is seventy-five years old, but still full of life and activity—capable of great endurance and incessant labor. No man enjoys to an equal extent the respect and confidence of the legislature. Though his opinions are called extreme, he contents himself with realizing, for the present, the good that is attainable. He is emphatically a progressive reformer; and the father of the House of Commons.

To the left of Mr. Hume you see a slim, thin-faced man, with spectacles, an anxious countenance, his hat on another seat before him, and in it a large paper rolled up. That is Edward Miall. He was educated for the Baptist ministry, and was called when very young to be a pastor. He relinquished his charge to become the conductor of a paper devoted to the abolition of the state church, and the complete political enfranchisement of the people. He made several unsuccessful attempts to go into Parliament, and at last succeeded Thomas Crawford in the representation of Rochdale, where in 1852 he was elected free of expense. He is one of the most democratic members of the legislature. Miall is an able writer and speaker—a very close and correct reasoner. He stands at the very head of the Nonconformist party in Great Britain; and *The Nonconformist,* of which he is editor, is the most radical journal in the United Kingdom.

Look at that short, thick-set man, with his hair parted on the crown of his head, a high and expansive forehead, and an uncommon bright eye. That is William Johnson Fox. He was a working weaver at Norwich; then went to Holton College, London, to be educated for the Orthodox Congregational ministry; afterwards embraced Unitarian views. He was invited to Finsbury Chapel, where for many years he lectured weekly upon a wide range of subjects, embracing literature, political science, theology, government and social economy. He is the writer of the articles signed "Publicola" in the *Weekly Dispatch,* a democratic newspaper. He has retired from his pulpit occupations, and supports himself exclusively by his pen, in connection with the liberal journals of the metropolis. Mr. Fox is a witty and vigorous writer, an animated and brilliant orator.

Yonder, on the right of us, sits Richard Cobden. Look at his thin, pale face, and spare-made frame. He started as a commercial traveller; was afterwards a calico-printer and merchant in Manchester. He was the expounder, in the Manchester Chamber of Commerce and in the town council, of the principles of free trade. In the council of the Anti-Corn-Law League,[18] he was the leader, and principal agitator of the question in public meetings throughout the kingdom. He was first elected for Stockport. When Sir Robert Peel's administration abolished the corn-laws, the prime minister avowed in the House of Commons that the great measure was in most part achieved by the unadorned eloquence of Richard Cobden. He is the representative of the non-intervention or political peace party; holding the right and duty of national defence, but opposing all alliances which are calculated to embroil the country in the affairs of other nations. His age is about fifty. He represents the largest constituency in the kingdom—the western division of Yorkshire, which contains thirty-seven thousand voters. Mr. Cobden has a reflective cast of mind; and is severely logical in his style, and very lucid in the treatment of his subjects. He may be termed the leader of the radical party in the House.

Three seats from Cobden you see that short, stout person, with his high head, large, round face, good-sized eyes. It is Macaulay, the poet, critic, historian and statesman. If you have not read his Essay on Milton, you should do so immediately; it is the finest thing of the kind in the language. Then there is his criticism on the Rev. R. Montgomery. Macaulay will never be forgiven by the divine for that onslaught upon his poetical reputation. That review did more to keep the reverend poet's works on the publisher's shelves than all other criticisms combined. Macaulay represents the city of Edinburgh.

Look at that tall man, apparently near seventy, with front teeth gone. That is Joseph Brotherton, the member for Salford. He has represented that constituency ever since 1832. He has always been a consistent liberal, and is a man of business. He is no orator, and seldom speaks, unless in favor of the adjournment of the House when the hour of midnight has arrived. At the commencement of every new session of Parliament he prepares a resolution that no business shall be entered upon after the hour of twelve at night, but has never been able to carry it. He is a teetotaller and a vegetarian, a member of the Peace Society, and a preacher in the small religious society to which he belongs.

In a seat behind Brotherton you see a young-looking man, with neat figure, white vest, frilled shirt, with gold studs, gold breast-pin, a gold chain round the neck, white kid glove on the right hand, the left bare with the exception of two gold rings. It is Samuel Morton Peto. He is of humble origin—has made a vast fortune as a builder and contractor for docks and railways. He is a Baptist, and contributes very largely to his own and other dissenting denominations. He has built several Baptist chapels in London and elsewhere. His appearance is that of a gentleman; and his style of speaking, though not elegant, yet pleasing.

Over on the same side with the liberals sits John Bright, the Quaker statesman, and leader of the Manchester school. He is the son of a Rochdale manufacturer, and first distinguished himself as an agitator in favor of the repeal of the corn-laws. He represents the city of Manchester, and has risen very rapidly. Mr. Cobden and he invariably act together, and will, doubtless, sooner or later, come into power together. Look at his robust and powerful frame, round and pleasing face. He is but little more than forty; an earnest and eloquent speaker, and commands the fixed attention of his audience.

See that exceedingly good-looking man just taking his seat. It is William Ewart Gladstone. He is the son of a Liverpool merchant, and represents the University of Oxford. He came into Parliament in 1832, under the auspices of the tory Duke of Newcastle. He was a disciple of the first Sir R. Peel, and was by that statesman introduced into official life. He has been Vice-president and President of the Board of Trade, and is now Chancellor of the Exchequer. Mr. Gladstone is only forty-four. When not engaged in speaking he is of rather unprepossessing appearance. His forehead appears low, but his eye is bright and penetrating. He is one of the ablest debaters in the House, and is master of a style of eloquence in which he is quite unapproached. As a reasoner he is subtle, and occasionally jesuitical; but, with a good cause and a conviction of the right, he rises to a lofty pitch of oratory, and may be termed the Wendell Phillips of the House of Commons.

There sits Disraeli, amongst the tories. Look at that Jewish face, those dark ringlets hanging round that marble brow. When on his feet he has a cat-like, stealthy step; always looks on the ground when walking. He is the son of the well-known author of the "Curiosities of Literature." His ancestors were Venetian Jews. He was himself born a Jew, and was initiated into the Hebrew faith. Subsequently he embraced Christianity. His literary works are numerous, consisting entirely of novels, with the exception of a biography of the late Lord George Bentinck, the leader of the protectionist party, to whose post Mr. Disraeli succeeded on the death of his friend and political chief. Mr. Disraeli has been all round the compass in politics. He is now professedly a conservative, but is believed to be willing to support any measures, however sweeping and democratical, if by so doing he could gratify his ambition—which is for office and power. He was the great thorn in the side of the late Sir R. Peel, and was never so much at home as when he could find a flaw in that distinguished statesman's political acts. He is an able debater and a finished orator, and in his speeches wrings applause even from his political opponents.

Cast your eyes to the opposite side of the House, and take a good view of that venerable man, full of years, just rising from his seat. See how erect he stands; he is above seventy years of age, and yet he does not seem to be forty. That is Lord Palmerston. Next to Joseph Hume, he is the oldest member in the House. He has been longer in office than any other living man. All parties have, by turns, claimed him, and he has belonged to all kinds of administrations; tory, conservative, whig, and coalition. He is a ready debater, and is a general favorite, as a speaker, for his wit and adroitness, but little trusted by any party as a statesman. His talents have secured him office, as he is useful as a minister, and dangerous as an opponent.

That is Lord Dudley Cutts Stuart speaking to Mr. Ewart. His lordship represents the populous and wealthy division of the district of Marylebone. He is a radical, the warm friend of the cause of Poland, Hungary and Turkey. He speaks often, but always with a degree of hesitation which makes it painful to listen to him. His solid frame, strongly-marked features, and unmercifully long eye-brows are in strange contrast to the delicate face of Mr. Ewart.

The latter is the representative for Dumfries, a Scotch borough. He belongs to a wealthy family, that has made its fortune by commerce. Mr. Ewart is a radical, a staunch advocate of the abolition of capital punishment, and a strenuous supporter of all measures for the intellectual improvement of the people.

Ah! we shall now have a speech. See that little man rising from his seat; look at his thin black hair, how it seems to stand up; hear that weak, but distant voice. O, how he repeats the ends of his sentences! It is Lord John Russell, the leader of the present administration. He is now asking for three million pounds sterling to carry on the war. He is a terse and perspicuous speaker, but avoids prolixity. He is much respected on both sides of the House. Though favorable to reform measures generally, he is nevertheless an upholder of aristocracy, and stands at the head and firmly by his order. He is brother to the present Duke of Bedford, and has twice been Premier; and, though on the sunny side of sixty, he has been in office, at different times, more than thirty years. He is a constitutional whig and conservative reformer. See how earnestly he speaks, and keeps his eyes on Disraeli! He is afraid of the Jew. Now he scratches the bald place on his head, and then opens that huge roll of paper, and looks over towards Lord Palmerston.

That full-faced, well-built man, with handsome countenance, just behind him, is Sir Joshua Walmesley. He is about the same age of Lord John; and is the representative for Leicester. He is a native of Liverpool, where for some years he was a poor teacher, but afterwards became wealthy in the corn trade. When mayor of his native town, he was knighted. He is a radical reformer, and always votes on the right side.

Lord John Russell has finished and taken his seat. Joseph Hume is up. He goes into figures; he is the arithmetician of the House of Commons. Mr. Hume is in the Commons what James N. Buffum is in our Anti-Slavery meetings, the *man of facts.* Watch the old man's eye as he looks over his papers. He is of no religious faith, and said, a short time since, that the world would be better off if all creeds were swept into the Thames. His motto is that of Pope:

> "For modes of faith let graceless zealots fight:
> His can't be wrong whose life is in the right."

Mr. Hume has not been tedious; he is done. Now for Disraeli. He is going to pick Lord John's speech to pieces, and he can do it better than any other man in the House. See how his ringlets shake as he gesticulates! and that sarcastic smile! He thinks the government has not been vigorous enough in its prosecution of the war. He finds fault with the inactivity of the Baltic fleet; the allied army has made no movement to suit him. The Jew looks over towards Lord John, and then makes a good hit. Lord John shakes his head; Disraeli has touched a tender point, and he smiles as the minister turns on his seat. The Jew is delighted beyond measure. "The Noble Lord shakes his head; am I to understand that he did not say what I have just repeated?" Lord John: "The Right Hon. Gentleman is mistaken; I did not say what he has attributed to me." Disraeli: "I am glad that the Noble Lord has denied what I thought he had said." An attack is made on another part of the minister's speech. Lord John shakes his head again. "Does the Noble Lord deny that, too?" Lord John: "No, I don't, but your criticism is unjust." Disraeli smiles again: he has the minister in his hands, and he shakes him well before he lets him go. What cares he for justice? Criticism is his forte; it was that that made him what he is in the House. The Jew concludes his speech amid considerable applause.

All eyes are turned towards the seat of the Chancellor of the Exchequer: a pause of a moment's duration, and the orator of the House rises to his feet. Those who have been reading *The Times* lay it down; all whispering stops, and the attention of the members is directed to Gladstone, as he begins. Disraeli rests his chin upon his hat, which lies upon his knee: he too is chained to his seat by the fascinating eloquence of the man of letters. Thunders of applause follow, in which all join but the Jew. Disraeli changes his position on his seat, first one leg crossed, and then the other, but he never smiles while his opponent is speaking. He sits like one of those marble figures in the British Museum. Disraeli has furnished more fun for *Punch* than any other man in the empire. When it was resolved to have a portrait of the late Sir R. Peel painted for the government, Mr. Gladstone ordered it to be taken from one that appeared in *Punch* during the lifetime of that great statesman. This was indeed a compliment to the sheet of fun. But now look at the Chancellor of the Exchequer. He is in the midst of his masterly speech, and silence reigns throughout the House.

> "His words of learned length and thundering sound
> Amazed the gazing rustics ranged around;
> And still they gazed, and still the wonder grew
> That one small head could carry all he knew."

Let us turn for a moment to the gallery in which we are seated. It is now near the hour of twelve at night. The question before the House is an interesting one, and has called together many distinguished persons as visitors. There sits the Hon. and Rev. Baptist W. Noel. He is one of the first of the Nonconformist ministers in the kingdom. He is about fifty years of age; very tall, and stands erect; has a fine figure, complexion fair, face long and rather pale, eyes blue and deeply set. He looks every inch the gentleman. Near by Mr. Noel you see the Rev. John Cumming. D.D. We stood more than an hour last Sunday in his chapel in Crown-court to hear him preach; and such a sermon we have seldom ever heard. Dr. Cumming does not look old. He has rather a bronzed complexion, with dark hair, eyes covered with spectacles. He is an eloquent man, and seems to be on good terms with himself. He is the most ultra Protestant we have ever heard and hates Rome with a perfect vengeance. Few men are more popular in an Exeter Hall meeting than Dr. Cumming. He is a most prolific writer; scarce a month passes by without something from his pen. But they are mostly works of a sectarian character, and cannot be of long or of lasting reputation.

Further along sits a man still more eloquent than Dr. Cumming. He is of dark complexion, black hair, light blue eyes, an intellectual countenance, and when standing looks tall. It is the Rev. Henry Melville. He is considered the finest preacher in the Church of England. There, too, is Washington Wilks, Esq., author of "The Half-century." His face is so covered with beard that I will not attempt a description; it may, however, be said that he has literally entered into the *Beard Movement*.

Come, it is time for us to leave the House of Commons. Stop a moment! Ah! there is one that I have not pointed out to you. Yonder he sits amongst the tories. It is Sir Edward Bulwer Lytton, the renowned novelist. Look at his trim, neat figure; his hair done up in the most approved manner; his clothes cut in the latest fashion. He has been in Paliament twenty-five years. Until the abolition of the corn-laws, he was a liberal; but as a land-owner he was opposed to free trade, and joined the protectionists. He has two country-seats, and lives in a style of oriental magnificence that is not equalled by any other man in the kingdom; and often gathers around him the brightest spirits of the age, and presses them into the service of his private theatre, of which he is very fond. In the House of Commons he is seldom heard, but is always listened to with profound attention when he rises to speak. He labors under the disadvantage of partial deafness. He is undoubtedly a man of refined taste, and pays a greater attention to the art of dress than any other public character I have ever seen. He has a splendid fortune, and his icome from the labors of his pen is very great. His title was given to him by the queen, and his rank as a baronet he owes to his high literary attainments. Now take a farewell view of this assembly of senators. You may go to other climes, and look upon the representatives of other nations, but you will never see the like again.

CHAPTER 23

"Take the spade of Perseverance,
  Dig the field of Progress wide;
Every bar to true instruction
  Carry out and cast aside."

The anniversary of West India emancipation was celebrated here on Monday last. But little notice of the intended meeting had been given, yet the capacious lecture-room of St. Martin's Hall was filled at an early hour with a most respectable audience, who appeared to have assembled for the sake of the cause.

Our old and well-tried friend, Geo. Thompson, Esq., was unanimously called to preside, and he opened the proceedings with one of his characteristic speeches. The meeting was then addressed by the Rev. Wm. Douglass, a colored clergyman of Philadelphia, in a most eloquent and feeling manner. Mr. Douglass is a man of fine native talent.

Francis W. Kellogg, of the United States, was the next speaker. Mr. Kellogg is an advocate of temperance, of some note, I believe, in his own country, and has been lecturing with considerable success in Great Britain. He is one of the most peculiar speakers I have ever heard. Born in Massachusetts, and brought up in the West, he has the intelligence of the one and the roughness of the other. He has the retentive memory of Wendell Phillips, the overpowering voice of Frederick Douglass, and the too rapid gestures of Dr. Delany. He speaks faster than any man I ever heard, except C. C. Burleigh. His speech, which lasted more than an hour, was one stream of fervid eloquence. He gave the audience a better idea of a real American stump orator than they ever had before. Altogether, he is the best specimen of the rough material out of which great public speakers

217

are manufactured that I have yet seen. Mr. Kellogg's denunciations of Clay and Webster (the dead lion and the living dog) reminded us of Wendell Phillips; his pictures of slavery called to memory Frederick Douglass in his palmiest days; and his rebuke of his own countrymen for their unchristian prejudice against color brought before us the favorite topic and best speeches of C. L. Remond. It was his maiden speech on the subject of slavery, yet it was the speech of the evening.

Hatred to oppression is so instilled into the minds of the people in Great Britain, that it needs but little to arouse their enthusiasm to its highest point; yet they can scarcely comprehend the real condition of the slaves of the United States. They have heard of the buying and selling of men, women and children, without any regard to the tenderest ties of nature; of the passage and execution of the infamous Fugitive Slave Law; and, as we walk through the streets of London, they occasionally meet an American slave, who reminds them of the fact that while their countrymen are boasting of their liberty, and offering an asylum to the exiled of other countries, they refuse it to their own citizens.

Much regret has been expressed on this side of the Atlantic that Kossouth should have kept so silent on the slavery question while in America,[19] and this act alone has, to a great extent, neutralized his further operations in this country. He certainly is not the man now that he was before his visit to the New World.

I seldom pass through the Strand, or other great thoroughfares of the metropolis, without meeting countrymen of mine. I encountered one, a short time since, under peculiar circumstances. It was one of those days commonly experienced in London, of half cloud and half sunshine, with just fog enough to give everything a gray appearance, that I was loitering through Drury Lane, and came upon a crowd of poor people and street beggars, who were being edified by an exhibition of Punch and Judy, on the one hand, and an organ-grinder, with a well-dressed and intelligent-looking monkey, on the other. Punch looked happy, and was performing with great alacrity, while the organ-grinder, with his loud-toned instrument, was furnishing music for the million. Pushing my way through the crowd, and taking the middle of the street for convenience' sake, I was leaving the infected district in greater haste than I entered it. I had scarcely taken my eyes off the motley group, when I observed a figure approaching me from the opposite direction, and walking with a somewhat hasty step. I have seen so much oddity in dress, and the general appearance of members of the human family, that my attention is seldom ever attracted by the uncivilized look of any one. But this being whom I was meeting, and whose appearance was such as I had not seen before, threw the monkey and his companions entirely in the shade. In fact, all that I had beheld in the Great Exhibition, of a ludicrous nature, dwindled away into utter insignificance when compared to this Robinson Crusoe looking man; for, after all, it turned out to be a man. He was of small stature, and, although not a cold day, his person was enveloped in a heavy over-coat, which looked as if it had seen some service, and had passed through the hands of some of the second-hand gentlemen of Brattle-street, Boston. The trousers I did not see, as they were benevolently covered by the long skirts of the above garment. A pair of patent-leather boots covered a small foot. The face was entirely hidden by a huge beard, apparently from ten to fifteen inches in length, and of a reddish color. Long, dark hair joined the beard, and upon the head was thrown, in a careless manner, one of those hats known in America as the wide-awake, but here as the billy-cock. A pair of bright eyes were entirely hid by the hair around the face. I was not more attracted by his appearance than astonished at the man's stopping before me, as if he knew me. I now observed something like smoke emanating from the long beard round the mouth. I was immediately seized by the individual by his right hand, while the left hand took from his mouth a pipe about three inches in length, stem included, and, in a sharp, shrill voice, sounding as if it came from the interior of a hogshead or from a sepulchre, he called me by my name. I stood for a moment and eyed the figure from head to foot, "from top to toe," to see if I could discover the resemblance of any one I had ever seen before. After satisfying myself that the object was new, I said, "Sir, you have the advantage of me." "Don't you know me?" he exclaimed, in a still louder voice. I looked again, and shook my head. "Why," said he, "it is C——." I stepped back a few feet, and viewed him once more from top to bottom, and replied, "You don't mean to say that this is H. C——?" "Yes, it is he, and nobody else." After taking another look, I said, "An't you mistaken, sir, about this being H. C——?" "No," said he, "I am sure I know myself." So I very reluctantly had to admit that I was standing in presence of the ex-editor of the "L. P. and H. of F." Indeed, one meets with strange faces in a walk through the streets of London. But I must turn again to the question of slavery.

Some months since a lady, apparently not more than fifty years of age, entered a small dwelling on the estate of the Earl of Lovelace, situated in the county of Surrey. After ascending a flight of stairs, and passing through a narrow passage, she found herself in a small but neat room, with plain furniture. On the table lay copies of the *Liberator* and *Frederick Douglass' Paper*. Near the window sat a young woman, busily engaged in sewing, with a spelling-book laying open on her lap. The light step of the stranger had not broken the silence enough to announce the approach of any one, and the young woman still sat at her task, unconscious that any one was near. A moment or two, and the lady was observed, when the diligent student hastily rose, and apologized for her apparent inattention. The stranger was soon seated, and in conversation with the young woman. The lady had often heard the word "slave," and knew something of its application, but had never before seen one of her own sex who had actually been born and brought up in a state of chattel slavery; and the one in whose company she now was so white, and had so much the appearance of an educated and well-bred lady, that she could scarcely realize that she was in the presence of an American slave. For more than an hour the illustrious lady and the poor exile sat and carried on a most familiar conversation. The thrilling story of the fugitive often brought tears to the eyes of the stranger. O, how I would that every half-bred, aristocratic, slave-holding, woman-whipping, negro-hating woman of America could have been present and heard what passed between these two distinguished persons! They would, for once, have seen one who, though moving in the most elevated and aristocratic society in Europe, felt it an honor to enter the small cottage and take a seat by the side of a poor, hunted and exiled American fugitive slave. Let it be rung in the ears of the thin-skinned aristocracy of the United States, who would rather receive a flogging from the cat-o'-nine-tails than to sit at the table of a negro, that Lady Noel Byron, widow of the great poet, felt it a peculiar pleasure to sit at the table and take tea with Ellen Craft. It must, indeed, be an interesting fact to the reader, and especially to those who are acquainted with the facts connected with the life and escape of William and Ellen Craft, to know that they are industrious students in a school, and attracting the attention of persons occupying the most influential positions in society. The wonderful escape of William and Ellen Craft is still fresh in the minds of all who take an interest in the cause of humanity; and their eluding the pursuit of the slave-hunters at Boston, and final escape from the Athens of the New World, will not be soon forgotten.

Every American should feel a degree of humiliation when the thought occurs to him that there is not a foot of soil over which the *Stars and Stripes* wave upon which Ellen Craft can stand and be protected by the constitution or laws of the country. Yet Ellen Craft is as white as most white women. Had she escaped from Austrian tyranny, and landed on the shores of America, her reception would have been scarcely less enthusiastic than that which greeted the arrival of Jenny Lind. But Ellen Craft had the misfortune to be born in one of the Slave States of the American Union, and that was enough to cause her to be driven into *exile* for daring to escape from American despotism.

CHAPTER 24

"——when I left the shore,
  The distant shore, which gave me birth,
I hardly thought to grieve once more,
  To quit another spot on earth."

What a change five years make in one's history! The summer of 1849 found me a stranger in a foreign land, unknown to its inhabitants; its laws, customs and history, were a blank to me. But how different the summer of 1854! During my sojourn I had travelled over nearly every railroad in England and Scotland, and had visited Ireland and Wales, besides spending some weeks on the continent. I had become so well acquainted with the British people and their history, that I had begun to fancy myself an Englishman by habit, if not by birth. The treatment which I had experienced at their hands had endeared them to me, and caused me to feel myself at home wherever I went. Under such circumstances, it was not strange that I commenced with palpitating heart the preparation to return to my *native land*. Native land! How harshly that word sounds to my ears! True, America was the land of my birth; my grandfather had taken part in her Revolution, had enriched the soil with his blood, yet upon this soil I had been worked as a slave. I seem still to hear the sound of the auctioneer's rough voice, as I stood on the block in the slave-market at St. Louis. I shall never forget the savage grin with which he welcomed a higher bid, when he thought that he had received the last offer. I had seen a mother sold and taken to the cotton-fields of the far South; three brothers had been bartered to the soul-driver in my presence; a dear sister had been sold to the negro-dealer, and driven away by him; I had seen the

221

rusty chains fastened upon her delicate wrists; the whip had been applied to my own person, and the marks of the brutal driver's lash were still on my body. Yet this was my native land, and to this land was I about to embark.

In Edinburgh, I had become acquainted with the Wighams; in Glasgow, the Patons and Smeals; in Manchester, the Langdons; in Newcastle, the Mawsons and Richardsons. To Miss Ellen Richardson, of this place, I was mainly indebted for the redemption of my body from slavery, and the privilege of again returning to my native country. I had also met, and become acquainted with, John Bishop Estlin, Esq., of Bristol, and his kind-hearted and accomplished daughter. Of the hundreds of British Abolitionists with whom I had the pleasure of shaking hands while abroad, I know of none whose hearts beat more fervently for the emancipation of the American slave than Mr. Estlin's. He is indeed a model Christian. His house, his heart and his purse, were always open to the needy, without any regard to sect, color or country. When those distinguished fugitive slaves, William and Ellen Craft, arrived in England, unnknown and without friends, Mr. Estlin wrote to me and said, "If the Crafts are in want, send to me. If you cannot find a home for them, let them come to Bristol, and I will keep them, at my expense, until something better turns up." And nobly did he keep his word. He put the two fugitives in school, and saw that they did not want for the means of support. I have known him to keep concealed what he had given to benevolent objects. To Mr. Estlin I am indebted for many acts of kindness; and now that the broad Atlantic lies between us, and in all probability we shall never again meet on earth, it is with heartfelt gratitude and pleasure that I make this mention of him.

And last, though not the least, I had become intimate with that most generous-hearted philanthropist, George Thompson, who never feels so well as when giving a welcome to an American fugitive slave. I had spent hours at the hospitable firesides of Harriet Martineau, R. D. Webb, and other distinguished authors. You will not, reader, think it strange that my heart became sad at the thought of leaving all these dear friends, to return to a country in which I had spent some of the best days of my life as a slave, and where I knew that prejudice would greet me on my arrival.

Most of the time I had resided in London. Its streets, parks, public buildings and its fog, had become "as familiar as household words." I had heard the deep, bass voice of the Bishop of London, in St. Paul's Cathedral. I had sat in Westminster Abbey, until I had lost all interest in the services, and then wandered about amongst the monuments, reading the epitaphs placed over the dead. Like others, I had been locked in the Temple Church, and compelled to wait till service was over, whether I liked it or not. I had spent days in the British Museum and National Gallery, and in all these I had been treated as a man. The "negro pew," which I had seen in the churches of America, was not to be found in the churches of London. There, too, were my daughters. They who had been denied education upon equal terms with children of a fairer complexion, in the United States, had been received in the London schools upon terms of perfect equality. They had accompanied me to most of the noted places in the metropolis. We had strolled through Regent-street, the Strand, Piccadilly and Oxford-street, so often, that sorrow came over me as the thought occurred to me that I should never behold them again.

Then the English manner of calling on friends before one's departure. I can meet an enemy with pleasure, but it is with regret that I part with a friend. As the time for me to leave drew near, I felt more clearly my identity with the English people. By and by the last hour arrived that I was to spend in London. The cab stood at the door, with my trunks on its top; and, bidding the household "good-by," I entered the vehicle, the driver raised his whip, and I looked for the last time on my old home in Cecil-street. As we turned into the Strand, Nelson's monument, in Trafalgar-square, greeted me on the left, and Somerset House on the right. I took a farewell look at Covent Garden Market, through whose walks I had often passed, and where I had spent many pleasant hours. My youngest daughter was in France, but the eldest met me at the dépôt, and after a few moments the bell rang, and away we went.

As the train was leaving the great metropolis of the world behind, I caught a last view of the dome of St. Paul's, and the old pile of Westminster Abbey.

In every town through which we passed on our way to Liverpool I could call to mind the name of some one whose acquaintance I had made, and whose hospitality I had shared. The steamer City of Manchester had her fires kindled when we arrived, and we went immediately on board. We found one hundred and seventy-five passengers in the cabin, and above five hundred in the steerage. After some delay, the ship weighed anchor, the machinery was put in motion, and, bidding Liverpool a long farewell, the vessel moved down the Mersey, and was in a short time out at sea. The steam tender accompanied the ship about thirty miles, during which time search was made throughout the Manchester to see that no "stow-aways" were on board. No vessel ever leaves an English port without some one trying to get his passage out without pay. When the crew are at work, or not on the watch, these persons come on board, hide themselves under the berths in the steerage cabin, or amongst the freight, until the vessel is out to sea, and then they come out. As they are always poor persons, without either baggage or money, they succeed in getting their passage without giving anything in return. As the tender was about quitting us to return to Liverpool, it came along-side to take on board those who had come with the vessel to see their friends off. Any number of white napkins were called into requisition, as friends were shaking hands with each other, and renewing their promises to write by the first post. One young man had come out to spend a few more hours with a handsome Scotch lass, with whom he, no doubt, had a matrimonial engagement. Another, an English lady, seemed much affected when the last bell of the tender rung, and the captain cried "All on board." Having no one to look after, I found time to survey others. The tender let go her cables amid three hearty cheers, and a deafening salute from the two-pounder on board the City of Manchester. A moment more, and the two steamers were leaving each other with rapid speed. The two young ladies of whom I have already made mention, together with many others, had their faces buried in their handkerchiefs, and appeared to be dying with grief. However, all of them seemed to get over it very soon. On the second day out at sea I saw the young English lady walking the quarter-deck with a fine-looking gentleman, and holding as tightly to his arm as if she had left no one behind; and as for the Scotch lass, she was seated on a settee with a countryman of hers, who had made her acquaintance on board, and, from all appearance, had entirely forgotten her first love. Such is the waywardness of man and woman, and the unfaithfulness of the human heart.

In the latter part of the second day a storm overtook us, and for the ten succeeding days we scarcely knew whether we were on our heads or our heels. The severest part of the gale was on the eighth and ninth nights out. On one of those evenings a fellow-roommate came in and said, "If you wish to see a little fun, go into the forward steerage." It was about eight o'clock, and most of the passengers were either in bed, or preparing for the night's rest, such as is to be had on board a ship in a gale of wind. This cabin contained about two hundred and fifty persons; some Germans, some Irish, and twenty-five or thirty Gypsies. Forty or fifty of these were on their knees in their berths, engaged in prayer. No camp-meeting ever presented a more noisy spectacle than did this cabin. The ship was rolling, and the sea running mountains high, and many of these passengers had given up all hope of ever seeing land again. The Gypsies were foremost amongst those who were praying; indeed, they seemed to fancy themselves in a camp-meeting, for many of them shouted at the top of their voices. One of them, known as the "Queen of the Gypsies," came to me and said, "O, Master! do get down and help us to ask God to stop the wind! You are a black man; may be he'll pay more attention to what you say. Now do, master do! and when the storm is over I will tell your fortune for nothing." At this juncture one of the chests which had been fastened to the floor broke away from its moorings, and came sliding acoss the cabin at the rate of about twenty miles per hour; soon another got loose, and these two locomotives broke up the prayer-meeting. Trunk after trunk became unfastened, until some eight or ten were crossing the cabin every time the vessel went over. At last the loose boxes upset the tables, on which were some of the passengers' eatables, and in a short time the whole cabin was in splendid confusion. The lamps, one after another, were knocked down and extinguished, so that the cabin was in total darkness. As I turned to retrace my steps, I heard the company joining in the prayer, and I was informed the next day that it was kept up during most of the night.

With all the watchfulness on the day of sailing, several persons succeeded in stowing themselves away. First one came out, and then another, until not less than five made their appearance on deck. As fast as these men were discovered they were put to work; so that labor, if not money, might be obtained for their passage. On the sixth day out I missed a small leather trunk, and search was immediately made in every direction, but no tidings of it could be found. However, after its being lost two days, I offered a reward for its recovery, and it was soon found, hid away in the forecastle. It had been broken open, and a few things, together with a little money, had been taken. The ships Chieftain and Harmony were the only vessels we met during the first ten days. An iceberg made its appearance while we were on the banks, but it was some distance to the larboard.

After a long passage of twenty days we arrived at the mouth of the Delaware, and took a pilot on board. The passengers were now all life; the Irish were basking in the sun, the Germans were singing, and the Gypsies were dancing. Some fifteen miles below Philadelphia, the officers came on board, to see that no sickness was on the vessel; and, after being passed by the doctors, each person began to get his luggage on deck, and prepare to go on shore. About four o'clock, on the twenty-sixth day of September, 1854, the City of Manchester hauled alongside the Philadelphia wharf, and the passengers all on the move; the Scotch lass clinging to the arm of her new Highland laddie, and the young English lady in company with her "fresh" lover. It is a dangerous thing to allow the Atlantic Ocean to separate one from his or her "affectionate friend." The City of Manchester, though not a fast steamer, is, nevertheless, a safe one. Her officers are men of experience and activity. Captain Wyly was always at his post; the first officer was an able seaman, and Mr. John Mirehouse, the second officer, was a most gentlemanly and obliging, as well as experienced officer. To this gentleman I am much indebted for kind attention shown me on the voyage. I had met him on a former occasion at Whitehaven. He is a stanch friend of humanity.

At Philadelphia I met with a most cordial reception at the hands of the Motts, J. M. M'Kim, the Stills, the Fortens, and that distinguished gentleman and friend of the slave, Robert Purvis, Esq. There is no colored man in this country to whom the Anti-slavery cause is more indebted than to Mr. Purvis. Endowed with a capacious and reflective mind, he is ever in search after truth; and, consequently, all reforms find in him an able and devoted advocate. Inheriting a large fortune, he has had the means, as well as the will, to do good. Few men in this country, either colored or white, possess the rare accomplishments of Robert Purvis. In no city in the Free States does the Anti-slavery movement have more bitter opponents than in Philadelphia. Close to two of our Southern States, and connected as it is in a commercial point of view, it could scarcely be otherwise. Colorphobia is more rampant there than in the pro-slavery, negro-hating city of New York. I was not destined to escape this unnatural and anti-christian prejudice. While walking through Chestnut-street, in company with two of my fellow-passengers, we hailed an omnibus going in the direction which we wished to go. It immediately stopped, and the white men were furnished with seats, but I was told that "We don't allow niggers to ride in here." It so happened that these two persons had rode in the same car with me from London to Liverpool. We had put up at the same hotel at the latter place, and had crossed the Atlantic in the same steamer. But as soon as we touch the soil of America we can no longer ride in the same conveyance, no longer eat at the same table, or be regarded with equal justice, by our thin-skinned democracy. During five years' residence in monarchical Europe I had enjoyed the rights allowed to all foreigners in the countries through which I passed; but on returning to my NATIVE LAND the influence of slavery meets me the first day that I am in the country. Had I been an escaped felon, like John Mitchell, no one would have questioned my right to a seat in a Philadelphia omnibus. Neither of the foreigners who were allowed to ride in this carriage had ever visited our country before. The constitution of these United States was as a blank to them; the Declaration of Independence, in all probability, they had never seen,—much less, read. But what mattered it? They were white, and that was enough. The fact of my being an American by birth could not be denied; that I had read and understood the constitution and laws, the most pro-slavery, negro-hating professor of Christianity would admit; but I was colored, and that was enough. I had partaken of the hospitality of noblemen in England, had sat at the table of the French Minister of Foreign Affairs; I had looked from the strangers' gallery down upon the great legislators of England, as they sat in the House of Commons; I had stood in the House of Lords, when Her Britannic Majesty prorogued her Parliament; I had eaten at the same table with Sir Edward Bulwer Lytton, Charles Dickens, Eliza Cook, Alfred Tennyson, and the son-in-law of Sir Walter Scott: the omnibuses of Paris, Edinburgh, Glasgow and Liverpool, had stopped to take me up; I had often entered the "Caledonia," "Bayswater," "Hammersmith," "Chelsea," "Bluebell," and other omnibuses that rattle over the pavements of Regent-street, Cheapside, and the west end of London,—but what mattered that? My face was not white, my hair was not straight; and, therefore, I must be excluded from a seat in a third-rate American omnibus. Slavery demanded that it should be so. I charge this prejudice to the pro-slavery pulpits of our land, which first set the example of proscription by erecting in their churches the "negro pew." I charge it to that hypocritical profession of democracy which will welcome fugitives from other countries, and drive its own into exile. I charge it to the recreant sons of the men who carried on the American revolutionary war, and who come together every fourth of July to boast of what their fathers did, while they, their sons, have become associated with bloodhounds, to be put at any moment on the track of the fugitive slave.

But I had returned to the country for the express purpose of joining in the glorious battle against slavery, of which this Negrophobia is a legitimate offspring. And why not meet it in its stronghold? I might have remained in a country where my manhood was never denied; I might have remained in ease in other climes; but what was ease and comfort abroad, while more than three millions of my countrymen were groaning in the prison-house of slavery in the Southern States? Yes, I came back to the land of my nativity, not to be a spectator, but a soldier—a soldier in this moral warfare against the most cruel system of oppression that ever blackened the character or hardened the heart of man. And the smiles of my old associates, and the approval of my course while abroad by my colored fellow-citizens, has amply compensated me for the twenty days' rough passage on my return.

OPINIONS OF THE BRITISH PRESS

"While all the world is reading 'Uncle Tom's Cabin,' it is quite possible that what a real fugitive slave has to say for himself may meet with less attention than it deserves. Mr. Brown's book is pleasingly written."—*The Critic*, Dec. 16, 1852.

"When he writes on the wrongs of his race, or the events of his own career, he is always interesting or amusing."—*The Athenæum*, Nov. 15, 1852.

"The appearance of this book is too remarkable a literary event to pass without a notice. At the moment when attention in this country is directed to the state of the colored people in America, the book appears with additional advantage; if nothing else were attained by its publication, it is well to have another proof of the capability of the negro intellect. Altogether, Mr. Brown has written a pleasing and amusing volume. Contrasted with the caricature and bombast of his white countryman Mr. Willis' description of 'People he has Met,' a comparison suggested by the similarity of the title, it is both in intellect and in style a superior performance, and we are glad to bear this testimony to the literary merit of a work by a negro author."—*The Literary Gazette*, Oct. 2, 1852.

"That a man who was a slave for the first twenty years of his life, and who has never had a day's schooling, should produce such a book as this, cannot but astonish those who speak disparagingly of the African race."—*The Weekly News and Chronicle*, Sept. 6, 1852.

"It is something new for a self-educated slave to publish such a work. It is really wonderful how one who has had to surmount so many difficulties in his literary career should have been able to produce a volume of so sparkling a character. The author is personally known to many of our readers, and therefore, we need not enlarge respecting his abilities or his merits. We recommend them to procure his book, and are induced to do so by the consideration that his main object in bringing out the work is to enable him to educate his family; an object at all times honorable and praiseworthy, but in one occupying the position of Wiliam Wells Brown eminently commendable, and in which every friend of humanity must wish him success."—*British Friend,* Aug. 1852.

"This remarkable book of a remarkable man cannot fail to add to the practical protests already entered in Britain against the absolute bondage of three millions of our fellow-creatures. The impressions of a self-educated son of slavery, here set forth, must hasten the period when the senseless and impious denial of common claims to a common humanity, on the score of color, shall be scouted with scorn in every civilized and Christian country. And when this shall be attained, among the means of destruction of the hideous abomination his compatriots will remember with respect and gratitude the doings and sayings of William Wells Brown. The volume consists of a sufficient variety of scenes, persons, arguments, inferences, speculations and opinions, to satisfy and amuse the most *exigent* of those who read *pour se desennuyer;* while those who look deeper into things, and view with anxious hope the progress of nations and of mankind, will feel that the good cause of humanity and freedom, of Christianity, enlightenment and brotherhood, cannot fail to be served by such a book as this."—*Morning Advertiser,* Sept. 10, 1852.

"He writes with ease and ability, and his intelligent observations upon the great question to which he has devoted and is devoting his life will be read with interest, and will command influence and respect."—*Daily News,* Sept. 24, 1852.

"The extraordinary excitement produced by 'Uncle Tom's Cabin' will, we hope, prepare the public of Great Britain and America for this lively book of travels by a real fugitive slave. Though he never had a day's schooling in his life, he has produced a literary work not unworthy of a highly-educated gentleman. Our readers will find in these letters much instruction, not a little entertainment, and the beatings of a manly heart, on behalf of a down-trodden race, with which they will not fail to sympathize."—*The Eclectic Review,* Nov. 1852.

"We have read this book with an unusual measure of interest. Seldom, indeed, have we met with anything more captivating. It somehow happens that all these fugitive slaves are persons of superior talents. The pith of the volume consists in narratives of voyages and journeys made by the author in England, Scotland, Ireland and France; and we can assure our readers that Mr. Brown has travelled to some purpose. The number of white men is not great who could have made more of the many things that came before them. There is in the work a vast amount of quotable matter, which, but for want of space, we should be glad to extract. As the volume, however, is published with a view to promote the benefit of the interesting fugitive, we deem it better to give a general opinion, by which curiosity may be whetted, than to gratify it by large citation. A book more worth the money has not, for a considerable time, come into our hands."—*British Banner,* Dec. 15, 1852.

"THREE YEARS IN EUROPE.—The remarkable man who is the author of this work is not unknown to many of our readers. He was received with kindness in this city, and honored with various marks of respect by many eminent characters in the sister country. Since his arrival Mr. Brown has contributed much to the press; and the work before us, though small and unpretending, is of a high character, and evinces a superior and cultivated mind."—*Dublin General Advertiser,* October 30, 1852.

"This is a thrilling book, independent of adventitious circumstances, which will enhance its popularity. The author of it is not a man in America, but a chattel, a thing to be bought, and sold, and whipped: but in Europe he is an author, and a successful one, too. He gives in this book an interesting and graphic description of a three years' residence in Europe. The book will no doubt obtain, as it well deserves, a rapid and wide popularity."—*Glasgow Examiner.*

"The above is the title of an intelligent and otherwise well-written book, in which the author details, in a pleasing and highly-interesting manner, an account of places he has seen and people he has met; and we take much pleasure in recommending it to our readers."—*Weekly Dispatch.*

"This is an interesting volume, ably written, bearing on every page the impress of honest purpose and noble aspiration. One is amused by the well-told anecdotes, and charmed with the painter-like descriptions of towns, cities and natural scenery. Indeed, our author gives many very recognizable sketches of the places he has seen and people he has met. His three years in Europe have been well spent. The work will be appreciated by all the friends of the negro."—*The Leader.*

"W. Wells Brown is no ordinary man, or he could not have so remarkably surmounted the many difficulties and impediments of his training as a slave. By dint of resolution, self-culture and force of character, he has rendered himself a popular lecturer to a British audience, and vigorous expositor of the evils and atrocities of that system whose chains he has shaken off so triumphantly and forever. We may safely pronounce William Wells Brown a remarkable man, and a full refutation of the doctrine of the inferiority of the negro."—*Glasgow Citizen.*

"We can assure those who are inclined to take up this volume that they will find it written with commendable care, as well as fluency, and will derive much pleasure from a perusal of it."—*Bristol Mercury.*

"The profound Anti-slavery feeling produced by 'Uncle Tom's Cabin' needed only such a book as this, which shows so forcibly the powers and capacity of the negro intellect, to deepen the impression. The work certainly exhibits a most favorable contrast to the more ambitious productions of many of his white countrymen, N. P. Willis among others."—*Caledonian Mercury.*

Endnotes

1. Reverend John B. Mahan, Brown's friend, was president of the institution which would become Oberlin College. In light of the radical principles on which Oberlin was founded fifteen years before—the school admitted women and blacks as students—it is no surprise that its president was involved with the peace movement, as well as the anti-slavery movement, and walked the streets of Halifax arm in arm with Brown.
2. John Philpot Curran (1750–1817), Robert Emmet (1778–1803), and Daniel O'Connell (1775–1847) were celebrated Irish patriots. They challenged the Act of Union (1801) in which Britain established the United Kingdom, incorporating the Irish Republic (1798) and eliminating its separate parliament.
3. The 1849 Paris Peace Congress was the second of four international peace congresses held between 1848 and 1851. The first was held in Brussels, Belgium in 1848. Later congresses were held in 1850 in Frankfort-on-Main, Germany, and in 1851 in London. Though originally inspired by religious and philosophical objections to war, the peace movements of the nineteenth century began to develop economic and political arguments against war at these international congresses.
4. Elihu Burritt (1810–1879), the "Learned Blacksmith," was one of the leading figures in the American Peace Society. In 1846 he organized the League of Universal Brotherhood which explicitly linked the peace and anti-slavery movements. It was presumably this added concern which led the American Peace Society to appreciate the symbolic value of selecting William Wells Brown as one of its official delegates to the Paris Peace Congress of 1849. Burritt was the principal organizer of both the Paris Congress and the Brussels Congress, the year before.
5. Victor Hugo (1802–1885) typifies the European notables with whom William Wells Brown hob-nobbed during his stay abroad. Now best known as the author of *Les Miserables* and *Notre Dame de Paris*, in his day—from the standpoint of the politics of culture—Hugo was best known as the author of the drama *Hernani*, whose performance in 1830 signaled the victory of Romanticism in French letters.
6. See William Wells Brown's own fulsome remarks about Cobden below

on pages 210–211. His importance at the Congress was due in part to the increasing emphasis on the economic roots of war.

7. Alexis de Tocqueville (1805–1859), author of the classic two volume *Democracy in America* (1835; 1840), is the most celebrated and influential foreign commentator on American life. His sociological insight and cultural sensitivity are best suggested in his discussion of the "Situation of the Black Population in the United States, and Dangers with which Its Presence Threatens the Whites" in chapter 18 of volume 1. Upon his return to France, de Tocqueville was elected to the *Academie des Sciences Morales et Politiques*. He sat in the French Chamber of Deputies and served on several occasions as Minister of Foreign Affairs. It was in that capacity that Brown encountered him in Paris in 1849.

8. George Thompson (1804–1878) was an important British anti-slavery spokesman and Member of Parliament who like a number of his countrymen had taken the opportunity to consider slavery at firsthand in the 1830s during a trip to the United States.

9. Clarissa (born 1836) and Josephine (born 1839) were Brown's daughters by his first wife, Elizabeth Schooner Brown, whom he married in 1834 and from whom he was estranged in 1845. In August 1851 Clarissa and Josephine would join Brown in France, where he enrolled them in a seminary for young women in Calais for the year.

10. The Calvinist John Knox (1505–1572) was both the leader of the Reformation in Scotland and its first historian.

11. The Crafts were a slave couple who made one of the most daring and dramatic escapes from bondage of which we have record. In a marvelous double disguise, the wife Ellen, light enough to pass for white, garbed herself as a man and posed as the owner of her husband William—ammunition for feminism, this! In a curious commentary on the deeper sources of human sympathy, the poignancy of their tale was felt at home and abroad to derive particularly from the fact that Ellen was to all appearances a white woman. William Wells Brown first described their escape in the *Liberator*, January 12, 1849, and was quick to have them accompany him on his anti-slavery lecture circuit, exploiting them—as, of course, he exploited himself—as living exhibits of the irrationality and iniquity of slavery.

12. Harriet Martineau (1802–1871) epitomized the woman of letters as cultural gadfly. Historian, biographer, journalist, translator, and essayist, she was also a feminist and an anti-slavery advocate. Like George Thompson, she had traveled through the United States in the 1830s studying slavery at first hand. Among her many works was *The Martyr Age of the United States of America, with an appeal on behalf*

of the Oberlin institute in aid of the abolition of slavery (Boston, 1838).

13. Alexander Crummell (1819–1898), an Episcopal clergyman, would later win wide recognition as a Liberian missionary, diplomat, and educator. Returning to the United States after the Civil War, he was acclaimed the wisest black man of his day. Late in his career, Crummell joined forces with W. E. B. Du Bois in 1897 to found the American Negro Academy, an organization of black savants.

14. Francois Dominique Toussaint L'Ouverture (1743–1803) masterminded a slave rebellion in the French West Indian colony of San Domingo which, following a twelve-year struggle against the armies of France, Spain, and Britain, led to the founding of the black nation of Haiti in 1803.

15. Thomas Babington Macaulay (1800–1859) was a celebrated historian, biographer, and essayist who is best known for his classic ten volume history of England.

16. Alfred Lord Tennyson (1809–1892), Poet Laureate under Queen Victoria, was the author of *In Memoriam* (1850), *Idylls of the King* (1859) and other works.

17. Theodore Parker (1810–1860), the largely self-taught son of a Massachusetts farmer, became a socially radical Congregationalist minister and one of the leaders of the so-called transcendentalist movement. Parker was more earthy and practical than his more celebrated transcendentalist colleague, the poet-essayist Ralph Waldo Emerson.

18. The Anti-Corn Law League was a lobbying organization of industrial employers and wage-earners in Manchester, England. It operated from 1838 to 1846. Made possible by the Reform Bill of 1832 which enfranchised members of the industrial middle classes, its objective was to force repeal of the Corn Laws, the tariffs on grain imports which kept the price of food high and artificially inflated the payroll costs of factory owners. The tariffs were raised to new heights in 1815, after the Napoleonic Wars, to protect the incomes of aristocratic landowners, who enjoyed political hegemony in Parliament before 1832 and continued to exercise great influence throughout English society. The repeal of the Corn Laws in 1846 represented a valedictory to an old regime in England that dated from the Glorious Revolution of 1689. It signalled the triumph of a new regime of free trade, and the coming of age of the English bourgeoisie.

19. Lajos [Louis] Kossuth (1802–1894) was a Hungarian freedom fighter who went into exile after the failed revolutions of 1848–1849. He traveled the United States and Europe, speaking widely to raise support for his cause.

Printed in the USA
CPSIA information can be obtained
at www.ICGtesting.com
LVHW030547020823
754017LV00003B/134